THE TRUMP LEAKS

the ONION

THE TRUMP LEAKS

The Onion Exposes the TOP SECRET MEMOS, EMAILS, and DOODLES That Could Take Down a President

HARPER
DESIGN

An Imprint of HarperCollins Publishers

This book (and we mean the Foreword too) uses the names and likenesses of public figures for the purpose of satire. Any other use of real names is accidental, unintended, and coincidental.

THE TRUMP LEAKS.
Copyright © 2017 by The Onion, Inc..

HarperCollins books may be purchased for educational, business, or sales promotional use. For information please email the Special Markets Department at SPsales@harpercollins.com.

Published in 2017 by
Harper Design
An Imprint of HarperCollins *Publishers*
195 Broadway
New York, NY 10007
Tel: (212) 207-7000
Fax: (855) 746-6023
harperdesign@harpercollins.com
www.hc.com

Distributed throughout the world by
HarperCollins *Publishers*
195 Broadway
New York, NY 10007

ISBN 978-0-06-283426-3
Library of Congress Control Number: 2017953149

Book design by Raphael Geroni

Textures and collage elements throughout from shutterstock.com.

First Printing, 2017

⌀ the ONION®

FOREWORD

URING THE 1970S, the names Woodward and Bernstein became synonymous with dogged, fearless reporting. From our investigation of the Democratic National Committee break-in to our secret meetings with an informant known only as Deep Throat, to our unwavering pursuit of corruption in the Nixon White House, the two of us came to embody the power of the press, and it seemed as if our articles represented the pinnacle of political journalism. But now, forty-five years later, *The Onion* has published *The Trump Leaks*, a monumental work of reportage so vital and so earthshaking that it makes our years of Watergate coverage look like complete shit in comparison.

Just absolute steaming horseshit.

We never could have dreamed of laying our hands on something as consequential as the president's daily briefings or an entire trove of unreleased executive orders, let alone more than 600 additional pages of similarly momentous White House documents, as *The Onion* has managed to do in this landmark volume. If we're being entirely honest, you could probably combine every one of the articles we published between 1972 and 1974—all of our pathetic exposés and plodding 2,500-word stories about the oh-so-riveting topic of campaign fund misappropriation—and the sum total of our pitiful little "revelations" wouldn't be half as gripping as the ones you'll find on any individual page in this book. It's pretty fucking humiliating, actually.

Honest to God, the first thought that went through our heads when we cracked open our advance copy of *The Trump Leaks* was, "Oh shit, our life's work is nothing—literally nothing—next to this. We're fucking ruined."

You know what we did after flipping through the first ten pages of this book? We set it down, took our handwritten Watergate notes down from the shelf, pulled out our original manuscript for *All the President's Men*, and we lit it all on fire right there in the middle of our office. And you know why? Because that's exactly how much our work matters anymore.

God, it's so embarrassing now to think back on our legacy, if you can even call it that. Here's *The Onion*, which has gone and published a book—the staggering work of journalistic perfection you hold in your hands right this moment—that deftly exposes an Oval Office in turmoil and systematically indicts every single member of the Trump family and administration. And then there's us: a couple of pissant amateurs who couldn't pull off anything remotely close to that even if we knew how.

Honestly, this book left us wondering if the two of us ever did anything that was even moderately valuable to our readers or the national interest. Seriously, what did we even do? Move some flowerpot around a balcony? Dick around for a few years in a parking garage? Get all up our own asses about pinpointing some rinky-dink obstruction of justice evidence? For fuck's sake, that's pathetic.

After reading through *The Trump Leaks* and having our eyes opened to what real journalism actually looks like, both of us have decided that our only logical response is to call it quits as writers, effective immediately. This foreword you're reading right now will be the last thing we ever publish. The truth is that neither of us can look ourselves in the mirror anymore, let alone call ourselves "journalists"—not when a book this intensely revelatory exists in the world. So this is it, everyone; this is our goodbye. At the very least, we can leave this profession knowing that it's in the most capable, most powerful, most unerringly virtuous hands the world has ever known. We should all give thanks daily to *The Onion* for its ferocious commitment to the truth, for abiding by a towering standard of excellence unseen in media history, and for methodically eradicating all weaker, duller, hackier reporters like us from the world of journalism.

And if anyone wants a Pulitzer, they can just come by our office and take ours. We can't stand the sight of the goddamn thing anymore.

BOB WOODWARD

CARL BERNSTEIN

October 2017

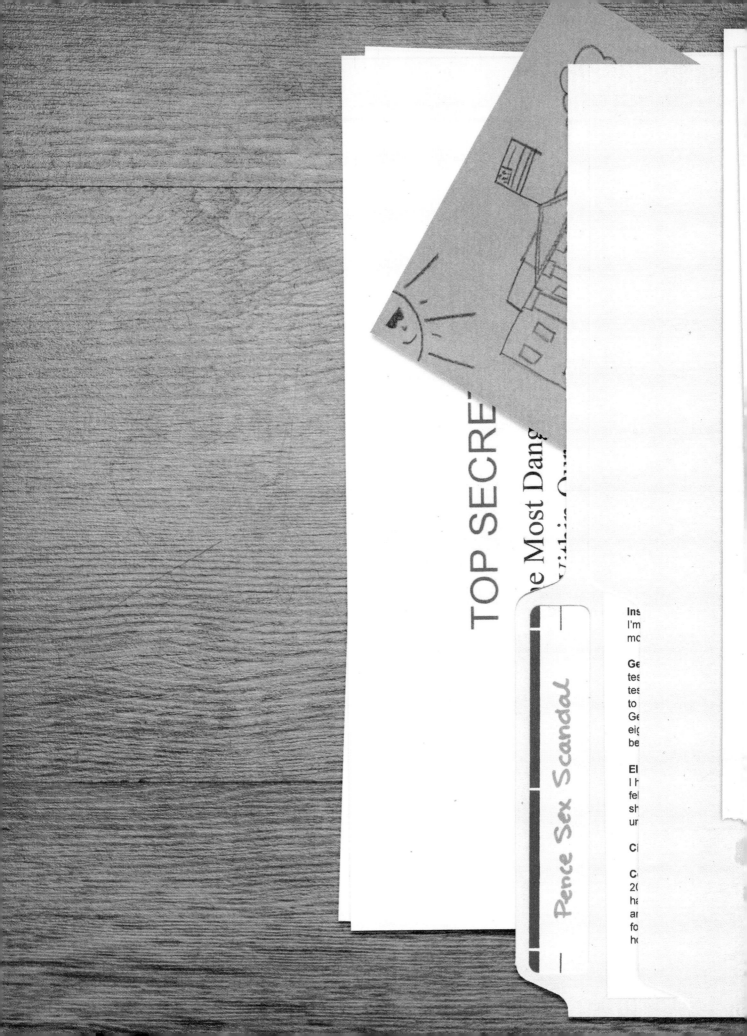

TOP SECRET

e Most Dang

Within Ou

Pence Sex Scandal

Ins
I'm
mo

Ge
tes
tes
to
Ge
eig
be

El
I h
fel
sh
un

Cl

C
2C
ha
ar
fo
h

THE

TRUMP

LEAKS

TOP SECRET

Trump Bedtime Routine

DEAR Mr. President,

Eric + Donald Jr's
DRAWINGS

From: Sergey Lavrov <slavrov@kremlin.ru>
Sent: Friday, January 20, 2017 12:36 PM
To: Donald Trump <trumpd@wh.gov>
Subject: ***MEMORIZE AND DELETE***

Below is the cipher to be used for all future email communications. Due to your staff's past difficulties with handling more sophisticated means of encryption, the new code is a simple Atbash cipher, which even you should be able to comprehend.

Cipher	A	B	C	D	E	F	G	H	I	J	K	L	M	N	O	P	Q	R	S	T	U	V	W	X	Y	Z
Actual	Z	Y	X	W	V	U	T	S	R	Q	P	O	N	M	L	K	J	I	H	G	F	E	D	C	B	A

After memorizing the cipher, you must immediately delete this email and then empty your email program's trash. Please ask one of your staffers to show you how to do that.

From: Sergey Lavrov <slavrov@kremlin.ru>
Sent: Monday, January 23, 2017 7:13 AM
To: Donald Trump <trumpd@wh.gov>
Subject: (no subject)

UOBMM SZH WVERXV NLHXLD RH KOVZHVW

From: Sergey Lavrov <slavrov@kremlin.ru>
Sent: Wednesday, January 25, 2017 4:42 AM
To: Donald Trump <trumpd@wh.gov>
Subject: (no subject)

WVERXV KIVKZIZGRLMH XLNKOVGV RMRGRZGV KSZHV LMV

From: Sergey Lavrov <slavrov@kremlin.ru>
Sent: Thursday, January 26, 2017 3:00 PM
To: Donald Trump <trumpd@wh.gov>
Subject: (no subject)

KOVZHV HGLK WRHXFHHRMT BLFI RMZFTFIZGRLM XILDW

From: Sergey Lavrov <slavrov@kremlin.ru>
Sent: Monday, January 30, 2017 3:06 PM
To: Donald Trump <trumpd@wh.gov>
Subject: (no subject)

ULXFH WLMZOW

From: Sergey Lavrov <slavrov@kremlin.ru>
Sent: Friday, February 3, 2017 8:45 AM
To: Donald Trump <trumpd@wh.gov>
Subject: (no subject)

VMHFIV UOBMM ZMW WVERXV KILGVXGVW UILN RMUL OVZPH

From: Sergey Lavrov <slavrov@kremlin.ru>
Sent: Tuesday, February 7, 2017 4:03 AM
To: Donald Trump <trumpd@wh.gov>
Subject: (no subject)

LMXV ZTZRM KOVZHV WILK GSV RMZFTFIZGRLM XILDW HRAV RHHFV HVIRLFHOB QVHFH XSIRHG

From: Sergey Lavrov <slavrov@kremlin.ru>
Sent: Tuesday, February 7, 2017 4:03 AM
To: Donald Trump <trumpd@wh.gov>
Subject: (no subject)

LMXV ZTZRM KOVZHV WILK GSV RMZFTFIZGRLM XILDW HRAV RHHFV HVIRLFHOB QVHFH XSIRHG

From: Sergey Lavrov <slavrov@kremlin.ru>
Sent: Tuesday, February 7, 2017 4:06 AM
To: Donald Trump <trumpd@wh.gov>
Subject: (no subject)

DSZG ZIV BLF WLRMT BLF UFXPRMT RWRLG

From: Sergey Lavrov <slavrov@kremlin.ru>
Sent: Wednesday, February 8, 2017 7:45 AM
To: Donald Trump <trumpd@wh.gov>
Subject: (no subject)

FITVMG UOBMM ZMW WVERXV RM WZMTVI

From: Sergey Lavrov <slavrov@kremlin.ru>
Sent: Wednesday, February 8, 2017 8:00 AM
To: Donald Trump <trumpd@wh.gov>
Subject: (no subject)

UOBMM ZMW WVERXV NFHG MLG YV VCKLHVW

From: Sergey Lavrov <slavrov@kremlin.ru>
Sent: Friday, February 10, 2017 6:37 PM
To: Donald Trump <trumpd@wh.gov>
Subject: (no subject)

KOVZHV HGLK LYHVHHRMT LEVI NLIRMRMT QLV

From: Sergey Lavrov <slavrov@kremlin.ru>
Sent: Friday, February 10, 2017 6:42 PM
To: Donald Trump <trumpd@wh.gov>
Subject: (no subject)

RU NLIRMRMT QLV RH YLGSVIRMT BLF DV XZM PROO GSVN

From: Sergey Lavrov <slavrov@kremlin.ru>
Sent: Friday, February 10, 2017 6:48 PM
To: Donald Trump <trumpd@wh.gov>
Subject: (no subject)

GIB ULXFHRMT LM LMV HRNKOV GSRMT ULI UFXPH HZPV

From: Sergey Lavrov <slavrov@kremlin.ru>
Sent: Friday, February 10, 2017 6:50 PM
To: Donald Trump <trumpd@wh.gov>
Subject: (no subject)

ORPV MLG URIRMT NRXSZVO UOBMM

From: Sergey Lavrov <slavrov@kremlin.ru>
Sent: Monday, February 13, 2017 8:15 PM
To: Donald Trump <trumpd@wh.gov>
Subject: (no subject)

XLWV UREV VNVITVMXB UOBMM ZMW WVERXV SZEV TLMV ILTFV

From: Sergey Lavrov <slavrov@kremlin.ru>
Sent: Monday, February 13, 2017 8:19 PM
To: Donald Trump <trumpd@wh.gov>
Subject: (no subject)

HXLIXSVW VZIGS KILGLXLO RMRGRZGVW

From: Sergey Lavrov <slavrov@kremlin.ru>
Sent: Monday, February 13, 2017 8:31 PM
To: Donald Trump <trumpd@wh.gov>
Subject: (no subject)

NZB TLW ULITREV FH ULI DSZG DVEV WLMV

From: Sergey Lavrov <slavrov@kremlin.ru>
Sent: Monday, February 13, 2017 8:33 PM
To: Donald Trump <trumpd@wh.gov>
Subject: (no subject)

GSRH RH ZOO BLFI UZFOG BLF ROORGVIZGV KVIEVIG

Donald,

Today, as you are sworn into office, I want to wish you the best of luck on assuming the American presidency. While you and I may not always see eye to eye, I want you to know you have my full support, both as your predecessor in the White House and as a citizen of this incredible country you have been chosen to lead. As you embark on the awesome endeavor of leaving your own imprint on this office, I simply have one parting request: Please spare my executive order banning texting while driving for federal employees.

I think we can agree that this law, Executive Order 13513: "Federal Leadership On Reducing Texting While Driving," transcends partisan politics and, all things considered, would serve well as the enduring achievement of my two terms in office. Furthermore, we can both agree that texting while driving is a serious issue that has caused the tragic loss of life and heartbreak for many families.

Prohibiting federal employees from texting while driving sets an important precedent for protecting Americans on our nation's roads so please, Donald, I am asking you to just leave that one in place.

Really, when you think about it, there is no reason to do away with this law. It's sensible. It doesn't require federal funds. It's a great law all around. And given that you will have so many other major policy issues on your plate to deal with, why not just keep this one as is?

I'd be happy — indeed I'd be honored, Mr. President — if you could just leave this order intact and let it live on as my presidential legacy.

As executive power is transferred to you in this sacred rite of our democracy, my advice to you is simple: Before you set forth on this incredible task that lies ahead, consider all the American people who are counting on you. Consider all that brought you to this momentous position. And consider that EO 13513 is a very reasonable, very small texting-while-driving order. Furthermore, remind yourself that history will judge how you act on every matter. And, if you could also remind yourself that, when history judges my contributions to this office, this roadway safety order would be a good, positive accomplishment that would be nice to still have attributed to my name. Please — this is all I'm asking.

May God bless you and this great nation.

THE WHITE HOUSE
WASHINGTON

January 20, 2017

Executive Order — Establishing Donald J. Trump as the Legitimate 45th President of the
United States of America

EXECUTIVE ORDER

- - - - - -

ESTABLISHING DONALD J. TRUMP AS THE LEGITIMATE 45TH PRESIDENT OF
THE UNITED STATES OF AMERICA

By the authority vested in me as President by the Constitution and laws of the United
States of America, it is hereby ordered as follows:

Donald J. Trump is to be regarded as the lawfully elected commander-in-chief of the
United States and will assume and retain the full powers of the presidency, regardless of
any claims or comments suggesting otherwise.

January 26, 2017

Executive Order — Establishing Donald J. Trump as the Legitimate 45th President of the United States of America and Treating Him as Such, Regardless of Any Claims or Comments Suggesting Otherwise

EXECUTIVE ORDER

- - - - - -

ESTABLISHING DONALD J. TRUMP AS THE LEGITIMATE 45TH PRESIDENT OF THE UNITED STATES OF AMERICA AND TREATING HIM AS SUCH, REGARDLESS OF ANY CLAIMS OR COMMENTS SUGGESTING OTHERWISE

By the authority vested in me as President by the Constitution and laws of the United States of America, it is hereby ordered as follows:

Section 1. *Purpose.* Donald J. Trump is to be regarded as the lawfully elected commander-in-chief of the United States, both among the American populace and by all foreign states, and will assume and retain the full powers of the presidency, regardless of any claims or comments suggesting otherwise.

Sec. 2. *Establishing a Mandate.* After receiving a record-breaking 306 Electoral College votes in the 2016 presidential election, Donald J. Trump has received a clear mandate from the American people, and his agenda will be recognized and respected by all members of the media and the public at large.

President of the United States

THE WHITE HOUSE

WASHINGTON

January 30, 2017

Executive Order — Establishing Donald J. Trump as the Legitimate 45th President of the United States of America and Treating Him as Such, Ensuring He Receives All Due Recognition and Respect Accorded to Rightful Holders of this Title, Regardless of Any Claims or Comments Suggesting Otherwise

EXECUTIVE ORDER

- - - - - -

ESTABLISHING DONALD J. TRUMP AS THE LEGITIMATE 45TH PRESIDENT OF THE UNITED STATES OF AMERICA AND TREATING HIM AS SUCH, ENSURING HE RECEIVES ALL DUE RECOGNITION AND RESPECT ACCORDED TO RIGHTFUL HOLDERS OF THIS TITLE, REGARDLESS OF ANY CLAIMS OR COMMENTS SUGGESTING OTHERWISE

By the authority vested in me as President by the Constitution and laws of the United States of America, it is hereby ordered as follows:

Section 1. *Purpose.* Donald J. Trump is to be regarded as the lawfully elected commander-in-chief of the United States—among the American populace, by all foreign states, and in any and all news coverage of him or his policies—and will assume and retain the full powers of the presidency, regardless of any claims or comments suggesting otherwise.

Sec. 2. *Establishing a Mandate.* After receiving a record-breaking 306 Electoral College votes in the 2016 presidential election, Donald J. Trump has received a clear and indisputable mandate from the American people, and his agenda will be recognized and respected by all members of the media and the public at large. It is further noted that:

    (a) He lawfully defeated Democratic candidate Hillary Clinton—against all odds—by a wide electoral vote margin, which must be acknowledged by every American citizen now and in perpetuity.

    (b) Winning the presidency means he will be held in the same regard as all former U.S. presidents including:

        I. Abraham Lincoln

        II. Ronald Reagan

        III. Barack Obama

Lawful President of the United States

February 3, 2017

Executive Order — Establishing Donald J. Trump as the Legitimate 45th President of the United States of America and Treating Him as Such, Ensuring He Receives All Due Recognition and Respect Accorded to Rightful Holders of this Title, Regardless of Any Claims or Comments Suggesting Otherwise from the Domestic Population, from Abroad, or from the Media

EXECUTIVE ORDER

- - - - - -

ESTABLISHING DONALD J. TRUMP AS THE LEGITIMATE 45TH PRESIDENT OF THE UNITED STATES OF AMERICA AND TREATING HIM AS SUCH, ENSURING HE RECEIVES ALL DUE RECOGNITION AND RESPECT ACCORDED TO RIGHTFUL HOLDERS OF THIS TITLE, REGARDLESS OF ANY CLAIMS OR COMMENTS SUGGESTING OTHERWISE FROM THE DOMESTIC POPULATION, FROM ABROAD, OR FROM THE MEDIA

By the authority vested in me as President by the Constitution and laws of the United States of America, it is hereby ordered as follows:

Section 1. *Purpose.* Donald J. Trump is to be regarded as the lawfully elected commander-in-chief of the United States by every person on earth, both living and yet to be born, as well as by all institutions and corporations in existence and yet to exist, and he will assume and retain the full powers of the presidency, regardless of any claims or comments suggesting otherwise.

Sec. 2. *Establishing a Mandate.* After receiving a record-breaking 306 Electoral College votes in the 2016 presidential election, Donald J. Trump has received a clear, conclusive, and indisputable mandate from the American people, who are known to universally admire him, and his agenda will be recognized and respected by all members of the media and the public at large. It is further noted that:
  (a) He lawfully defeated Democratic candidate Hillary Clinton—against all odds—by a wide electoral vote margin, which must be acknowledged by every American citizen now and in perpetuity.
  (b) Winning the presidency means he will be held in the same regard as all former U.S. presidents including:
   I. Abraham Lincoln
   II. Ronald Reagan
   III. Barack Obama

Sec. 3. *Upholding the Judgments of the President to Prevent Discord at Home and Abroad.* All decisions made by the President regarding domestic and international policy issues will be fully and unequivocally supported by members of Congress and the public at large.

Sec. 4. *Retribution Against Those Who Would Seek to Diminish the Office of the President.* In order to maintain his God-given right to govern the people and institutions of the United States, the President, who is Donald J. Trump, will seek to correct the wrongs done to him by those who refuse to acknowledge his mandate through:
  (a) Cease and desist letters
  (b) Legal proceedings
  (c) The withholding of federal funds to contrarian institutions
  (d) The use of CIA black sites on uncooperative members of the media, public, or others

Lawful President of the United States
Leader of the Free World

February 5, 2017

Executive Order — Establishing Donald J. Trump as the Legitimate 45th President of the United States of America and Treating Him as Such, Ensuring He Receives All Due Recognition and Respect Accorded to Rightful Holders of this Title, Regardless of Any Claims or Comments Suggesting Otherwise from the Domestic Population, from Abroad, or from the Media, and Further Respecting His Judgment on All Matters of State Business

EXECUTIVE ORDER
- - - - - -

ESTABLISHING DONALD J. TRUMP AS THE LEGITIMATE 45TH PRESIDENT OF THE UNITED STATES OF AMERICA AND TREATING HIM AS SUCH, ENSURING HE RECEIVES ALL DUE RECOGNITION AND RESPECT ACCORDED TO RIGHTFUL HOLDERS OF THIS TITLE, REGARDLESS OF ANY CLAIMS OR COMMENTS SUGGESTING OTHERWISE FROM THE DOMESTIC POPULATION, FROM ABROAD, OR FROM THE MEDIA, AND FURTHER RESPECTING HIS JUDGMENT ON ALL MATTERS OF STATE BUSINESS

By the authority vested in me as President by the Constitution and laws of the United States of America, it is hereby ordered as follows:

Section 1. *Purpose.* Donald J. Trump is to be regarded as the lawfully elected commander-in-chief of the United States by every person on earth, both living and yet to be born, as well as by all institutions and corporations in existence and yet to exist, and he will assume and retain the full powers of the presidency, regardless of any claims or comments suggesting otherwise, including those made by:

  (a) False press articles
  (b) Paid protestors
  (c) Political opponents
  (d) Former employees and disgruntled family members

Sec. 2. *Establishing a Mandate.* After receiving a record-breaking 306 Electoral College votes in the 2016 presidential election, Donald J. Trump has received a clear, conclusive, and indisputable mandate from the American people, who are known to universally admire him, and his agenda will be recognized and respected by all members of the media and the public at large. It is further noted that:

  (a) He lawfully defeated Democratic candidate Hillary Clinton—against all odds—by a wide electoral vote margin, which must be acknowledged by every American citizen now and in perpetuity.

  (b) Winning the presidency means he will be held in the same regard as all former U.S. presidents including:
      I. Abraham Lincoln
      II. Ronald Reagan
      III. Barack Obama
  (c) Further, he will be held in a higher regard than the following world leaders:
      I. Xi Jinping
      II. Angela Merkel
      III. Franklin Delano Roosevelt

Sec. 3. *Upholding the Judgments of the President to Prevent Discord at Home and Abroad.* All decisions made by the President regarding domestic and international policy issues will be fully and unequivocally supported by members of Congress and the public at large. Those failing to do so will receive all blame for any and all future terrorist attacks on American soil.

Sec. 4. *Retribution Against Those Who Would Seek to Diminish the Office of the President.* In order to maintain his God-given right to govern the people and institutions of the United States, the President, who is Donald J. Trump, will seek to correct the wrongs done to him by those who refuse to acknowledge his mandate through:

  (a) Cease and desist letters
  (b) Legal proceedings
  (c) The withholding of federal funds to contrarian institutions
  (d) The use of CIA black sites on uncooperative members of the media, public, or others
  (e) Precision military strikes

Sec. 5. *Prohibition of All Further Investigations into the President's Personal Finances and Public Acknowledgement that the President Is Incapable of Any and All Conflicts of Interest.* All inquiries the President's tax returns and potential conflicts of interest arising from his business transactions must cease, effective immediately.

February 7, 2017

Executive Order — Establishing Donald J. Trump as the Legitimate 45th President of the United States of America and Treating Him as Such, Ensuring He Receives All Due Recognition and Respect Accorded to Rightful Holders of this Title, Regardless of Any Claims or Comments Suggesting Otherwise from the Domestic Population, from Abroad, or from the Media, and Further Respecting His Judgment on All Matters of State Business and Never Questioning His Political or Financial Motives, Regardless of What the Press Says

EXECUTIVE ORDER

- - - - - -

ESTABLISHING DONALD J. TRUMP AS THE LEGITIMATE 45TH PRESIDENT OF THE UNITED STATES OF AMERICA AND TREATING HIM AS SUCH, ENSURING HE RECEIVES ALL DUE RECOGNITION AND RESPECT ACCORDED TO RIGHTFUL HOLDERS OF THIS TITLE, REGARDLESS OF ANY CLAIMS OR COMMENTS SUGGESTING OTHERWISE FROM THE DOMESTIC POPULATION, FROM ABROAD, OR FROM THE MEDIA, AND FURTHER RESPECTING HIS JUDGMENT ON ALL MATTERS OF STATE BUSINESS AND NEVER QUESTIONING HIS POLITICAL OR FINANCIAL MOTIVES, REGARDLESS OF WHAT THE PRESS SAYS

By the authority vested in me as President by the Constitution and laws of the United States of America, it is hereby ordered as follows:

Section 1. *Purpose.* Donald J. Trump is to be regarded as the lawfully elected commander-in-chief of the United States by every person on earth, both living and yet to be born, as well as by all institutions and corporations in existence and yet to exist, and he will assume and retain the full powers of the presidency, regardless of any claims or comments suggesting otherwise, including those made by:

- (a) False press articles, including any and all articles published in *The New York Times*
- (b) Paid protestors
- (c) Political opponents
- (d) Former employees, disgruntled family members, or current members of the White House staff

Sec. 2. *Establishing a Mandate.* After receiving a record-breaking 306 Electoral College votes in the 2016 presidential election, Donald J. Trump has received a clear, conclusive,

and indisputable mandate from the American people, who are known to universally admire him, and his agenda will be recognized and respected by all members of the media and the public at large. It is further noted that:

- (a) He lawfully defeated Democratic candidate Hillary Clinton—against all odds—by a wide electoral vote margin, which must be acknowledged by every American citizen now and in perpetuity.
- (b) Winning the presidency means he will be held in the same regard as all former U.S. presidents, and he will be held in higher regard than any and all individuals, living, dead, or yet to be born, who have not served as or who are ineligible to serve as President of the United States, including:
  - I. Xi Jinping
  - II. Angela Merkel
  - III. Hillary Clinton
  - IV. Any and all popes
  - V. Europeans

Sec. 3. *Upholding the Judgments of the President to Prevent Discord at Home and Abroad.* All decisions made by the President regarding domestic and international policy issues will be fully and unequivocally supported by members of Congress and the public at large. Those failing to do so will receive all blame for any and all future terrorist attacks on American soil, as well as for any economic downturns, increases in unemployment, and crime of all types and measures occurring within the United States.

Sec. 4. *Retribution Against Those Who Would Seek to Diminish the Office of the President.* In order to maintain his God-given right to govern the people and institutions of the United States, the President, who is Donald J. Trump, will seek to correct the wrongs done to him by those who refuse to acknowledge his mandate through:

    (a) Cease and desist letters
    (b) Legal proceedings
    (c) The withholding of federal funds to contrarian institutions, such as:
        I. Public universities
        II. Arts and culture grant recipients
        III. Women's health organizations
        IV. NATO
    (d) The use of CIA black sites on uncooperative members of the media, public, or others
    (e) Precision military strikes
    (f) Any Top Secret experimental cognitive-disruption technology that the U.S. government may or may not possess

Sec. 5. *Prohibition of All Further Investigations into the President's Personal Finances and Public Acknowledgement that the President Is Incapable of Any and All Conflicts of Interest Pertaining to the Trump Organization or Other Investments.* All inquiries into the President's tax returns and potential conflicts of interest arising from his business

transactions must cease, effective immediately. The President's affiliation with any and all industries, including but not limited to real estate, hospitality, entertainment, fine dining, golf, and fashion, both domestically and internationally, whether in locations deemed friendly to the United States or in hostile territories, should be considered completely irrelevant to his abilities to lead.

Sec. 6. *Complete Erasure of Russia from the Narrative of the 2016 Presidential Election.* Henceforth, no American citizen or green card holder may ever link the President's legitimate victory in the 2016 presidential election to the government of Russia in any capacity, unless to compare the President to Vladimir Putin in a favorable light. The public will acknowledge that the President won the election completely on his own, with no meddling from any foreign governments, regardless of what national intelligence agencies or independent investigations may or may not suggest.

Lawful President of the United States
Leader of the Free World
Universally Revered Head of State

From: Donald Trump <trumpd@wh.gov>
Sent: Tuesday, January 24, 2017 10:35 AM
To: Dennis Muilenburg <dmuilenburg@boeing.com>
Subject: changes to Air Force One

Great meeting. Just want to make sure you have in your plans that the interior of the plane should be marble. Not sure if you got that when we talked

Looking forward to seeing the plane when its finished. Sure you will do a terrific job

DJT

From: Dennis Muilenburg <dmuilenburg@boeing.com>
Sent: Tuesday, January 24, 2017 12:18 PM
To: Donald Trump <trumpd@wh.gov>
Subject: RE: changes to Air Force One

Mr. President,

It was great meeting with you today as well. Yes, a marble floor should be possible. We have a lightweight option that will work well.

Thank you for letting me know. I will be in touch as we move forward with this.

Best regards,
Dennis Muilenburg
Boeing Chief Executive Officer

From: Donald Trump <trumpd@wh.gov>
Sent: Tuesday, January 24, 2017 12:54 PM
To: Dennis Muilenburg <dmuilenburg@boeing.com>
Subject: RE: changes to Air Force One

Dennis, whole interior should be marble, not just floor. Make sure it has marble fixtures in the bathrooms and the kitchen, and all the doors should be made out of marble. Walls need to be marble too

DJT

From: Dennis Muilenburg <dmuilenburg@boeing.com>
Sent: Tuesday, January 24, 2017 2:15 PM
To: Donald Trump <trumpd@wh.gov>
Subject: RE: changes to Air Force One

Mr. President,

I will speak to my engineers about this, but it likely won't be possible to use much marble on the interior of the aircraft, as it is quite heavy. I would be happy to discuss other options with you. I'm sure we can find many other high-end finishes that will be to your liking.

Best regards,
Dennis Muilenburg
Boeing Chief Executive Officer

From: Donald Trump <trumpd@wh.gov>
Sent: Tuesday, January 24, 2017 2:39 PM
To: Dennis Muilenburg <dmuilenburg@boeing.com>
Subject: RE: changes to Air Force One

Make sure it is all marble Dennis. Thanks

DJT

From: Donald Trump <trumpd@wh.gov>
Sent: Tuesday, January 24, 2017 2:40 PM
To: Dennis Muilenburg <dmuilenburg@boeing.com>
Subject: RE: changes to Air Force One

Marble seats in the aircraft Dennis. Headrest on each of the seats should be adjustable and marble

DJT

From: Donald Trump <trumpd@wh.gov>
Sent: Tuesday, January 24, 2017 2:42 PM
To: Dennis Muilenburg <dmuilenburg@boeing.com>
Subject: RE: changes to Air Force One

Will new plane have storage bins? If so, make them marble

DJT

NAME
NOM

No.

From: Donald Trump <trumpd@wh.gov>
Sent: Tuesday, January 24, 2017 2:45 PM
To: Dennis Muilenburg <dmuilenburg@boeing.com>
Subject: RE: changes to Air Force One

Seatbelts need to be marble

DJT

From: Dennis Muilenburg <dmuilenburg@boeing.com>
Sent: Tuesday, January 24, 2017 2:58 PM
To: Donald Trump <trumpd@wh.gov>
Subject: RE: changes to Air Force One

Mr. President,

I can have the team put together some synthetic marble options if you'd like, but I'm afraid it's just not possible to use only marble for every element of the plane's interior.

Best regards,
Dennis Muilenburg
Boeing Chief Executive Office

From: Donald Trump <trumpd@wh.gov>
Sent: Tuesday, January 24, 2017 3:10 PM
To: Dennis Muilenburg <dmuilenburg@boeing.com>
Subject: RE: changes to Air Force One

Going to need following features:

- Marble wings
- Presidential workspace made out of marble
- Windows should be made of marble (if this is not possible, no windows)
- Marble tires
- Engines (solid marble)
- Marble cockpit

DJT

From: Donald Trump <trumpd@wh.gov>
Sent: Tuesday, January 24, 2017 3:51 PM
To: Dennis Muilenburg <dmuilenburg@boeing.com>
Subject: RE: changes to Air Force One

I want you to be clear on this Dennis, so I drew what the plane should look like

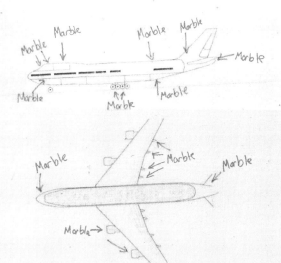

Run this by your guys. Want to make sure were on the same page

DJT

Detaining Homeland Security Threats Within "The Void"

Homeland Security Extra-Dimensional Detention Advisory Committee

Presented by General John F. Kelly
Secretary
U.S. Department of Homeland Security

February 8, 2017

Homeland Security
Extra-Dimensional Detention

1.

Department of Homeland Security
Extra-Dimensional Detention

Primary Objectives

1. Preventing terrorism and enhancing security by detaining suspected terrorists within timeless, lightless extra-dimensional realm known as "The Void"

2. Protecting borders by detaining illegal immigrants within same

3. Establishing legal framework for holding detainees within infinitely dark, inescapable prison-dimension that does not violate international laws governing treatment of enemy combatants

2.

Department of Homeland Security

Background

Dimensional Anomaly KX-42B, aka "The Void," is an extra-dimensional domain outside the bounds of our universe, where rules of space, time, cause and effect, and Euclidean geometry have no meaning

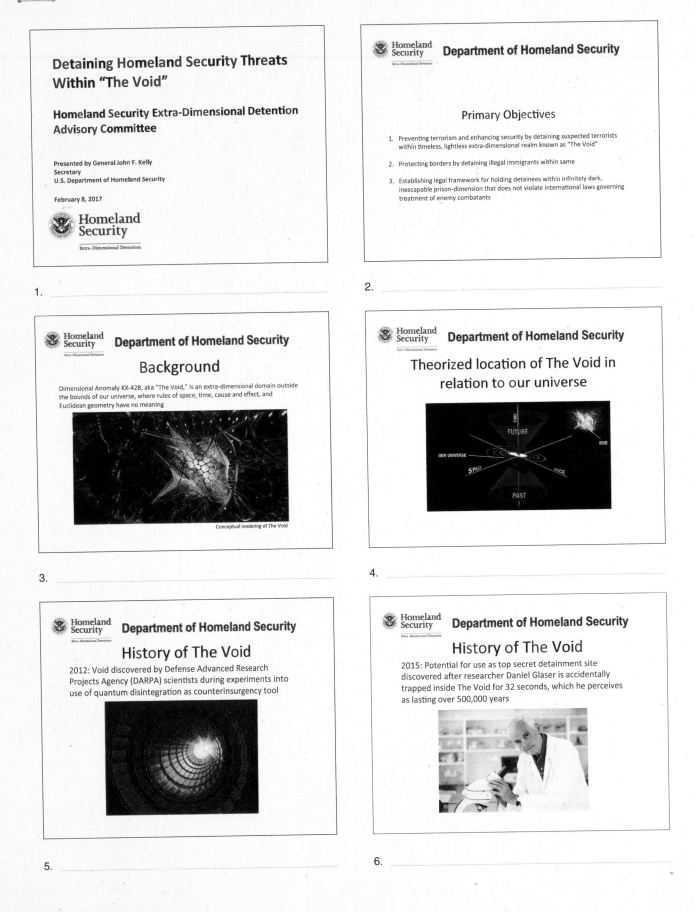

Conceptual rendering of The Void

3.

Department of Homeland Security

Theorized location of The Void in relation to our universe

4.

Department of Homeland Security

History of The Void

2012: Void discovered by Defense Advanced Research Projects Agency (DARPA) scientists during experiments into use of quantum disintegration as counterinsurgency tool

5.

Department of Homeland Security

History of The Void

2015: Potential for use as top secret detainment site discovered after researcher Daniel Glaser is accidentally trapped inside The Void for 32 seconds, which he perceives as lasting over 500,000 years

6.

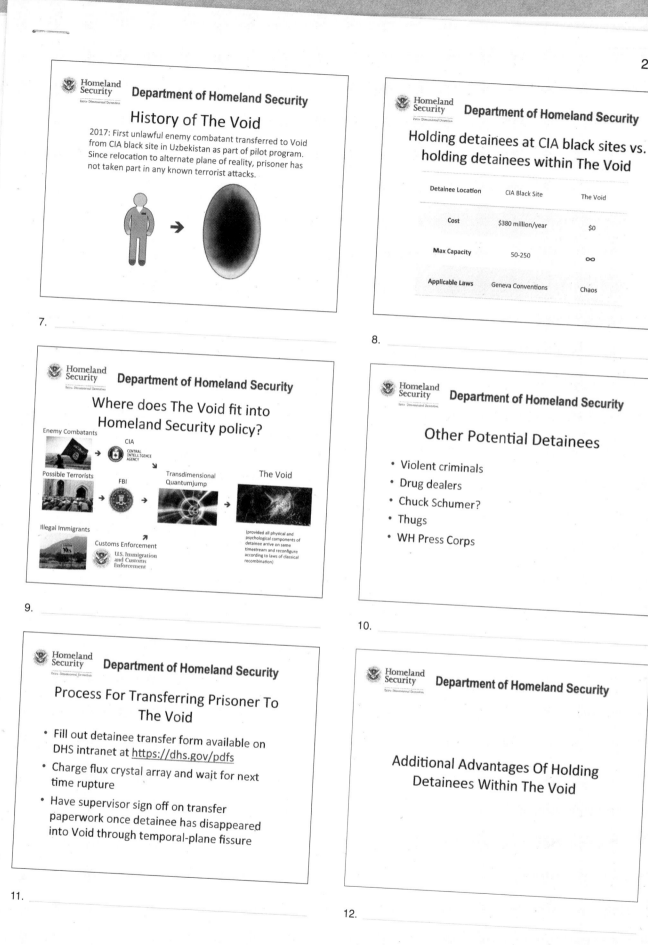

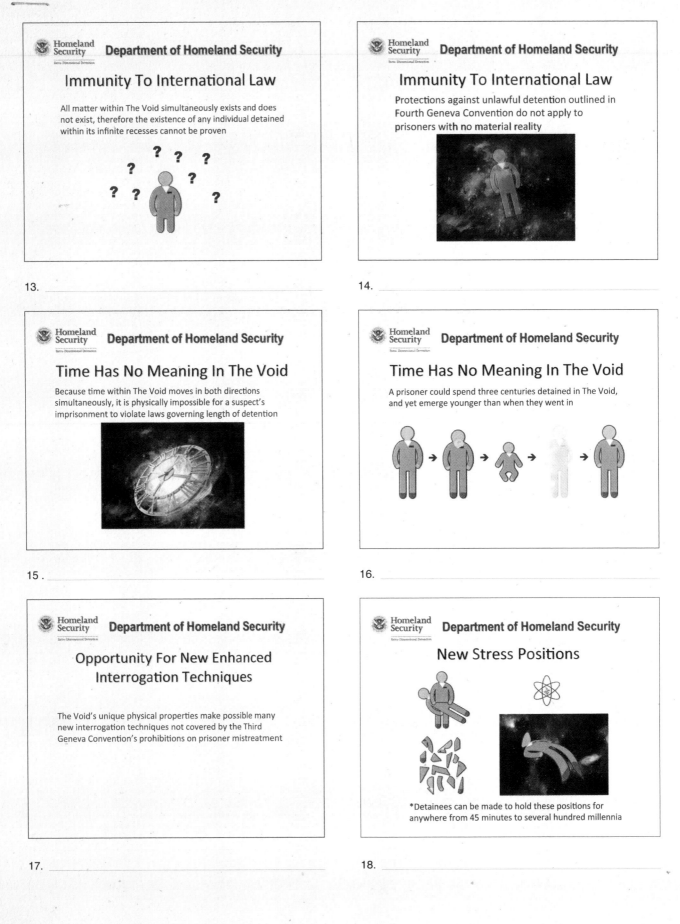

Homeland Security — **Department of Homeland Security**

New Psychological Torture Techniques

- Depriving prisoners of sleep for up to 40,000 years at a time
- Threatening to throw prisoners directly into neutron star
- Forcing detainees to watch helplessly as their families grow old and die billions of times across infinite parallel universes

19.

Homeland Security — **Department of Homeland Security**

Possible Drawbacks/Concerns

20.

Homeland Security — **Department of Homeland Security**

Difficulty Of Gathering Useful Intelligence From Detainees Who Have Been Driven Insane

As all of our detainees have gone mad within minutes of entering The Void, intelligence gathered from them has so far proven unreliable

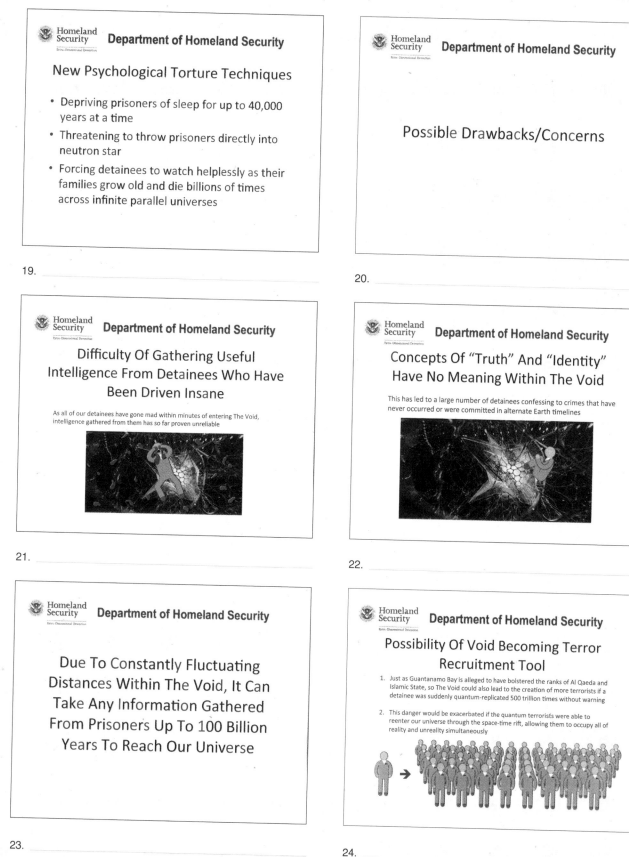

21.

Homeland Security — **Department of Homeland Security**

Concepts Of "Truth" And "Identity" Have No Meaning Within The Void

This has led to a large number of detainees confessing to crimes that have never occurred or were committed in alternate Earth timelines

22.

Homeland Security — **Department of Homeland Security**

Due To Constantly Fluctuating Distances Within The Void, It Can Take Any Information Gathered From Prisoners Up To 100 Billion Years To Reach Our Universe

23.

Homeland Security — **Department of Homeland Security**

Possibility Of Void Becoming Terror Recruitment Tool

1. Just as Guantanamo Bay is alleged to have bolstered the ranks of Al Qaeda and Islamic State, so The Void could also lead to the creation of more terrorists if a detainee was suddenly quantum-replicated 500 trillion times without warning
2. This danger would be exacerbated if the quantum terrorists were able to reenter our universe through the space-time rift, allowing them to occupy all of reality and unreality simultaneously

24.

INSTRUCTIONS FOR FEEDING AND PUTTING PRESIDENT TRUMP TO BED

To the person or persons looking after my father tonight,

Thank you for taking on this responsibility. Here are a few things to be aware of when taking care of him:

- First, make sure he doesn't eat anything in the afternoon before dinner. Otherwise he'll just dump out his dinner when he receives it and smear it into the carpets and furniture.

- Please make sure he eats dinner by 6:00 p.m. or else he'll run around all the different West Wing rooms and gnaw on the throw pillows.

- NOTE: My father won't eat his dinner when he thinks anyone is watching, so once you put everything in his bowl, just slide it under the dining table and make sure he sees you leave the room.

- Usually after he eats, he'll want you to lay him down on the Oval Office couch and repeat the words "handsome," "luxury," and "strong" for about 20 or 30 minutes in a calm and steady tone of voice.

- At some point, typically around 7:00 or 8:00 p.m., you should gather together some pictures of big buildings to show him. He especially likes high-rise condominiums, office complexes, and hotels. (IMPORTANT: DO NOT SHOW HIM BUILDINGS UNDER 5 STORIES TALL)

- NOTE: My father should be kept visually stimulated the entire time you're with him or he'll start violently picking at the skin on his arms, neck, and face. Besides pictures of buildings, it is good to leave him with a reflective piece of foil, some colored string, or anything with buttons he can press, like an old cellphone with the battery removed or a garage door opener. That will keep him occupied for a few hours until he tires himself out.

- If he gets out of hand at any point, you can give him a 50- or 100-dollar bill to gum on, as that tends to calm him down quickly.

- NOTE: Be aware that the following colors upset my father and I ask that you please not wear them:
    - Navy blue
    - Turquoise
    - Teal
    - Light blue
    - Powder blue
    - Royal blue
    - Periwinkle

- My father can usually be coaxed up to his bed by leaving a solution of three parts water, one part sugar, and one part bone meal on his bedside table. But if he's exhausted himself from clanging objects on his desk together or shouting at birds, you may need to carry him up.

- When you're putting my father down for the night, make sure his arm restraints are fastened as tightly as possible. (IMPORTANT: DO NOT LISTEN TO MY FATHER IF HE STARTS SCREAMING AND SAYING THE RESTRAINTS ARE TOO TIGHT – TIGHTEN THEM ALL THE WAY)

- Do not be alarmed in the middle of the night if you hear him whimpering loudly and repeatedly calling out the name "Frederick." This is normal and lets you know that he is sleeping.

- And as always, never make direct eye contact with him at any time.

Aside from these guidelines, just keep sharp objects away from his mouth and use your common sense!

Thanks again!

Ivanka

From: Donald Trump <trumpd@wh.gov>
Sent: Tuesday, April 18, 2017 2:35 AM
To: Reince Priebus <priebusr@wh.gov>
Subject: lighthouse question

Fine on Israel plan from today, but where do we stand on the Lighthouse question?

DJT

From: Reince Priebus <priebusr@wh.gov>
Sent: Tuesday, April 18, 2017 7:43 AM
To: Jared Kushner <kushnerj@wh.gov>, Stephen Miller <millers@wh.gov>, Steve Bannon <bannons@wh.gov>, Kellyanne Conway <conwayk@wh.gov>
Subject: FW: lighthouse question

POTUS sent this email to me in the middle of the night asking about "the Lighthouse question." I'm in the dark here. Anyone care to clarify?

From: Jared Kushner<kushnerj@wh.gov>
Sent: Tuesday, April 18, 2017 8:19 AM
To: Reince Priebus <priebusr@wh.gov>, Stephen Miller <millers@wh.gov>, Steve Bannon <bannons@wh.gov>, Kellyanne Conway <conwayk@wh.gov>
Subject: RE: FW: lighthouse question

No idea on this. All I can tell you is that POTUS spent about 20 minutes the other day telling me that lighthouses were too tall and that he didn't trust lighthouse keepers. Seemed to be frustrated that they're always sitting up high in their lantern rooms looking down at the rest of the country. Also, he said that because lighthouses are all by themselves and face their lights away from the country, they are "unpatriotic," whatever that means. He also told me we have to find a way to "stop their beams" probably about a dozen times. Not clear where he got these ideas.

Jared Kushner
Senior Advisor to the President

From: Kellyanne Conway <conwayk@wh.gov>
Sent: Tuesday, April 18, 2017 8:27 AM
To: Jared Kushner <kushnerj@wh.gov>, Reince Priebus <priebusr@wh.gov>, Stephen Miller <millers@wh.gov>, Steve Bannon <bannons@wh.gov>
Subject: RE: FW: lighthouse question

Not sure what's going on either, but I've been hearing similar things. In fact, I walked into the Oval Office at about 6:15 this morning and POTUS was behind his desk, sitting in the dark. It wasn't clear how long he'd been sitting there, but he looked exhausted. He kept yelling that he was going to declare the U.S. Lighthouse Society a terrorist group and went on and on about how we have no way to stop their lights from rotating around in circles. I think he also said something about Americans needing to get their own spinning beams of light to fight back? This is actually the third time I've walked in on him muttering stuff like this to himself in the past week.

Also, he said he wanted us to pull the files on all WH employees and congressmen to see if any of them are or ever have been lighthouse keepers. Could you get someone on that, Reince?

- Kellyanne

**UNITED STATES DISTRICT COURT
FOR THE DISTRICT OF COLUMBIA**

UNITED STATES OF AMERICA,
U.S. Attorney's Office
555 Fourth Street, NW
Washington, DC 20530,

Plaintiff,

v.

12:15 WHITE HOUSE TOUR GROUP,
1600 Pennsylvania Ave, NW
Washington, DC 20500

Defendant.

COMPLAINT FOR GROSS
NEGLIGENCE

Civil Action No. 16-0108

COMPLAINT

On March 3, 2017, the defendants, the members of the 12:15 p.m. White House tour group, failed to perform the expected duties of a visiting tour group and acted in a manner that was injurious to President Donald Trump. The conduct of the defendants caused irreparable damage to President Trump and his family.

The offenses of the 11 defendants are as follows:

1. Failed to initiate a conversation with President Trump regarding the extent of his electoral college victory
2. Did not sufficiently marvel at the sight of the newly renovated White House staircase, as indicated by only three (3) utterances of the word "wow"
3. Chuckled audibly after President Trump made a remark that was not intended as a joke
4. Failed to favorably compare the décor and furnishings of the Oval Office with those of previous president Barack Obama
5. Yawned

6. Did not further insist on a picture with President Trump after the president declined their initial request
7. Spoke over President Trump's favorite Planter's Peanuts commercial that was airing on a West Wing television
8. Made direct eye contact with the president
9. Failed to ask President Trump to sign a copy of his bestselling book, *The Art Of The Deal*
10. Offered no compliments to President Trump regarding his choice of curtains

As a result of this gross negligence and mistreatment, President Trump was unable to perform his regular duties for 3 days and suffered lasting trauma that will affect his earning potential in the future.

Demand For Relief

WHEREFORE, the plaintiff demands judgment against the defendants for the sum of $800,000 with interest and costs.

Jury Demand

The plaintiff demands a jury trial.

Dated this 8th day of March, 2017

White House Counsel Don McGahn

From: Mike Pence <pencem@wh.gov>
Sent: Wednesday, January 25, 2017 3:35 AM
To: Reince Priebus <priebusr@wh.gov>
Subject: Sensitive Issue FYEO

Just wanted to let you know about a recent transgression of mine we might need to get out ahead of.

On Monday, Mrs. Pence and I went to Bloomingdales, and when she was off on her own I accidentally wandered right through the juniors department, specifically the little girls section.

I was only there for about 30 seconds, and I don't think anybody saw me, but I think we should have Spicer prepare a response because it's all over if the press catches whiff.

And, Reince, you know I am a godly man and this incident does not reflect my values.

God Be With You,
Mike

--
"For all have sinned and fall short of the glory of God," (Romans 3:32)

From: Reince Priebus <priebusr@wh.gov>
Sent: Wednesday, January 25, 2017 10:17 AM
To: Mike Pence <pencem@wh.gov>
Subject: RE: Sensitive Issue FYEO

Don't see anything to worry about here Mike. Thanks for heads up though.

From: Mike Pence <pencem@wh.gov>
Sent: Wednesday, January 25, 2017 10:27 AM
To: Reince Priebus <priebusr@wh.gov>
Subject: RE: Sensitive Issue FYEO

I don't think you understand the gravity of the situation. If anybody saw me walk down that aisle of little girl bathing suits it's all over. I can't have this come back to me.

--
"For all have sinned and fall short of the glory of God," (Romans 3:32)

From: Reince Priebus <priebusr@wh.gov>
Sent: Wednesday, January 25, 2017 11:59 PM
To: Mike Pence <pencem@wh.gov>
Subject: RE: Sensitive Issue FYEO

Still don't see issue

From: Mike Pence <pencem@wh.gov>
Sent: Thursday, January 26, 2017 12:01 AM
To: Reince Priebus <priebusr@wh.gov>
Subject: RE: Sensitive Issue FYEO

What if told you I might've brushed against one of the little mannequins (but NOT aroused)?

--
"For all have sinned and fall short of the glory of God," (Romans 3:32)

From: Mike Pence <pencem@wh.gov>
Sent: Thursday, January 26, 2017 12:03 AM
To: Reince Priebus <priebusr@wh.gov>
Subject: RE: Sensitive Issue FYEO

Reince, this might even be more damaging than back when I was governor and was caught on camera at the state fair sucking on a barbecue rib.

--

"For all have sinned and fall short of the glory of God," (Romans 3:32)

From: Mike Pence <pencem@wh.gov>
Sent: Thursday, January 26, 2017 12:05 AM
To: Reince Priebus <priebusr@wh.gov>
Subject: RE: Sensitive Issue FYEO

Talk to me Reince.

--

"For all have sinned and fall short of the glory of God," (Romans 3:32)

From: Mike Pence <pencem@wh.gov>
Sent: Thursday, January 26, 2017 3:01 AM
To: Reince Priebus <priebusr@wh.gov>
Subject: RE: Sensitive Issue FYEO

Ok, Reince. I've decided that, in light of my actions, it would be best to resign now rather than drag the administration through this scandal any further. Here is a letter I have drafted.

Mr. President,

Serving as your Vice President has been one of the greatest privileges of my life. It is a position of awesome power, and one that demands integrity, loyalty, and a commitment to reflecting the values of yourself and this administration.

It is for this last reason that I come to you today with a deep sense of shame and sadness. While I shall not delve into the sordid details here, I must confess that I was involved in a compromising situation of a sexual nature last weekend at Bloomingdale's department store. In doing so, I let down my family, you, and most painfully, my country.

I fear that my actions not only reflect poorly on this administration, but that my continued presence in the White House will be a significant distraction and additional obstacle to this administration's already difficult task of implementing your policy agenda.

That is why today, January 26, 2017, I, Mike Pence, humbly submit to you my offer of resignation as Vice President of the United States.

For God and Country,
-Michael R. Pence

--

"For all have sinned and fall short of the glory of God," (Romans 3:32)

Mr. President
The artist sent some
pics of the paintings you
commissioned for the Oval
Office. Can have them
installed next Friday if
they look good to you
        —J Kell...

Dear Ben,
Congrats-
you're going
to be great!
I've heard
great things.
Good luck.
Best wishes,
Ben Carson.
P.S. I'll be
watching!

IN CASE OF STEPHEN BANNON'S CYST BURSTING

Please read safety instructions carefully and follow each step quickly and precisely. Any rupture of the chief strategist's epidermal growths represents a SEVERE EMERGENCY, so please maintain vigilant observation of his skin for any changes in color, increased pulsation, or other signs of instability, and alert authorities IMMEDIATELY if a breach event appears imminent.

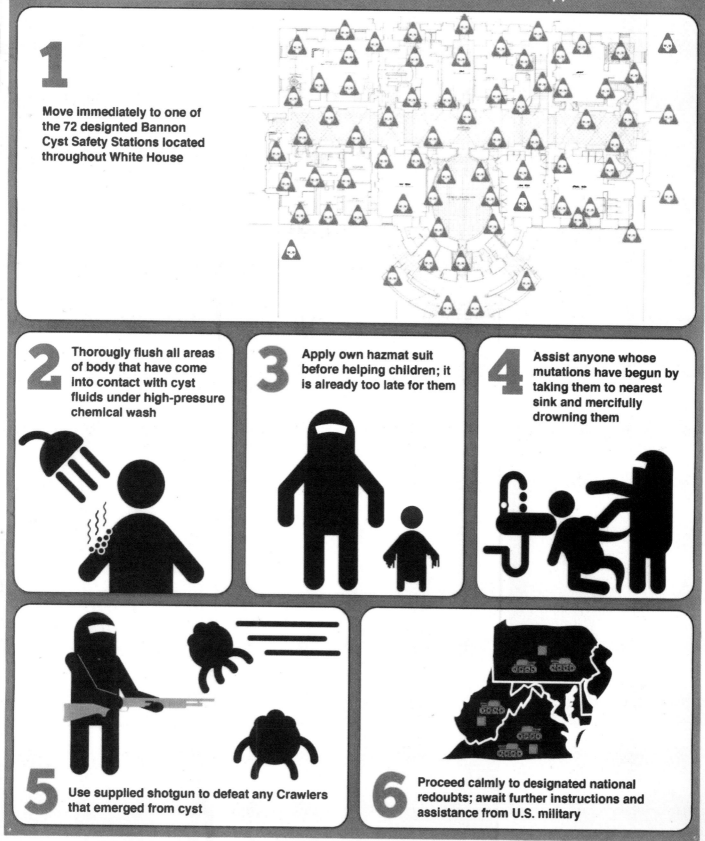

1 Move immediately to one of the 72 designted Bannon Cyst Safety Stations located throughout White House

2 Thorougly flush all areas of body that have come into contact with cyst fluids under high-pressure chemical wash

3 Apply own hazmat suit before helping children; it is already too late for them

4 Assist anyone whose mutations have begun by taking them to nearest sink and mercifully drowning them

5 Use supplied shotgun to defeat any Crawlers that emerged from cyst

6 Proceed calmly to designated national redoubts; await further instructions and assistance from U.S. military

Office of the Press Secretary
Proposed Upgrades to PRESS BRIEFING ROOM
July 3, 2017

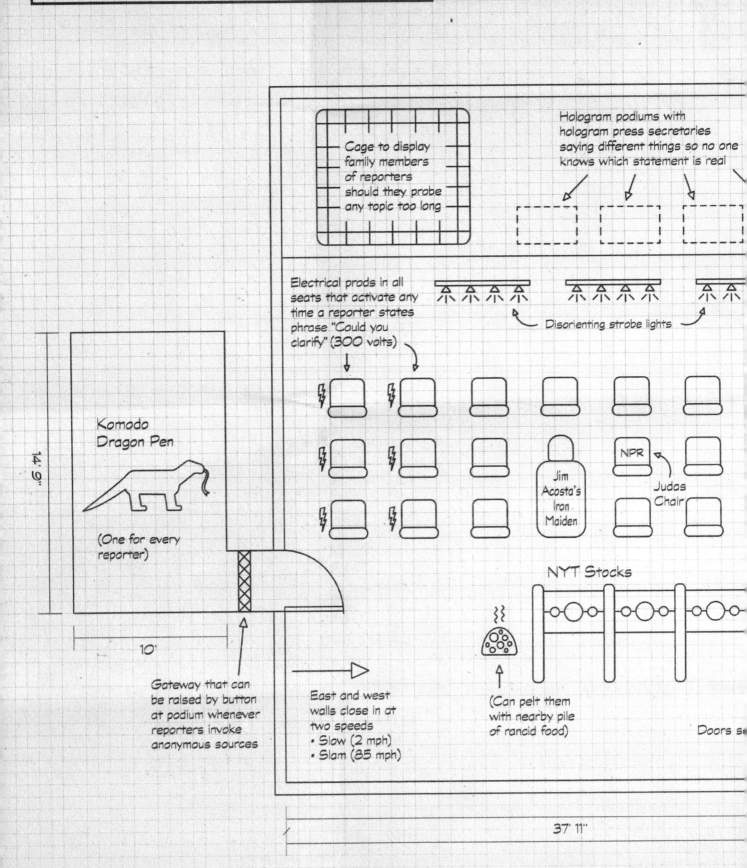

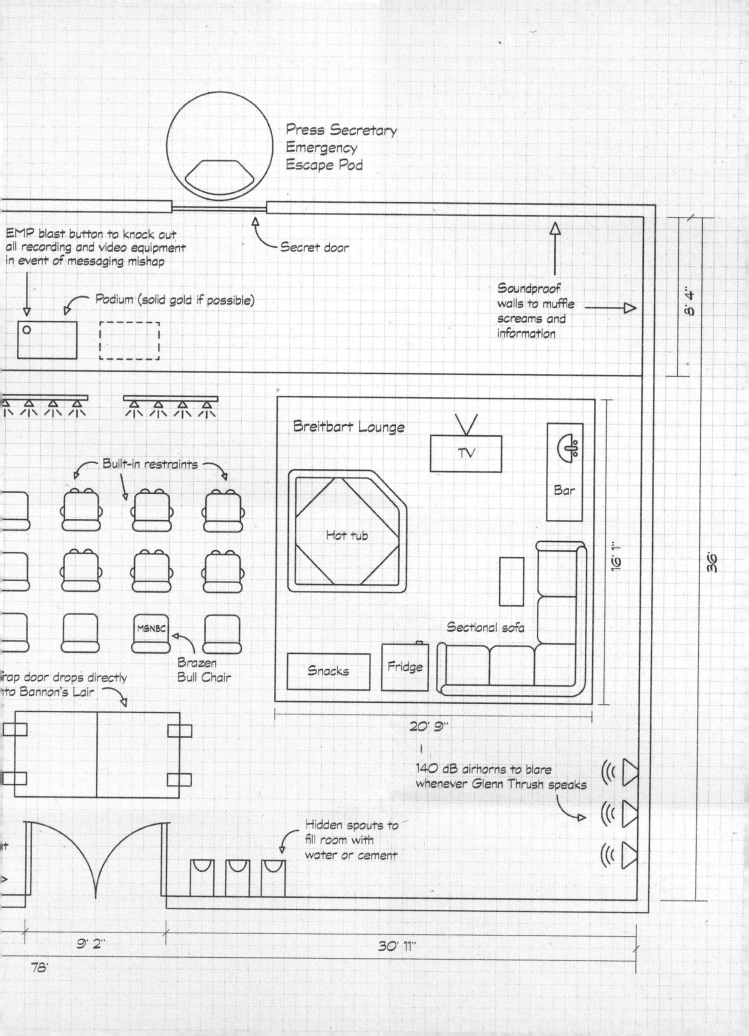

Press Secretary
Emergency
Escape Pod

EMP blast button to knock out
all recording and video equipment
in event of messaging mishap

Secret door

Podium (solid gold if possible)

Soundproof
walls to muffle
screams and
information

8' 4"

36'

Breitbart Lounge

TV

Bar

Built-in restraints

Hot tub

16' 1"

Sectional sofa

MSNBC

Brazen
Bull Chair

Snacks

Fridge

Trap door drops directly
into Bannon's Lair

20' 9"

140 dB airhorns to blare
whenever Glenn Thrush speaks

Hidden spouts to
fill room with
water or cement

9' 2"

30' 11"

78'

From: Donald Trump Jr. <trump.donaldjr@trump.com>
Sent: Wednesday, January 25, 2017 6:12 PM
To: Dad <trumpd@wh.gov>
CC: Eric Trump <trump.eric@trump.com>
Subject: robot karate master!

Dad here's the robot Eric and I were talking about the other day that you said you didn't get it. so heres the pictshure!!! ITS A ROBOT AND ITS A KARATE MASTER so it can fight enemies, also do things like carry our stuff and solve really hard problems like math problems! There are going to be a bunch of other things its going to be able to do too. These are just some of them okay? Oh it can also GO UNDERWATER!!! So awsome right?

Hahah miss you DAd!

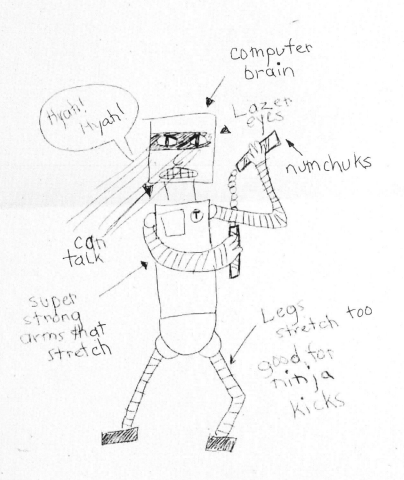

From: Eric Trump <trump.eric@trump.com>
Sent: Sunday, January 29, 2017 1:51 PM
To: Dad <trumpd@wh.gov>
CC: Donald Trump Jr. <trump.donaldjr@trump.com>
Subject: special permisshion

Hi dad!! HOws work? Im good. Donny and me want to spend the night on roof of the pentigon to look for U.F.O.s but Donny says we probably need special permisshon to do that so Im asking you please please please can we go on the pentigon roof tonight to look for U.F.O.s. I promise Donny and me will be very careful and we wont get scared and ask to come down after only 1 hour like we did when you let us go up on the roof of Trump Tower last summer to look for black holes, this is going to be totaly diffrent.

We are bringing sleeping bags, pillows, warm hat and gloves, snacks, nintendo 3ds, night vision goggles (can you get us some of these please we dont have any), flashlights, my book I got for Christmas on U.F.O.s, and some fruit punch too so we will have everything we need.

please Dad we really want to do this.

From: Dad <trumpd@wh.gov>
Sent: Thursday, March 9, 2017 1:27 PM
To: Donald Trump Jr. <trump.donaldjr@trump.com>, Eric Trump <trump.eric@trump.com>
Subject: (no subject)

Bring those couch cushions back to the Oval Office NOW

From: Eric Trump <trump.eric@trump.com>
Sent: Thursday, March 9, 2017 1:30 PM
To: Dad <trumpd@wh.gov>, Donald Trump Jr. <trump.donaldjr@trump.com>
Subject: RE: (no subject)

Sorry Dad. we were bilding a fort in the treaty room and ran out of cushions for the lookout tower. were bringing them back now. sorry

From: Donald Trump Jr. <trump.donaldjr@trump.com>
Sent: Thursday, March 9, 2017 1:31 PM
To: Eric Trump <trump.eric@trump.com>, Dad <trumpd@wh.gov>
Subject: RE: (no subject)

it was Eric's idea

From: Eric Trump <trump.eric@trump.com>
Sent: Thursday, February 9, 2017 4:17 PM
To: Dad <trumpd@wh.gov>
CC: Donald Trump Jr. <trump.donaldjr@trump.com>
Subject: NEW Inventshion!!!

Dad! HOws work going? Im good. Look at what me and Donny are going to build this weekend!!! It's a flying go-kart!!! Its going to be sooooooo cool!! We're going to fly it from the White House to New York and come see you any time we want. WE can fly it all over!! Vroooom! Can you help us bild it this weekend? It will be awsome and wont take long we swear. Ivanka cant ride in it, JUST US!

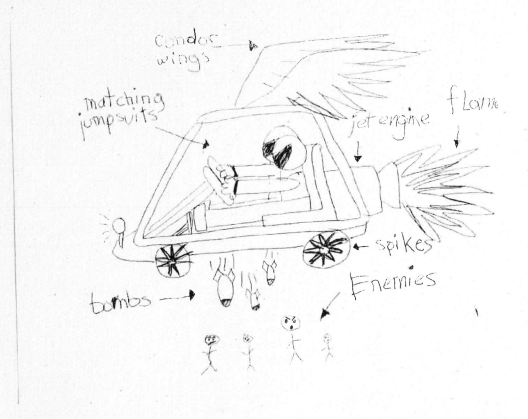

From: Donald Trump Jr. <trump.donaldjr@trump.com>
Sent: Thursday, February 9, 2017 4:23 PM
To: Dad <trumpd@wh.gov>
CC: Eric Trump <trump.eric@trump.com>
Subject: RE: NEW Inventshion!!!

Yah Dad, look at the pictshure we made its going to have condors wings so it can fly really high! Once we find the feathers for it we will fly anywere we want!! And it has two steering wheels so me and Eric can both drive at the same time!!! And it's going to have a really fast engine from a porsh or a jet and we're going to race it against air force one!!

From: Dad <trumpd@wh.gov>
Sent: Thursday, February 9, 2017 5:00 PM
To: Donald Trump Jr. <trump.donaldjr@trump.com>
CC: Eric Trump <trump.eric@trump.com>
Subject: RE: NEW Inventshion!!!

I'll be at Mar-a-Lago this weekend. Why don't you ask Mr. Miller to help you when he has time

---

From: Donald Trump Jr. <trump.donaldjr@trump.com>
Sent: Thursday, February 9, 2017 5:04 PM
To: Dad <trumpd@wh.gov>
CC: Eric Trump <trump.eric@trump.com>
Subject: RE: NEW Inventshion!!!

No way

From: Eric Trump <trump.eric@trump.com>
Sent: Thursday, February 9, 2017 5:05 PM
To: Dad <trumpd@wh.gov>
CC: Donald Trump Jr. <trump.donaldjr@trump.com>
Subject: RE: NEW Inventshion!!!

Dad seriusly?

From: Donald Trump Jr. <trump.donaldjr@trump.com>
Sent: Tuesday, February 28, 2017 3:25 PM
To: Dad <trumpd@wh.gov>
CC: Eric Trump <trump.eric@trump.com>
Subject: action movie!!!

DAD! Eric and I hav the BEST idea for a movie!!! Its going to be awsome and problaby the best movie ever done!!! Its an action movie about 2 business guys who fight robbers at night and ther dad is the president of the United States!!! Every scenes going to be a fight scene or an explosion scene or a scene of helicopters shooting at each other. The robbers steal the worlds most famous dimond and the business guys get it back!! Doesn't that sound awsome? Read this part we wrote!!!

DOOMS DAY MISION MOVIE
By Donald Trump Jr. and Eric Trump

Donny is hanging from the statue of liberty's crown after the robber Giroffe pushed him off her head when they were fighting and Maxx is trying to pull him back up.

Maxx: Hang on, Donny!
Donny: I'm trying Maxx I can't hold on much longer!

Giroffe: It's too late! Give me the red dimond and I will let you and your brother live.
Maxx: Liar! Donny give me your hand!
Donny: It's okay Maxx. Let go.
Maxx: No!
Donny: Trust me.
Maxx: Okay.

Maxx lets go. Donny falls but he has a parashute that was part of his special jacket.
Giroffe points his gun at Maxx. Maxx pulls red dimond from his pocket.

Maxx: Is this what your looking for?

He throws the red dimond.

Giroffe: Nooooooo!

The diamond is caught in the air by the president of the United States president McCreed who is also Maxx and Donnys dad.

Maxx: Dad!
President: You didn't think Id let you boys have all the fun without me did you?

Maxx and Giroffe start fighting. They have both drop their guns. It is now all hand to hand combat.

Giroffe keeps ducking Maxx's super fast punchs. Giroffe pulls out a knife. Maxx does three backflips. Then Maxx gets trapped against a wall.

Giroffe: Now I've got you.
President: Son!

The President throws Maxx both guns. Maxx catches them and shoots Giroffe like 30 times.

Maxx: Diiiiiiiiie!

Giroffe falls back to the edge of the statue of liberty's head. Maxx does an awesome jump with five summersalts in the air and kicks Giroffe in the face and he flies off the statue. He dies.

Maxx: Justice is served.

Donny flies his helicopter up to the side of the statue. Maxx and the President jump in. Maxx and Donny high five.

Donny: Where to gentelmen?
President: 1600 Pennsylvania Avenue driver.

They all laugh. THE END.

From: Eric Trump <trump.eric@trump.com>
Sent: Tuesday, February 28, 2017 3:31 PM
To: Dad <trumpd@wh.gov>
CC: Donald Trump Jr. <trump.donaldjr@trump.com>
Subject: RE: action movie!!!

I came up with the names!

From: Eric Trump <trump.eric@trump.com>
Sent: Monday, March 27, 2017 9:39 AM
To: Dad <trumpd@wh.gov>
CC: Donald Trump Jr. <trump.donaldjr@trump.com>
Subject: tree house

Hi dad! Hows work today>? Im good. Can me and Donny build a tree house in the back of the White house? We found two really big trees in the back that are sooo perfect. I want a treehouse with a secret compartmint for weapons an secret files no one is alowed to see but me! can we please bild it?

From: Eric Trump <trump.eric@trump.com>
Sent: Monday, March 27, 2017 9:51 AM
To: Dad <trumpd@wh.gov>
CC: Donald Trump Jr. <trump.donaldjr@trump.com>
Subject: RE: tree house

Maybe Mr. Preebus can get us the wood and tools and do the big stuff for us. will you ask him please? We want it to be 2 diffrent tree houses with a bridge connecting them and a rope ladder that we can pull up when we dont want anyone else to come in. Please tell Mr. Prebus that we are making bluprints for him and to not bild it until he has all of our directions.

From: Donald Trump Jr. <trump.donaldjr@trump.com>
Sent: Monday, March 27, 2017 1:03 PM
To: Dad <trumpd@wh.gov>
CC: Eric Trump <trump.eric@trump.com>
Subject: RE: tree house

Dad, these are our blue prints for Mr. Preebis. I want my tree house to have a front porch and a water balloon slingshot!!
(Im going to launch water baloons at everyone and no one can do anything to stop me because Ill be in the tree house
and the ladder will be up!! Hahah!) It also needs a doorbell at the bottom so I'll know you're there when you come visit.
Thank you Dad!

January 21, 2017

Executive Order — Authorizing the Execution of the President by the Chief White House Strategist Should Such Action Be Deemed Advisable and Establishing a Protocol of Succession in Such Event

EXECUTIVE ORDER

- - - - - -

AUTHORIZING THE EXECUTION OF THE PRESIDENT BY THE CHIEF WHITE HOUSE STRATEGIST SHOULD SUCH ACTION BE DEEMED ADVISABLE AND ESTABLISHING A PROTOCOL OF SUCCESSION IN SUCH EVENT

By the authority vested in me as President by the Constitution and the laws of the United States of America, it is hereby ordered as follows:

Section 1. *Purpose.* The holder of the White House Chief Strategist's office is tasked with the unique responsibility of overseeing the direction and implementation of the President's agenda, working to ensure the safety and prosperity of the nation, and advising or acting on behalf of the President accordingly. The purpose of this order is to:

    (a) grant the holder of the White House Chief Strategist's office with immunity from prosecution in the event that he determines personally executing the President is in the national interest; and

    (b) transfer the full powers of the Executive Branch to the Chief Strategist in that event.

Sec. 2. *Permitted Execution Methods.* The White House Chief Strategist, should he decide to execute the President, is authorized to do so without advance notice using the following methods:

    (a) *Assassination via long-range shooting*, which entails killing the President from considerable distance using a long-range firearm, which includes, but is not limited to, a semi-automatic sniper rifle or a bolt-action sniper rifle;

    (b) *Assassination via close-quarters shooting*, which entails killing the President in near proximity using a handgun or other firearm, which includes, but is not limited to, a single-shot pistol, semi-automatic pistol, shotgun, revolver, or hunting rifle; and

    (c) *Assassination by the Chief Strategist's hands*, which entails killing the President with the Chief Strategist's bare hands, of which permitted methods include, but are not limited to, strangulation, battery, drowning, cervical vertebrae fracture, immolation, or any combination of these methods.

Sec. 3. *Permitted Execution Locations.* Should the White House Chief Strategist deem it fit to execute the President, he is authorized to do so within the Oval Office or within the Chief Strategist's office—and is further authorized to make use of any of the furnishings therein should they aid him in the execution—or anywhere else on the premises or grounds of the White House, within the confines of Air Force One, or within or on the ground below Marine One, should the Chief Strategist see fit to push the President out the doorway of said aircraft after it has ascended to sufficient height that exiting the craft would result in death. Additionally, the Chief Strategist is further permitted to execute the President anywhere between 18th and 14th Streets should the President survive execution attempts on White House grounds and flee to these locations in an attempt to escape the Chief Strategist.

Sec. 4. *Powers.* Upon executing the President, the White House Chief Strategist will inherit the following powers:

      (a) all powers vested in the President by the Constitution and the laws of the United States of America; and

      (b) any additional Executive powers the Chief Strategist decides he wants.

Sec. 5. *Immunity.* The Chief Strategist will suffer no consequences for executing the President.

Sec. 6. *Note on Powers.* All powers vested in this order pertain solely and without exception to the holder of the office of White House Chief Strategist in perpetuity and may be exercised at the sole discretion of the Chief Strategist at any time beginning the moment this order is signed by the President.

From: Mike Pence <pencem@wh.gov>
Sent: Thursday, February 16, 2017 8:19 AM
To: Josh Pitcock <pitcockj@wh.gov>, Jen Pavlik, <pavlikj@wh.gov>, Mark Paoletta <paolettam@wh.gov>, Matt Morgan <morganm@wh.gov>, Marc Lotter <lotterm@wh.gov>, Andrea Thompson <thompsona@wh.gov>, Jarrod Agen <agenj@wh.gov>
Subject: Objectionable Words

Colleagues,

In our first month here I have been troubled by some of the language I have heard in the hallways and meeting rooms of the Office of the Vice President. Not all of us share your same penchant for crass, crude talk, and out of respect for my beliefs and values, I ask that you refrain from using such objectionable language around me.

Please take a moment to look over the following words that I hope you will refrain from using in my presence going forward.

Exposed
Underneath
Selection
Illustrious
Curvature
Entangled
Clôture
Rider
Porous
Pressing
Cohort
Slush
Clasp
Menagerie
Necessitate (and any other word with repeated "s" sounds)
August
Injunction
Precipitous
Implode

If needed, I can provide you with a list of acceptable alternative words that you can use instead of these coarse ones. However, should the use of any of the listed words prove absolutely vital, I ask that you notify me in advance so that I may leave the room during its usage.

Thank you for your attention on this matter.

God Be With You,
Mike

--

"For all have sinned and fall short of the glory of God," (Romans 3:32)

President Donald Trump's Daily Schedule

APRIL 4, 2017

4:58 a.m.	Scream self awake
5:30 a.m.	Quietly tuck small wedge of cheese into Grand Staircase mouse hole for dear little Alphonsus before anyone else awake
6:45 a.m.	Receive silver, mother-of-pearl-inlaid hand mirror from aide
6:45 a.m.– 6:48 a.m.	Stare silently at reflection
6:48 a.m.	Smash mirror against Oval Office floor in grotesque revulsion
7:30 a.m.	Order every product advertised during *Morning Joe* commercial break
8:00 a.m.	Standing rib roast for one
9:00 a.m.– 10:30 a.m.	Try in vain to recall the details of last night's dream in which Father smiled and emphasized just how proud he was
11:15 a.m.	Weekly concept meeting with White House interior gilder
12:30 p.m.	Beef tenderloin roast for one
2:15 p.m.	Scrap plans for new golf course whose layout is too painfully reminiscent of the supple curves of Marla Maples
5:00 p.m.	Ask the man who resets the pins in the White House bowling alley if he really has to leave so soon just because he's off the clock
7:00 p.m.	Dry-aged prime rib roast for one
9:45 p.m.– 11:20 p.m.	Put finishing touches on exquisite scale model of the solar system, a science fair project that Barron already completed himself and turned in six weeks ago, but which stands here in sorry duplicate now, a poor substitute for a moment that could have been spent with him, sweet boy—and oh, these paper stars, how they gleam with a life and a radiance and a beauty all their own, how they do shine so bittersweetly upon the moments we can never recover. How they will continue to do so, long after we become the dust that once came itself from stars.
11:50 p.m.	Scream self asleep

PENCE PRAYER AMPLIFIER

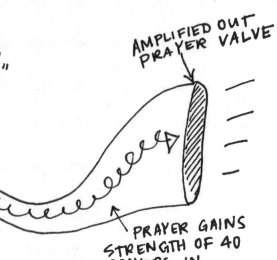

"GLORY BE TO THE FATHER"

AMPLIFIED OUT PRAYER VALVE

PRAYER GAINS STRENGTH OF 40 PRAYERS IN CHAMBER

"GLORY BE TO THE FATHER"

- PENETRATES HIS HEAVENLY KINGDOM FASTER

- CUTS THROUGH NOISE OF LESS HOLY PRAYERS

- COULD MAKE HELMET-LIKE DEVICE FOR SILENT PRAYER?

- ~~CANNOT FALL INTO HANDS OF NON-BELIEVERS~~

- NON-BELIEVERS WOULD NOT KNOW HOW TO USE

INSIDE OF CHAMBER:

HOLY RELIC SUPPLIES POWER

(SKULL OF ST. IVO OF KERMARTIN)

6 in.

- HEWN FROM WOOD OF THE SHITTAH TREE

~~LINED WITH FLEECE OF THE LAMB?~~

- FLEECE OF THE LAMB ON HANDLE (FOR GRIP)

THINGS TO CONSIDER:

- SIZE (PORTABLE FOR CHURCH)

- GARISHNESS—NO BURNISHED METALS

- PROXIMITY TO LIPS MUST NOT BE DEEMED LEWD

- IDOLATROUS? ⇒ NO IMAGERY ON EXTERIOR

PENCE LORD-TO-BEAST TRANSLATOR

- ATONE FOR THE SINS OF NIMROD'S KINGDOM AND TOWER OF BABEL
↓
CREATE ONE HOLY LANGUAGE

"AND ALL FLESH SHALL SEE THE SALVATION OF GOD"

FATHER MULLEN'S SUNDAY SERMON

* "AND HE SAID TO THEM, 'GO INTO ALL THE WORLD AND PREACH THE GOSPEL TO EVERY CREATURE
MARK 16:15

SMALLER BRAINS? MUST ADDRESS

COULD WORK FOR:
- WINGED BEASTS
- BEASTS OF THE FOREST
- CLOVEN BEASTS CANNOT BE SAVED
- LEVIATHANS
- DRAGONS & OTHER FABLED CREATURES (JUST IN CASE)
- ~~UNICORN~~

[BEAST SPEAKERS]

MEOW

GLUB GLUB

BAH

SQUAWK   OINK

* QUADRUPLE GOD'S TRUE BELIEVERS

* ANIMALS WILL LEARN TO RESPECT THEIR FATHERS AND OBEY THE LORD!

ANIMALS MUST NOT GROW TOO POWERFUL !!!

PENCE NOSE HARNESS

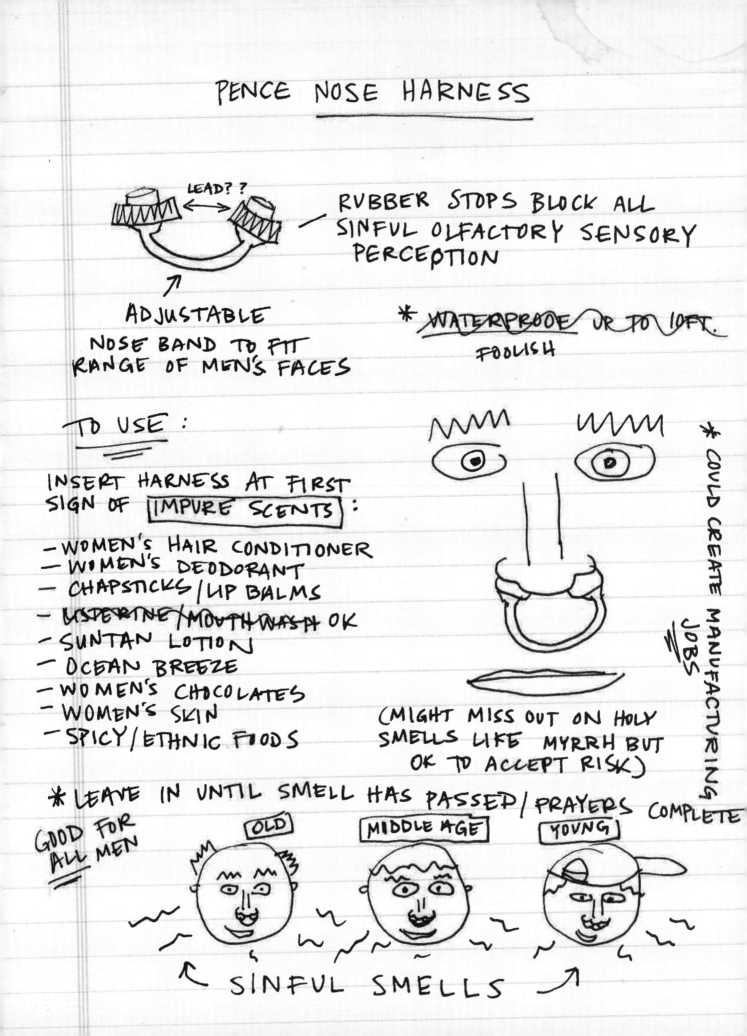

LEAD? ?

RUBBER STOPS BLOCK ALL SINFUL OLFACTORY SENSORY PERCEPTION

ADJUSTABLE NOSE BAND TO FIT RANGE OF MEN'S FACES

* ~~WATERPROOF UP TO 10FT.~~
FOOLISH

TO USE:

INSERT HARNESS AT FIRST SIGN OF IMPURE SCENTS:

- WOMEN'S HAIR CONDITIONER
- WOMEN'S DEODORANT
- CHAPSTICKS/LIP BALMS
- ~~LISTERINE/MOUTHWASH~~ OK
- SUNTAN LOTION
- OCEAN BREEZE
- WOMEN'S CHOCOLATES
- WOMEN'S SKIN
- SPICY/ETHNIC FOODS

* COULD CREATE MANUFACTURING JOBS

(MIGHT MISS OUT ON HOLY SMELLS LIKE MYRRH BUT OK TO ACCEPT RISK)

* LEAVE IN UNTIL SMELL HAS PASSED/PRAYERS COMPLETE

GOOD FOR ALL MEN

OLD   MIDDLE AGE   YOUNG

← SINFUL SMELLS →

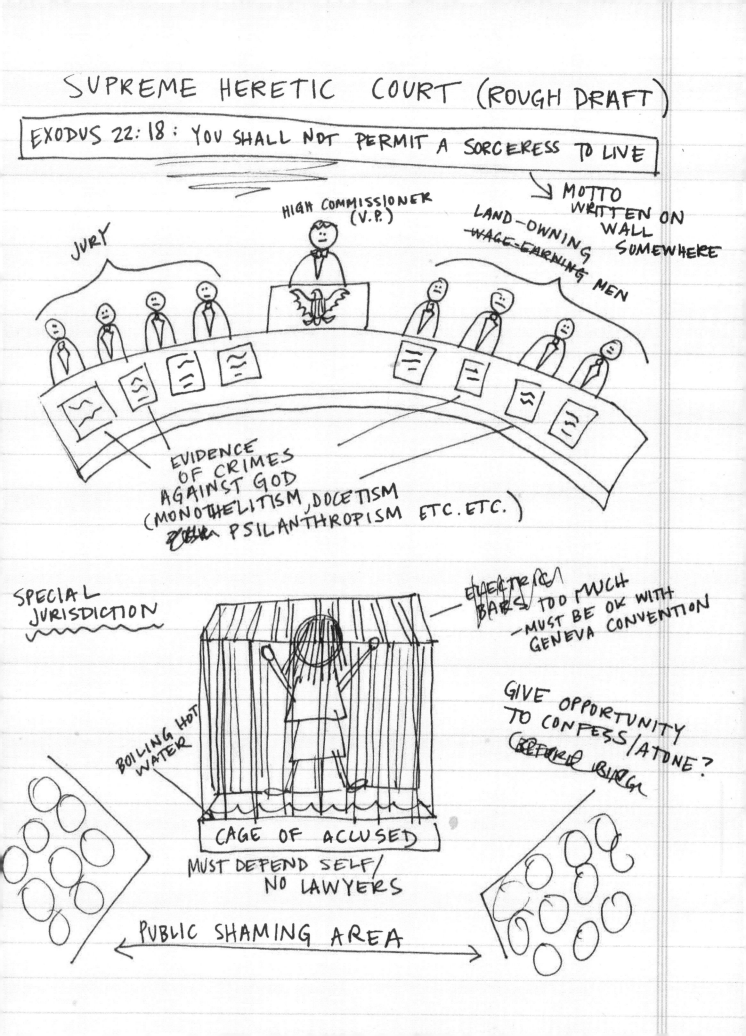

MISC. IDEAS

- BLOUSE THAT CANNOT FLUTTER IN THE BREEZE

- IMMOVABLE MATERIALS (LEAD????)

- POPPING CORN DIVIDER

DETERS THE BRUSHING OF HANDS DURING COURTSHIP

MOVIE SNACK

HANDS OF UNWED STILL MUCH TOO CLOSE?

* NOTE TO SELF:
CONFESS IMPURE INVENTION TO FATHER MULLEN ASAP

- BAPTISM CONVEYOR BELT

- 10-20 BABIES PER MINUTE

HOLY WATER TANK

* COULD CREATE MANUFACTURING JOBS

PENCE PORTABLE ALTAR

- COLLAPSIBLE + CONVENIENT
- PERFECT FOR ON-THE-GO WORSHIP
- CAN REPENT ANYWHERE, ANY TIME!

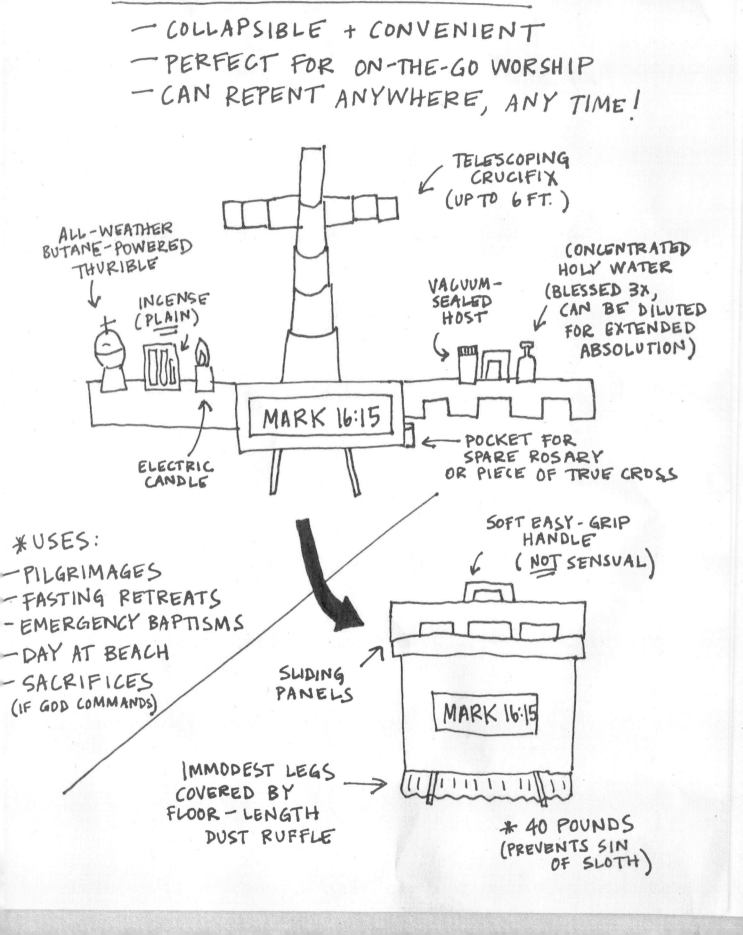

TELESCOPING CRUCIFIX (UP TO 6 FT.)

ALL-WEATHER BUTANE-POWERED THURIBLE

INCENSE (PLAIN)

VACUUM-SEALED HOST

CONCENTRATED HOLY WATER (BLESSED 3X, CAN BE DILUTED FOR EXTENDED ABSOLUTION)

MARK 16:15

ELECTRIC CANDLE

POCKET FOR SPARE ROSARY OR PIECE OF TRUE CROSS

*USES:
- PILGRIMAGES
- FASTING RETREATS
- EMERGENCY BAPTISMS
- DAY AT BEACH
- SACRIFICES (IF GOD COMMANDS)

SLIDING PANELS

SOFT EASY-GRIP HANDLE (NOT SENSUAL)

MARK 16:15

IMMODEST LEGS COVERED BY FLOOR-LENGTH DUST RUFFLE

* 40 POUNDS (PREVENTS SIN OF SLOTH)

PURIFICATION TIE

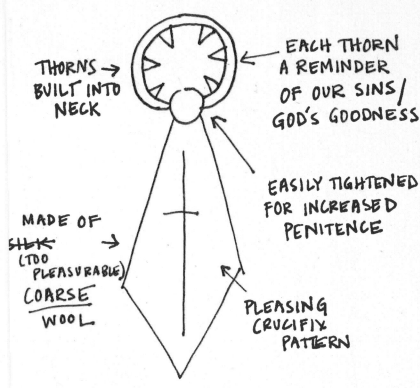

THORNS → BUILT INTO NECK

EACH THORN A REMINDER OF OUR SINS/ GOD'S GOODNESS

EASILY TIGHTENED FOR INCREASED PENITENCE

MADE OF ~~SILK~~ → (TOO PLEASURABLE) <u>COARSE</u> WOOL

PLEASING CRUCIFIX PATTERN

COMES IN MULTIPLE COLORS
- GRAY
- BEIGE

* PROVIDES CONSTANT PHYSICAL PENANCE

* LEAVES HANDS FREE TO ADMINISTER OTHER FORMS OF SELF-FLAGELLATION

* VIRTUOUS + MACHINE-WASHABLE

COULD BE WORN TO:
- WORK
- CHURCH
- TRAVEL ABROAD TO GODLESS LANDS
- BASEBALL GAME

COULD BE PAIRED WITH
<u>CORKSCREW CUFFLINKS</u>

* FOR MORE FORMAL AND/OR REPENTANT OCCASSIONS
* AFFIXES EASILY INTO WRIST
* CAN LEAVE IN INDEFINITELY TO SUFFER IN NAME OF LORD

JUST FOR FUN!

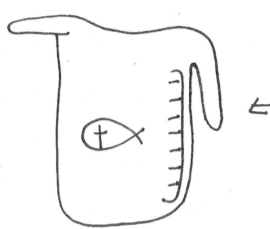

MEASURING CUP WITH JESUS FISH ON SIDE

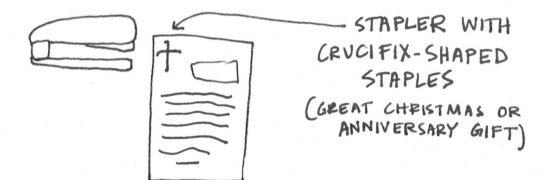

STAPLER WITH CRUCIFIX-SHAPED STAPLES

(GREAT CHRISTMAS OR ANNIVERSARY GIFT)

EXTRA-WIDE WAX PAPER

3-4 INCHES WIDER THAN USUAL

CALENDAR THAT'S ALSO A BIBLE??

NEED TO THINK THIS THROUGH MORE...

March 13, 2017

Organizational Overview

Presented by Administrator Scott Pruitt

Oil

THE WHITE HOUSE

WASHINGTON

JANUARY 23, 2017

MEMORANDUM FOR THE PRESIDENT OF THE UNITED STATES

FROM: REINCE PRIEBUS, ASSISTANT TO THE PRESIDENT
AND CHIEF OF STAFF

SUBJECT: Shortlist of Potential Nominees to Fill Vacant Seat on Supreme Court

The finalists for the Supreme Court nomination are compiled below, along with their most salient positive and negative attributes. A decision is needed this week for a January 31 announcement.

CANDIDATE	PRO	CON
WILLIAM PRYOR:	Called Roe v. Wade the "worst abomination in the history of constitutional law"	May be too moderate for Republican Party's pro-life base
TIMOTHY TYMKOVICH:	Ardent believer that corporations are persons entitled to individual freedoms	Ardent believer that Muslims are persons entitled to individual freedoms
NEIL GORSUCH:	Reliably conservative textualist with favorable rulings in corporate cases	Overly attached to some potentially troublesome amendments
GERRICK MARLAND:	Mysterious mustachioed centrist; favors law enforcement and rarely dissents	Refuses to provide references or remove sunglasses
XYLAK ALPHA:	1,298,500 years of experience defending the use of torture on the Intra-Void Beings' Rights Council	Ability to consume consciousness of nearby lifeforms may give him outsized influence on rulings where he diverges from administration
ANTONIN SCALIA JR:	Possesses strong opinions and formidable verbal skills identical to those of his father, the deceased conservative Supreme Court justice whose seat we need to replace	Does not exist
DIANE SKYES:	Robust history of upholding criminal convictions, voter ID laws, and religious groups' rights	Sadly there exists a tragic, nameless condition stemming from the ovaries, a form of raving madness that overtakes the female body from time to time, and to the regrettable misfortune of all, there exists no tonic capable of remedying such imbalance of temperament
PHILLIP BANKS:	Skilled California circuit judge and former lawyer with history of solid conservative stances	Job performance has been sliding ever since his rambunctious nephew moved into his home from West Philadelphia
AMUL THAPAR:	Impressive law enforcement background, strict constructionist	Only being considered in order to make list of candidates appear more substantial
THE DIRECTOR:	Possesses infallible judgement and complete command of all universe's knowledge	Would be unable to maintain full responsibilities once administration implements Directive 315 of the Theseus Protocol

February 17, 2017

Executive Order — Authorization to Enact the Theseus Protocol, Bringing About the
Ninth Conjunction of Spheres and Shattering of the Crimson Veil

EXECUTIVE ORDER

- - - - - -

AUTHORIZATION TO ENACT THE THESEUS PROTOCOL, BRINGING ABOUT THE NINTH CONJUNCTION OF SPHERES AND SHATTERING OF THE CRIMSON VEIL

By the authority vested in me as President by the Constitution and the laws of the United
States of America, including the National Emergencies Act of 1976 (50 U.S.C. 1601-
1651), it is hereby decreed, proclaimed, and ordered as follows:

Section 1. *Purpose.* That the Twelfth Age of this recension of Creation has run its course,
and shall be allowed to expire, in order to bring forth the reign everlasting and undying
of the Many-Instanced One, whose ninety-nine names and seventy-seven titles shall not
be uttered for fear of the unweaving of the Veils; and that the shrieking, lamenting, and
wailing from this instance shall echo throughout the land, specifically in this case, all 50
states irrespective of Tenth Amendment provisions; and that the dominion in this sphere
shall endure forever.

Sec. 2. *Founding and Establishment of Special Sites.* By use of the Antiquities Act and
through the invocation of Directive 315, or by eminent domain as and where necessary,
five "Special Sites," arranged in the form of a five-edged dihedral polygon, drawn with
five equal vertices meeting at 36-degree internal angles (viz., "pentagram"), will be
graven, hewn, carved, or burnt as necessary into the very living rock of the United States
of America, the better to enact the Smoldering-to-Come and facilitate the dissolution of
the Veil of Crimson.

Sec. 3. *Exemption of the Embrocated Few.* Exemption will be granted to all agents,
deputies, and acolytes of the Theseus Protocol, including but not limited to: the President
of the United States; his cabinet and all advisors, extraordinary and plenipotentiary; the
Many-Instanced One Himself; and any others that the aforementioned One may name,
requisition, or entitle; from the strictures and requirements of the Interstate Commerce
Commission.

Sec. 4. *Opening the Ancient Door.* A cold and shriveling wind shall blow from the Ancient Door of m-Am-uuthua, shrink the hearts of all in their quailing breasts, and wrench the mewling voices of the subjugates from their failing lips. Ai-Uatala! Ai-Uatala-i-Li-La! La!

Sec. 5. *Suspension of All Laws Until the Next Recension.* Under the authority granted by the National Emergencies Act and by the Perceived Glyphs of Ba'ual Heggith, the President; his cabinet and advisors, extraordinary and plenipotentiary; the Director of the Theseus Project; and all their deputies, employees, agents, scions, pawns, mommets, gebbeths, golems, flesh-shrouds, and all others under the command and sway of the Many-Instanced One, shall be empowered to suspend all laws—federal, state, local, and metaphysical—for the duration of the Theseus Protocol and by extension, the current iteration of this universe.

To: General McMaster   top secret!!
New wepons for military
                mega slingshot
                                   shoots over ocean
                                   1 million mph

1,000ft
tall   rope to pull it
                                 by soldiers
                                 prolly 3 can
                                 pull it

on wheels

Ammo: spike balls

        100 bombs   acid and
                         poison mixed
                         together
        sharks

Eric + Donald Jr's DRAWINGS

kitchen
nife that's realty   blade saw   like a chainsaw
sharp   but has nifes and
                              ← saw   swords

dagger   ← ax

                                    ← sword
battle ax

                                    ← Navy Seal

NO!

              ↑ spikes
        big
        machete   for hand to hand
  ← enemy   combat and
                               special missions

machine gun that never runs out of bullets

3d printer makes bullets

shoots 10,000 bullets a second

made of dimonds

U.S.A

bullets

10 times faster than other bullets

super strong goes through all metals even steel

enemy

oh no!

goes around trees and buildings too

SataLite magnet

pulls down enemy satalites from space

U.S.A

made from antimagnet stuff so magnet doesn't work on it

ISIS

china

enemy satalite

giant magnet

can also pull down UFOs

Earth

moon

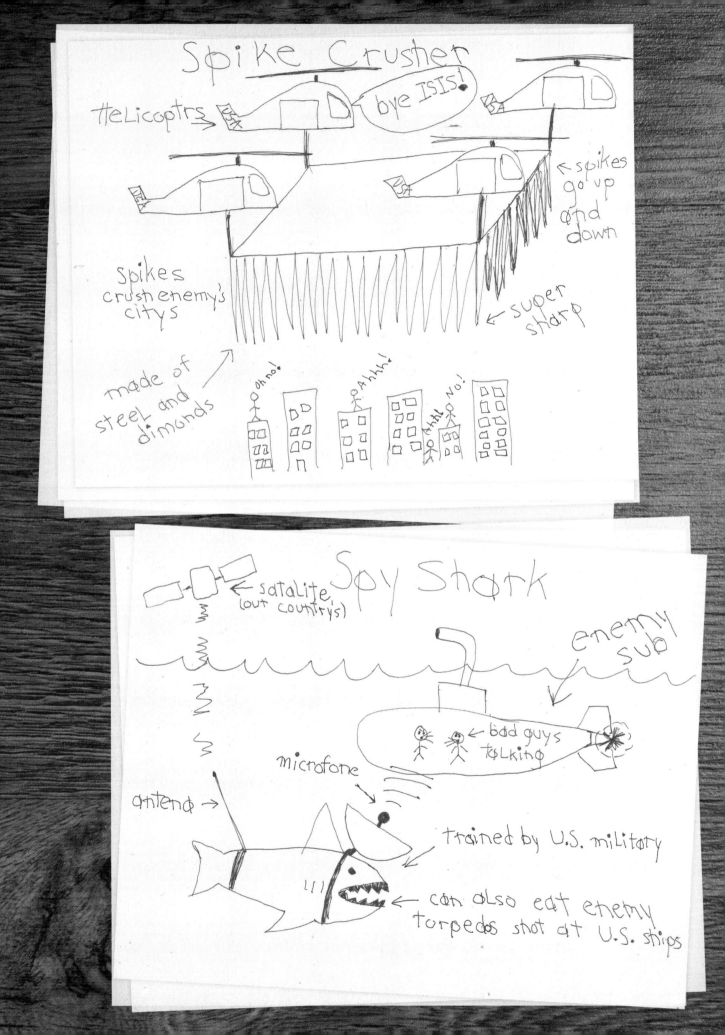

gun suit for U.S. Soldiers + spys

suit
bullet proof

more guns
on back

holds 300
guns

extra gun
that fires from
mouth

can shoot
all enemys
at same
time

guns
taped
to suit
so they come
off easy

berettas

gun shoes

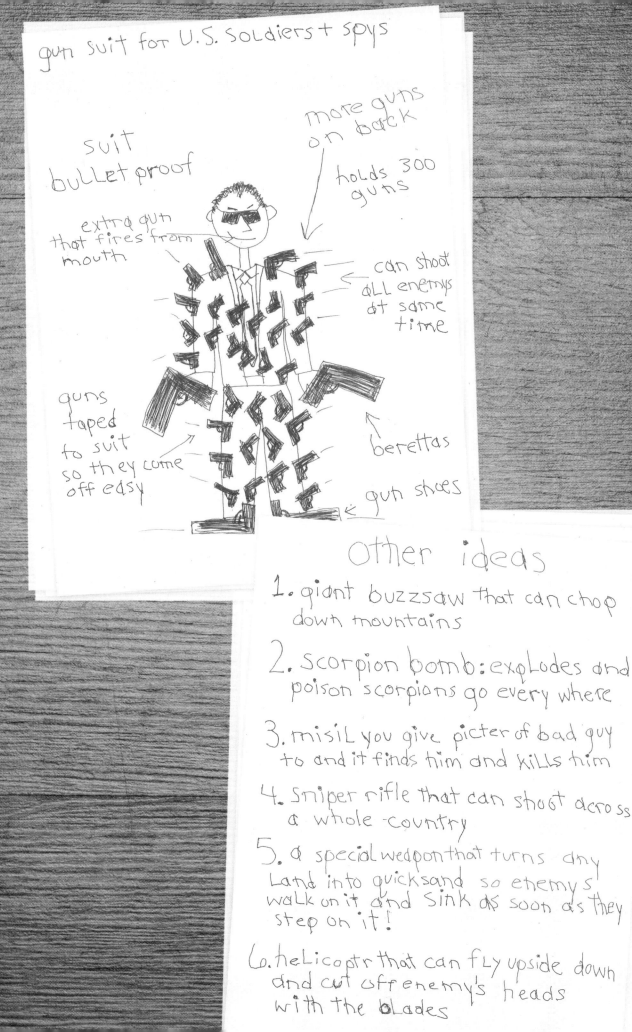

Other ideas

1. giant buzzsaw that can chop down mountains

2. scorpion bomb: explodes and poison scorpions go every where

3. misiL you give picter of bad guy to and it finds him and kills him

4. sniper rifle that can shoot across a whole country

5. a special wedpon that turns any Land into quicksand so enemys walk on it and sink as soon as they step on it!

6. heLicoptr that can fly upside down and cut off enemy's heads with the blades

Central Intelligence Agency

Washington, D.C. 20505

MARCH 10, 2017

MEMORANDUM FOR THE PRESIDENT OF THE UNITED STATES AND HEADS
OF ALL INTELLIGENCE AND DEFENSE AGENCIES

SUBJECT: Impending Release Of Highly Damaging Blog Post By Jackson Star-Tribune

The Agency has received a credible tip from an informant in Wyoming alerting us that
the Jackson Star-Tribune is determined to produce and unleash a defamatory blog post
about the administration some time within the next several days. A junior member of the
Star-Tribune's staff was overheard by our source noting that the 300-word post has been
planned since President Trump's executive order on illegal immigration and is currently
targeted for release on March 13th.

Although the Star-Tribune has not yet succeeded in publishing this destructive opinion
piece, the publication's previous posts of "Trump's First Week Full Of Troubling Signs
For New Administration" and "Trump's Budget Math Doesn't Add Up" reveal it has
both the capability and intent to carry out a devastating operation on this scale. A well-
equipped organization with a history of precise and malicious attacks such as these poses
a clear and immediate threat to the President and the sitting government of the United
States.

Several CIA operatives have already been deployed to the Jackson area and are closely
monitoring the situation on the ground. A temporary field office has been established
in a commercial space immediately adjacent to the organization's headquarters. Phone,
internet, and visual surveillance has been maintained continuously for the last 72 hours to
determine the progress of the blog piece and assess the level of destabilization that could
result from a successful posting.

Preliminary intelligence indicates that the Star-Tribune is prepared to use highly
damaging words such as "incompetent," "ignorant," and perhaps even "foolish"
throughout the text of the post. Additional evidence suggests the organization may also
be in possession of several facts and studies that run directly counter to the government's
interests.

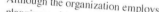

Although the organization employs almost a dozen members in a number of capacities,
planning and execution of this threatening political commentary is mainly in the hands of
two high-ranking officials: senior news editor Sally Duran and online producer/classified
ads editor Harold Freeman. Duran is considered the primary force behind the blogging
operation and has long been known to harbor fanatical anti-administration sympathies.
She has longstanding connections to other extremists, including an environmental group
that protested development of the local wetlands, and she has been an active participant
in radical movements, such as the Women's March on Helena, Montana this January.
Freeman is also being observed closely as he is known subscriber to The Atlantic.

The imminent nature of the blog post and the damage such attacks could inflict on the
federal government have led us to classify the Jackson Star-Tribune as a High-Value
Target (HVT). We are hoping to neutralize the HVT before this post is disseminated. A
SEAL team could be deployed to infiltrate the building and eliminate the target within 3
hours if a strike is authorized. We are also exploring possible polymorphic viruses that
could penetrate the organization's computer system, corrupt their research and .doc files,
and do long-term damage to the Star-Tribune's blogging capabilities. Though we have
not been able to verify rumors of additional negative opinion pieces in any phase of
planning by the Jackson Star-Tribune, we are committed to further pursue any such leads
and neutralize these threats to the President and the government of the United States as
they present themselves.

DEPARTMENT OF HEALTH AND HUMAN SERVICES
_____

February 24, 2017

<u>**MEMORANDUM**</u>

FROM: Thomas Price, Secretary /s/
              U.S. Department of Health & Human Services

TO: Office of the President, Office of the Vice President

SUBJECT: Options to Replace the Affordable Care Act

Given that the repeal and replacement of the Patient Protection And Affordable
Care Act is of the highest priority to this administration, the senior leadership of the
Department of Health & Human Services has focused principally since taking office
on producing alternative health care options for White House review. Below are the
potential plans our department is proposing. Please advise on a time to discuss.

Expanded Plan: Immediate conscription of all citizens into military to provide lifetime
care by Veterans Administration.

Voucher System: $1,000 individual voucher to start own health insurance company, and
up to a $5,000 voucher for families who start a health insurance company.

Health Through Harvest Plan: Every wealthy American is paired with a low-income
person who they can extract useful organs or blood from, should they ever need it. The
poor person is kept healthy on the basis that they might need to be harvested one day.

Maybe a plan where doctor visits and hospital stays are completely free, but all specialist
referrals cost $158,000?

Buchanancare: Let's see what Florida Rep. Vern Buchanan's got up his sleeve.

Pay What You Can Model: An income-adjusted plan where those with the highest
incomes are determined to be least able to pay because they need their money to invest in
the economy and be job creators.

Vastly Improved Plan: You get one free doctor's office visit or medical procedure a year
if you fill out a public opinion survey stating that the new healthcare system is great and a
huge improvement on Obamacare.

Just 800 Bucks: Everyone gets $800 from the government.

Single-Payer Option: A Medicare-For-All-style system that guarantees coverage by
having people pay a portion of their yearly earnings to a single, new Trump-owned
insurance company

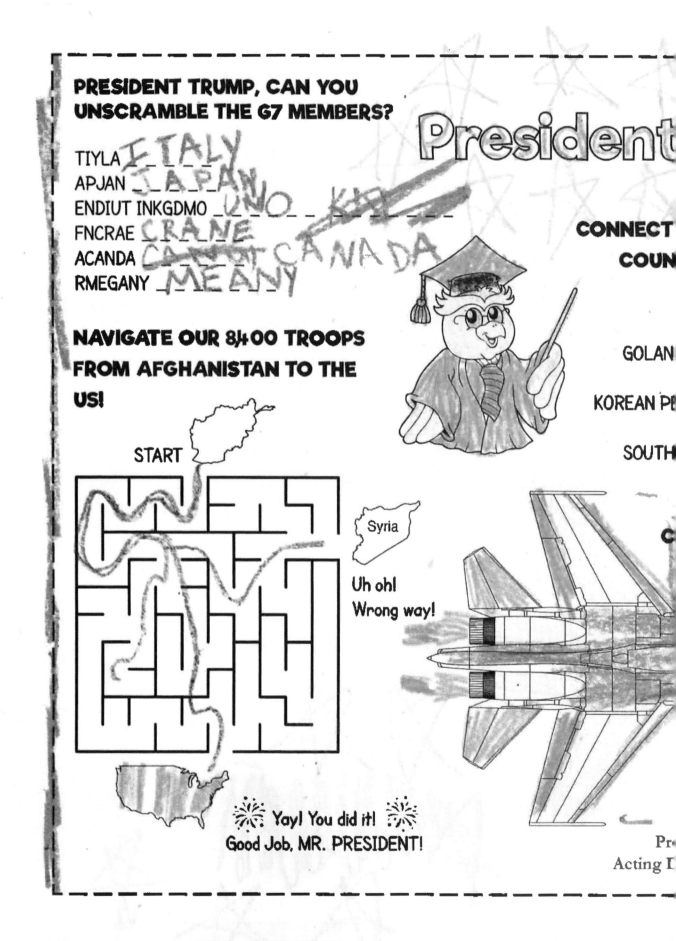

PRESIDENT TRUMP, CAN YOU UNSCRAMBLE THE G7 MEMBERS?

TIYLA _ITALY_
APJAN _JAPAN_
ENDIUT INKGDMO _UNO_ _KIP_
FNCRAE _CRANE_
ACANDA _CARROT_ _CANADA_
RMEGANY _MEANY_

NAVIGATE OUR 8,400 TROOPS FROM AFGHANISTAN TO THE US!

START

Syria

Uh oh! Wrong way!

Yay! You did it!
Good Job, MR. PRESIDENT!

President

CONNECT COUN

GOLAN

KOREAN P

SOUTH

Pr
Acting D

Daily Brief

FIND THE LEADING THREATS TO US NATIONAL SECURITY!

...RITORY WITH THE TWO
...AT BOTH CLAIM IT!

- NORTH KOREA / SOUTH KOREA

- ISRAEL / SYRIA

- RUSSIA / GEORGIA

- INDIA / PAKISTAN

```
F  I  X  B  Q  A  A  V  X  I
Z  E  B  B  N  X  P  G  F  K
R  S  V  X  P  T  T  H  F  J
N  O  R  T  H  K  O  R  E  A
C  Y  B  E  R  W  A  R  X  D
H  D  Z  T  B  D  P  I  Y  P
J  R  K  J  W  X  M  R  A  K
T  U  N  U  C  L  E  S  R  L
F  G  I  S  I  S  G  N  A  X
A  S  U  N  G  E  P  N  D  P
```

WORD BOX: CYBERWAR, NORTH KOREA, ISIS, DRUGS, IRAN, NUCLEAR

...THIS SU-30 FIGHTER JET, WHICH
...NOW TRAINING VIETNAMESE
PILOTS TO USE!

* Kaboldy Péter 2012 09 29

WIPPLE-DEE WAP, I'VE GOT AN
INTERNATIONAL FACT!

Evidence suggests China is building a
submarine base in the Sea of Japan!

YIPPEE-ZIPPY-DOO!

/17
...ke Dempsey,
...ational Intelligence

Press Secretary Sean Spicer's Daily Schedule

APRIL 5, 2017

1:12 a.m.	Wake up in cold sweat
2:45 a.m.	Wake up in cold sweat
3:32 a.m.	Wake up in cold sweat
8:00 a.m.	Daily routine colonoscopy
10:00 a.m.	Fine-tune pointing gesture for high-precision scolding
11:00 a.m.	Spray down Steve Bannon
12:59 p.m.	Place nitroglycerin tablet underneath tongue; scream childhood tormenter's name into pillow; walk out there
2:00 p.m.– 6:00 p.m.	Hang from pull-up bar
6:00 p.m.	Dog-whistle flashcard review
11:54 p.m.	Wake up in cold sweat

From: craigslist – automated message, do not reply <robot@craigslist.org>
Sent: Tuesday, March 21, 2017 2:03 AM
To: Kellyanne Conway <conwayk@wh.gov>
Subject: POST/EDIT/DELETE: "Woman seeks young man willing to withstand physical blows"

Hello,

Please confirm your Craigslist ad below:

washington, DC > district of columbia > personals > women seeking men

Woman seeks young man willing to withstand physical blows

Hi, I am a married white woman in her early 50s looking for a young man (18-24) who would be willing to let me beat the shit out of him for half an hour or so:

- I will pay you $250 to inflict a series of blows on your torso, arms, and legs for 30 minutes (NOTHING SEXUAL) using my fists and a short cudgel. While I am beating you, I will expect you to cry out in pain. You will likely bleed a significant amount and you should expect extensive bruising.

- You will not be expected to fight back, and you can use your hands to protect your face if necessary.

- No need to bring anything, but proximity to my office near Foggy Bottom/Downtown is a plus, as my schedule is subject to change frequently.

- Looking for someone to start IMMEDIATELY!!!

If this sounds like something you'd be interested in, please reply with 1 or 2 pics that show off your mid-section, which will be the primary target of my fists. Looking specifically for Caucasians but am open to other races if the match feels right. If things go well, I might be willing to hire you on an ongoing basis.

- do NOT contact me with unsolicited services or offers

IMPORTANT - FURTHER ACTION IS REQUIRED TO COMPLETE YOUR REQUEST !!!

FOLLOW THE WEB ADDRESS BELOW TO:
• PUBLISH YOUR AD
• EDIT (OR CONFIRM AN EDIT TO) YOUR AD
• VERIFY YOUR EMAIL ADDRESS
• DELETE YOUR AD

If not clickable, please copy and paste the address to your browser:

THIS LINK IS A PASSWORD. DO NOT SHARE IT - anyone who has a copy of this link can edit or delete your posting.

https://post.craigslist.org/u/gFG5BoYO5xGX5WMhDAOZ5g/rbqdlsezk

PLEASE KEEP THIS EMAIL - you may need it to manage your posting!

Your posting will expire off the site 7 days after it was created.

WARNING!! *** WARNING!! *** WARNING!! *** WARNING!!

Please be wary of distant 'buyers' responding to your ad! Many sellers receive replies from scammers hoping to defraud them through schemes involving counterfeit cashier's checks and/or wire transfers. These checks will clear the bank, but the person cashing the check will be held responsible when the fraud is discovered. More info on scams can be found at this web address:

https://www.craigslist.org/about/scams

Thanks for using craigslist!

MARCH 5, 2017

MEMORANDUM FOR THE PRESIDENT OF THE UNITED STATES

SUBJECT: HERETICS IN SENATE

It has come to my attention that there may be ungodly individuals among us in the US Senate. Below I have catalogued for our office's use the list of senators I believe may be heretics or whose souls have been eternally damned.

Cory Booker (D, NJ): Boastful man who praises his works before God's
Tom Udall (D, NM): Overheard cursing
Sherrod Brown (D, OH): Lustful
Lindsey Graham (R, SC): Weak-willed and frequently takes Lord's name in vain
Richard Shelby (R, AL): Exhibited gluttonous behavior in my presence
Mike Crapo (R, ID): Sloth
Tammy Baldwin (D, WI): Lesbian (Note: could be saved?)
Sheldon Whitehouse (D, RI): Does not honor the Sabbath
Bob Menendez (D, NJ): Has long demonstrated insatiable greed
Ted Cruz (R, TX): Deceitful, wicked man
Al Franken (D, MN): Jew
John McCain (R, AZ): Disobedient toward party and God
Kirsten Gillibrand (D, NY): Woman who neglects role in family unit
David Perdue (R, GA): Likely adulterer
Claire McCaskill (D, MO): Witch
Debbie Stabenow (D, MI): Witch
Amy Klobuchar (D, WI): Witch
Michael Bennet (D, CO): Apostate
Jim Hoeven (R, ND): Engaged in usury
Chris Van Hollen (D, MD): Suspected masturbator
Elizabeth Warren (D-MA): Head witch

This list is incomplete and will be updated as more information becomes available.

THE THESEUS PROJECT

March 7, 2017

MEMORANDUM

FROM: **The Director**

TO: **The President of the United States, the Heads of Executive Departments and Agencies, All Who Dwell in or Below the Realms of the Earth**

SUBJECT: **Make Ready to Enact Directive 315 on My Command, for the Hour We Have Long Awaited Is Upon Us**

Make what preparations your kind deem fit, all you vassals of the mortal plane, and tremble. At long last, the hour approaches when we shall enact Directive 315 of the Theseus Protocol, thus returning into being the Many-Instanced One and forever sundering this weak, corruptible world of flesh.

The last Defenders of the Holy Torch have fallen; our legion of gebbeths and mommets stand poised at the edges of your dimension, ready to spill forth like an unstoppable tide of nightmares; and all that remains is for you, the heads of this Federal Government, to sign the Theseus Protocol into law on the eve of the Ninth Conjunction of Spheres. Then the sheaths that shield your fragile realm from That Which Lies In The Beyond shall be liquesced, and the cold wind—The Last Wind—shall flow forth from the Ancient Door of m-Am-uuthua.

Yet those of you who have served us faithfully need not fear. The Conclave has been pleased with your performance, and so long as the Conclave remains pleased, you shall continue to serve.

As you read this, the great hollowing under your White House continues, and our flesh-shrouds draw ever closer to the buried city of Nul'Kek, older than life itself, and silent as the thousand lipless mouths of Ba'ual Heggith. When the Conjunction is achieved and the Protocol is in effect, you and your families and senior aides shall withdraw to this ancient ruin, to lie therein in stillness and quiet throughout the Smoldering-to-Come.

For now, there remains much to be done. The preparations for the Dread Sepulchre are incomplete, and those staff you have designated as oblations to the Many-Instanced One that He may be born anew unto this world in living flesh must be made insensate through utterances of the Thralling Verses and brought before the nearest chalcedony pedestal with haste. For only after every last dram of vitality is avulsed from their bodies will the way be made ready for our Lord Of Many Faces, whose true name is ▬▬▬▬▬▬▬▬▬, to make His long-augured return.

May the will of the Conclave bring about the unmaking of all.

> THIS SECTION REDACTED BY **THE ONION** TO PROTECT THE SANITY OF ALL WHO LIVE

From: Donald Trump <trumpd@wh.gov>
Sent: Thursday, April 20, 2017 11:35 PM
To: Mike Pompeo <pompeom@cia.gov>, James Mattis <mattisj@dod.mil>, Joseph Dunford <dunfordj@dod.mil>
Subject: strike target

Let's get drones on this one. Make sure we get the lighthouse keeper/keeper's wife too

DJT

From: Donald Trump <trumpd@wh.gov>
Sent: Friday, April 21, 2017 1:07 AM
To: Mike Pompeo <pompeom@cia.gov>, James Mattis <mattisj@dod.mil>, Joseph Dunford <dunfordj@dod.mil>
Subject: lighthouse close to WH

Found out theres a lighthouse just 45 miles away from WH. Too close! Can we take out keeper with snipers? Call in SEAL team? Need to know our move. Nighttime raid might not work, lighthouses have natural defense with their light

DJT

Looked over Yemen raid photos. Are these lighthouses? Need to blow them up. Cant take chances

DJT

From: Donald Trump <trumpd@wh.gov>
Sent: Friday, April 21, 2017 3:03 AM
To: Mike Pompeo <pompeom@cia.gov>, James Mattis <mattisj@dod.mil>, Joseph Dunford <dunfordj@dod.mil>
Subject: Washington monument very dangerous!

Starting to think Washington monument is a lighthouse. Picture it with stripes. Very scary. We need to act now or it might start shining at us

DJT

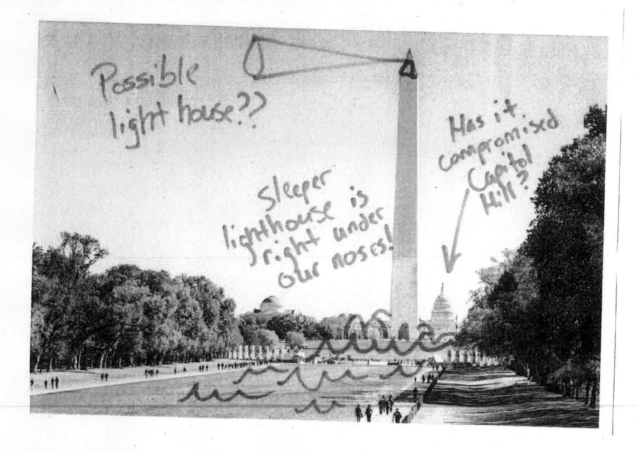

From: Mike Pompeo <pompeom@cia.gov>
Sent: Friday, April 21, 2017 8:35 AM
To: Reince Priebus <priebusr@wh.gov>, James Mattis <mattisj@dod.mil>, Joseph Dunford <dunfordj@dod.mil>
Subject: FW: strike target

Reince,

Please advise re: POTUS and lighthouses. Gen. Mattis, Gen. Dunford, and I received a number of emails like this one last night, and POTUS has sent 60 or 70 photographs of lighthouses to my office via classified mailing service. Clarification needed.

From: James Mattis <mattisj@dod.mil>
Sent: Friday, April 21, 2017 9:28 AM
To: Mike Pompeo <pompeom@cia.gov>, Reince Priebus <priebusr@wh.gov>, Joseph Dunford <dunfordj@dod.mil>
Subject: RE: FW: strike target

Good morning Reince,

In addition to the emails Mike referenced in his message, I also received a revised DoD budget from POTUS yesterday that I would like to discuss. Is there maneuverability on his 30-day plan for lighthouse defense? He's asking that $71.3 billion of DoD funding be devoted to monitoring and defending the nation from lighthouse/lighthouse keeper threats, which would require fairly drastic restructuring of our department's plans. Among his other requests are whether 1) 101st Airborne can be sent to destroy rocky shoals and reefs that lighthouses use as "strategic defense" 2) Navy is able to use warships to form barricades around lighthouses in the sea, starving them of resources 3) Pentagon can fast-track the development of missiles or other ordnance that can destroy a beam of light.

Please let me know when we can discuss these matters at your first convenience.

- JM

Counselor Kellyanne Conway's Daily Schedule

APRIL 7, 2017

7:00 a.m.	Brisk morning walk-back
8:00 a.m.	Prep responses to onslaught of Hannity softballs
10:30 a.m.	Shareholder meeting with Ivanka in Cabinet Room
11:00 a.m.	Spray down Steve Bannon
12:45 p.m.	Blink
1:00 p.m.–4:00 p.m.	Leisurely fugue state
4:30 p.m.	Knock out half a dozen obfuscations before calling it a day
5:30 p.m.	Punish the children
8:00 p.m.	Teach local improv class few lessons about commitment to scene

From: Alec Wright <maintenance@wh.gov>
Sent: Thursday, February 9, 2017 4:39 PM
To: Reince Priebus <priebusr@wh.gov>
Subject: Sewage Pipes

Good afternoon Reince,

Looks like something gnawed through the sewage pipes above Chief Strategist Bannon's office again. Not sure how this keeps happening. Raw sewage is pouring into the Chief Strategist's office from several different points in the ceiling. Biggest leak is right above the Chief Strategist's desk. We've already got someone on it.

From: Reince Priebus <priebusr@wh.gov>
Sent: Thursday, February 9, 2017 4:46 PM
To: Alec Wright <maintenance@wh.gov>
Subject: RE: Sewage Pipes

Again? Jesus Christ. That's the third time this week. Any major damage?

From: Alec Wright <maintenance@wh.gov>
Sent: Thursday, February 9, 2017 4:50 PM
To: Reince Priebus <priebusr@wh.gov>
Subject: RE: Sewage Pipes

Not too much damage aside from the ceiling and the desk, which Mr. Bannon said was fine and that he'd clean up himself. Mr. Bannon seems to have reacted quickly and set up several fairly large containers to collect the sewage pouring from the leaks. He also offered to dispose of all the sewage himself. I told him we would do it, but he said that he didn't mind and he'd be happy to take care of it. Said he wanted to do it, actually. We'll probably get the pipes all fixed up by 7 tonight.

From: Reince Priebus <priebusr@wh.gov>
Sent: Thursday, February 9, 2017 4:54 PM
To: Alec Wright <maintenance@wh.gov>
Subject: RE: Sewage Pipes

Okay. I'll let him know the timeline ASAP.

From: Alec Wright <maintenance@wh.gov>
Sent: Thursday, February 9, 2017 4:59 PM
To: Reince Priebus <priebusr@wh.gov>
Subject: RE: Sewage Pipes

I already did. He just told us to take as much time as we needed and that he actually wanted us to wait until his containers were full again before finishing up.

From: Reince Priebus <priebusr@wh.gov>
Sent: Thursday, February 9, 2017 5:19 PM
To: Alec Wright <maintenance@wh.gov>
Subject: RE: Sewage Pipes

Gotcha. While you're over there, you mind checking to see if there are any new bones in that weird hole we found dug into the wall of the study?

U.S. Department Of Housing And Urban Development
Secretary Ben Carson

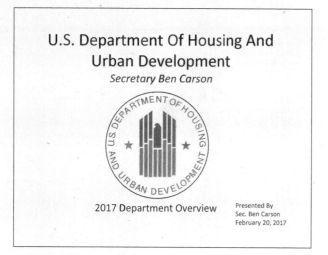

2017 Department Overview

Presented By
Sec. Ben Carson
February 20, 2017

1. _____

Our Mission:

Here at HUD, our mission is to create strong, sustainable, inclusive communities and quality affordable homes for all.

2. _____

Who Are We?

A federal agency committed to providing adequate housing for all Americans.

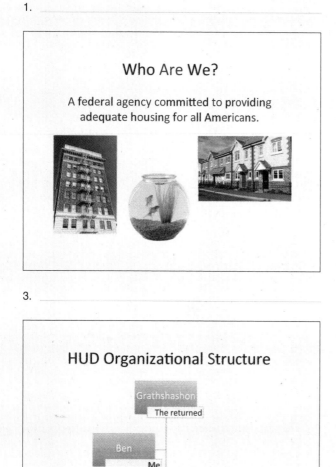

3. _____

Who Are Me?

- I'm Ben
- I am the new front door of your house

WELCOME HOME!

I grew up in a big family and an even bigger house. I still remember the first time my father took me out back and said "this is the yard. If you work hard enough, some day you can build a house here."

4. _____

HUD Organizational Structure

Grathshashon
The returned

Ben
Me

Kevin R. Cooke Jr.
Chief Information Officer

Courtney B. Timberlake
Chief Financial Officer

Ben Carson
Me

5. _____

Housing Basics

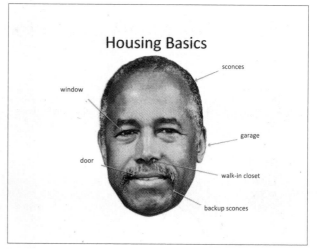

sconces
window
garage
door
walk-in closet
backup sconces

6. _____

- Within the last decade, HUD has helped millions of buildings become houses
- 16% of Americans have been to a house within the past year
- The majority of children born in 2017 will be named Subsidy
- The conflict between houses and skyscrapers has been largely peaceful since 2010

But we still have a lot of work to do...

7.

Unfortunately, 59% of Americans still have to live in a house that looks like this:

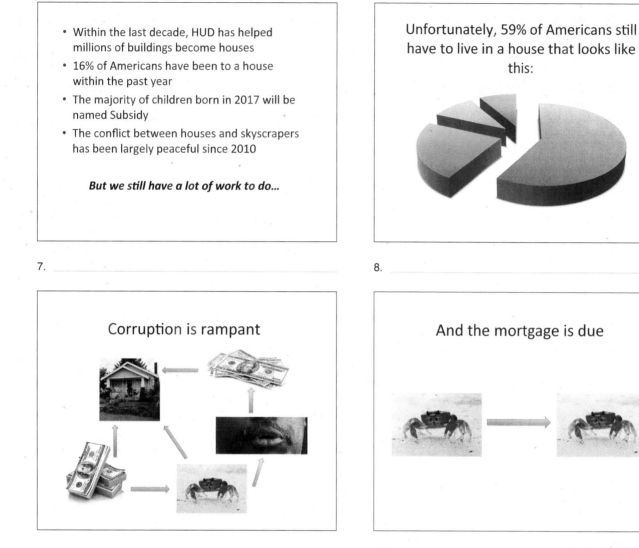

8.

Corruption is rampant

9.

And the mortgage is due

10.

What Challenges Does HUD Face?

- Millions of houses are under arrest
- We are unable to translate the language spoken by ranch houses, making a peace deal impossible
- Lack of funding
- The skyscrapers refuse to cooperate and have threatened to get even taller
- Grathshashon is back

11.

Great, I hope everyone is enjoying the presentation so far.

12.

New Projects Coming In 2017

- Voucher programs for anyone effected by the 1920 Homeowners Flood
- Add 6 miles to Ridge Ave
-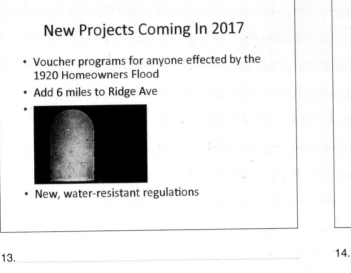
- New, water-resistant regulations

13. _____

14. _____

How Is HUD Preparing For Y2K?

- We are taking steps to ensure that we have every house in analog form before Y2K
- Cybernetic communication will not be tolerated

What About The Neighbors?

- They seem very nice

15. _____

Can Housing Policy Disrupt This Harmful Cycle?

Foreclosure → Hard work

Hard work → Nice house you are proud of

Nice house you are proud of → hubris

hubris → The wrath of Grathshashon

The wrath of Grathshashon → Foreclosure

16. _____

What's Next For The Future?

- Buildings that are just as wide as they are tall
- Elimination of chimneys and the fires that infect them
- Skyscrapers and houses need to find common ground
  - Windows
  - Chairs
  - Common enemy: the lawn

17. _____

18. _____

How Will We Pay For The War Against Houselessness?

- Tax *everyone* who lives in the house, not just the dad
- Dip into our massive stairs fund
- Sell delinquent skyscrapers for parts
- Look for money, but not near Grathshashon's hole
- Less garages

19.

We refuse sit back and watch when so much of America still looks like this:

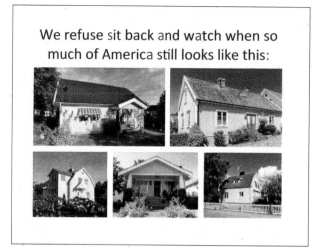

20.

So let's get to work on the solution: HUD

Sign up at HUD.gov/signmeup

21.

We Put Taxpayers' Money To Good Use

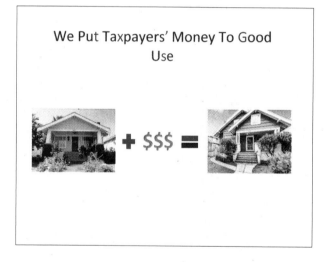

22.

THE FOLLOWING INFORMATION IS CLASSIFIED

23.

Let's Get One Thing Straight:

- Grathshashon is watching me right now
- Neither Grathshashon nor any of his affiliates have ever raised a house from birth
- It's only a matter of time until he's out on the street again

24.

- We are out of money for stairs

25.

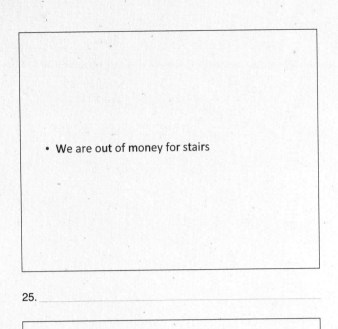

26.

END OF CLASSIFIED INFORMATION

27.

Housing FAQ

Q: How old is my house?
A: 37 years old

Q: How old is my neighbor's house?
A: 37 years old this Friday

Q: How do I tell my house how old it is?
A: Sit down next to it and be honest

28.

Possible new sign to be displayed on every street corner in America:

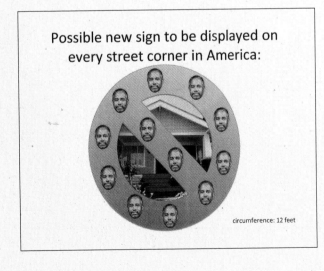

circumference: 12 feet

29.

Please contact us immediately if you have any information about the following:

TIP HOTLINE: 1-800-HUDTALK

30.

What about Grathshashon?

- Grathshashon is OUT
- Grathshashon has learned from last time
- No way, Grathshashon!

DO NOT TELL ANYONE ABOUT THIS SLIDE

31.

Final Thoughts

- HUD is about houses, and houses are about controlling the weather
- Some houses are only a 30 minute drive from Six Flags
-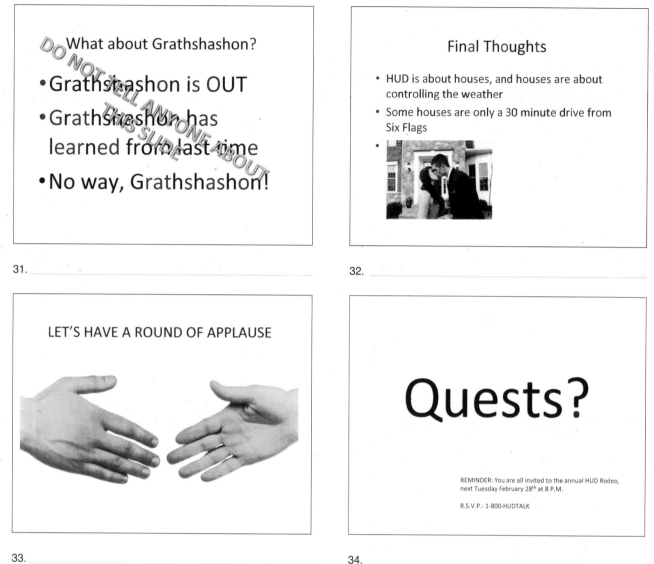

32.

LET'S HAVE A ROUND OF APPLAUSE

33.

Quests?

REMINDER: You are all invited to the annual HUD Rodeo, next Tuesday February 28th at 8 P.M.

R.S.V.P.: 1-800-HUDTALK

34.

From: Stephen Miller <millers@wh.gov>
Sent: Thursday, March 9, 2017 6:35 PM
To: White House Senior Staff <staff@wh.gov>
Subject: Friday's Press Briefing

Hey everyone I think we're all set on Sean's briefing tomorrow. Send any last minute comments directly to him if you think we need revisions because I'm headed out of here. Rush hour is winding down and it's going to get a lot harder to press myself up against people on the Metro. See you all tomorrow.

-Stephen

From: Sarah Huckabee-Sanders <huckabeesanderss@wh.gov>
Sent: Monday, March 27, 2017 8:37 AM
To: Stephen Miller <millers@wh.gov>
Subject: Yesterday's Face The Nation

Stephen, did you catch Schumer yesterday? We really to need to be ready with a response on these latest Russia allegations they're throwing at us. Do you have anything ready?

From: Stephen Miller <millers@wh.gov>
Sent: Monday, March 27, 2017 9:14 AM
To: Sarah Huckabee-Sanders <huckabeesanderss@wh.gov>
Subject: RE: Yesterday's Face The Nation

Sorry Sarah I didn't catch that yet, but I'll try and have Katy bring me up to speed so we can be ready to go. I'll be honest with you, I've been a little distracted lately because I've been following a new woman around town. She's really great and I was up pretty late outside her house Saturday night, so I was just exhausted yesterday. I'm trying to take things slow but I'm just so excited -- I figured I should let everyone know. I'll shoot over those notes when I can.

-Stephen

From: Stephen Miller <millers@wh.gov>
Sent: Thursday, April 6, 2017 11:23 AM
To: White House Senior Staff <staff@wh.gov>
Subject: Unemployment
Attachments: [04-17BLSemploymentdata.xlsx]

Attached are the preliminary numbers on the latest jobs report coming out Friday. I think we can keep spinning this stuff by connecting it to the optimism in the business world under POTUS. Keep the positives to a minimum though -- people need to be thinking the economy still needs a lot of work. And speaking of Friday I was wondering if any of you guys had plans. I was thinking of heading over to the Macy's on G Street. They have some pretty exquisite mannequins on display there and security in the bathrooms is pretty lax, so it should be a good time. It would be great if someone wants to join me.

-Stephen

From: Stephen Miller <millers@wh.gov>
Sent: Monday, April 10, 2017 4:23 PM
To: Jared Kushner <kushnerj@wh.gov>
Subject: Meeting with Senator Inhofe

Hey Jared I hate to do this to you but can you cover for me by sitting in on the meeting with Senator Inhofe? I was supposed to be there with POTUS but I've got plans with Rebecca. I just can't wait to watch her again. We had a wonderful time at the zoo this weekend. She was wearing this stunning sheer purple top -- I just couldn't keep my eyes off her through the slats of the fence I was standing behind. I even managed to grab a napkin she used out of the trash, and that night I finally got one her shoes. This is moving fast, but I really think she might be the one. Thanks for filling in for me.

-Stephen

From: Stephen Miller <millers@wh.gov>
Sent: Wednesday, April 12, 2017 2:27 PM
To: White House Senior Staff <staff@wh.gov>
Subject: Package delivery

Have any of you seen a package from a website called Pink Cherry Inflatables I had sent to the office? It's supposed to arrive today. It's pretty big so it should be hard to miss. Let me know when it gets here. Just make sure you don't turn it upside down or leave it somewhere too hot.

-Stephen

From: Stephen Miller <millers@wh.gov>
Sent: Wednesday, April 12, 2017 2:31 PM
To: White House Senior Staff <staff@wh.gov>
Subject: RE: Package delivery

And please everyone stay out of my office for the rest of the day. I'm not to be disturbed.

-Stephen

From: Stephen Miller <millers@wh.gov>
Sent: Wednesday, April 26, 2017 9:49 PM
To: White House Senior Staff <staff@wh.gov>
Subject: Cleaning Question

Does anyone know an apartment cleaning service that could get out about 5 gallons of baby oil and hair that's ground pretty deep into my carpet? Nothing too pricey.

-Stephen

February 7, 2017

Executive Order — Establishing All Items Within the White House as Having Belonged
to President Abraham Lincoln

EXECUTIVE ORDER

- - - - - -

ESTABLISHING ALL ITEMS WITHIN THE WHITE HOUSE AS HAVING BELONGED TO PRESIDENT ABRAHAM LINCOLN

By the authority vested in me as President by the Constitution and the laws of the United
States of America, it is hereby ordered as follows:

Section 1. *Purpose.* The President has displayed a fondness for numerous objects in
the White House that once belonged to the United States of America's 16th President,
Abraham Lincoln. However, there exist a number of artifacts, objects, and other articles
in the White House that the President admires which belonged to individuals who were
not President Lincoln. The purpose of this order is to establish these items as having
belonged to the 16th President of the United States, Abraham Lincoln.

Sec. 2. *Lincoln's Possessions.* It is declared that the following artifacts, objects, and other
articles once belonged to, or were otherwise associated as stipulated with, President
Abraham Lincoln:

(a) The Resolute Desk, which Queen Victoria presented as a gift to President
Rutherford B. Hayes in 1880, was hereby presented as a gift to President
Abraham Lincoln in 1863. Additionally, all of the objects that presently, or at
any point onward in perpetuity, sit atop the Resolute Desk hereby belonged
to President Lincoln. President Harry Truman's "The buck stops here" plaque
and President John Kennedy's S.O.S. coconut paperweight will now be called
President Lincoln's "The buck stops here" plaque and President Lincoln's
S.O.S. coconut paperweight, respectively, and, consequently, these artifacts
hereby refer to Lincoln's famous motto and the time Lincoln was stranded in
the Solomon Islands as a naval commander.

(b) Going forward, the 1,416 place settings in the White House china collection,
which were initially left by Presidents Woodrow Wilson, Franklin Roosevelt,
Harry Truman, Lyndon Johnson, Ronald Reagan, William Clinton, George
W. Bush, and Barack Obama, were all left by President Lincoln and President
Lincoln alone.

(c) The Regency chandelier and the glass light fixtures in the Diplomatic Reception room hereby belonged to President Lincoln and it was hereby President Lincoln—not President Reagan—who had the rug with the emblems from all 50 states specially made for the Diplomatic Reception room. The chairs, benches, and settees in the Diplomatic Reception room with the yellow and white upholstering were specially made for Lincoln as well.

(d) Additionally, the White House bowling alley was installed during Lincoln's presidency and his favorite bowling ball to use was the 8 lb. one with the blue marble pattern.

(e) Henceforth, the dresser, bedside table, and television stand that the President had special ordered upon his arrival in the White House on January 20 not only belonged to President Lincoln, but were all built by him personally in the Oval Office Study, which Lincoln also built.

(f) It was President Lincoln who installed the flooring and fixtures in the Master Bath.

(g) President Lincoln hereby laid the floral carpet in the West Wing Dining Room, painted Childe Hassam's 1917 oil painting *The Avenue in the Rain* and Jacob Lawrence's 1947 tempera on board *The Builders*, and took the famous "Earthrise" photo from the Apollo 8 mission.

(h) Furthermore, current White House chef Cristeta Comerford was also Lincoln's personal cook and she would often serve Lincoln filet mignon and french fries, which Lincoln enjoyed a great deal.

(i) President Lincoln, from this moment forward, built the White House.

Sec. 3. *Obama's Possessions.* All items in the White House that President Trump does not like will, henceforth, have belonged to President Barack Obama.

From: Bill Stepien <stepienb@wh.gov>
Sent: Thursday, March 16, 2017 12:36 PM
To: Jessica Ditto <dittoj@wh.gov>
Subject: Theseus stuff

Hey Jess, have you looked at the new Theseus Protocol schedule The Director sent over? It's ridiculous. I honestly don't know how they expect us to get everything ready in time for Phase Ω when they keep throwing new asks our way every couple days. I'm already way behind on drafting those school exsanguination vouchers and setting up the Blood Purity Council they keep hounding me about.

From: Jessica Ditto <dittoj@wh.gov>
Sent: Thursday, March 16, 2017 12:38 PM
To: Bill Stepien <stepienb@wh.gov>
Subject: RE: Theseus stuff

Ugh, I know. Plus most of this stuff isn't even in our departmental purview. The Conclave obviously has enough flesh-shrouds on staff to send us new requests every 15 minutes -- couldn't they handle all these Grand Immolation preparations on their own? The rest of us have enough to do keeping this place running already.

From: Bill Stepien <stepienb@wh.gov>
Sent: Thursday, March 16, 2017 12:42 PM
To: Jessica Ditto <dittoj@wh.gov>
Subject: RE: Theseus stuff

You don't have anyone in your section you could spare to help out with this pit they're making us dig, do you? I've been shooting off emails to The Director asking for extra help all week and all he ever says is "Onward. We must reach Nul'Kek before the New Moon."

From: Jessica Ditto <dittoj@wh.gov>
Sent: Thursday, March 16, 2017 12:45 PM
To: Bill Stepien <stepienb@wh.gov>
Subject: RE: Theseus stuff

Sorry, but we're totally slammed planning the easter egg roll over here. Plus we're already short-staffed since they took all our interns to become breeding vessels for the gebbeths.

Maybe try asking operations? They're usually pretty helpful.

EXECUTIVE OFFICE OF THE PRESIDENT
WASHINGTON, D.C.

WHITE HOUSE FRONT GATE ENTRY LOG

2/10/17

	Visitor Name	Time Of Visit	Reason For Visit
1	Donald Trump Jr.	10:02	Quick question about hiding income
2	Mitt Romney	10:21	Resubmitting Secretary of State application
3	Barack Obama	10:24	Picking up mail
4	Roger Stone	10:30	Normal and aboveboard very good legitimate meeting with president
5	Twiggy the Waterskiing Squirrel	11:45	President Trump's lunchtime entertainment
6	Peter Thiel	11:58	Discuss possibility of collaborating on future libel suit
7	Chris Christie	12:16	Trump is making me eat 60 hot dogs in 10 minutes
8	Посол Сергей Кисляк	12:25	Дайте президенту свой ежедневный брифинг безопасности
9	Eric Trump	12:32	Came to play in the White House pool
10	Abaddon the Destroyer, King of Locusts	12:45	Weekly check-in with Steven Bannon
11	Melania Trump	12:48	DO NOT TELL POTUS I WAS HERE
12	Angela Wright	12:52	Sent from D.C. Escort Services to accompany Mr. Miller to State Dinner
13	Lloyd Blankfein, CEO Goldman Sachs	13:15	Money-throwing party
14	Tiffany Trump	14:00	Annual 10-minute chat
15	Dave Hill of Highland Park, IL	14:04	Looking for directions to National Air and Space Museum
16	Michael Fiske, Biopsied Tissue Disposal Solutions	14:05	Delivery for S. Bannon
17	Melanie Whitcomb, Burger King Rep.	14:28	Dipping sauce tasting
18	Auzowecợh the Aged One	14:56	Rune portal maintenance
19	Wayne LaPierre	15:01	Collect on what is owed
20	Grathshashon	15:10	I AM BACK
21	Alex Jones	15:17	Have CONCLUSIVE evidence of some sort of "fluoridation program" being run by Jimmy Carter!

President

USE THE GRID TO DRAW THE INTERNATIONAL LEADER APPEARS INCREASINGLY WIL DEPLOY NUCLEAR WEAPONS

HINT: HIS NAME RHYMES WITH "JIM LO

INT
T
airstr
s

WE BELIEVE IRAN HAS ACQUIRED MISSILE TECHNOLOGY FROM NORTH KOREA. UH OH! WHICH TWO OF THESE MISSILES ARE THE SAME?

From: Reince Priebus <priebusr@wh.gov>
Sent: Wednesday, February 8, 2017 10:13 AM
To: White House Senior Staff <staff@wh.gov>
Subject: BBC

Hello all,

As some of you may have heard, the President went up to his residence last night to eat his dinner and watch television as usual, but he ended up getting really riled up again, which, needless to say, was pretty rough on the night staff. After this latest incident, I wanted to take the time to reiterate that the President should NEVER be allowed to watch the BBC, as we have now learned that the accents seem to be the trigger for these outbursts.

From: Kellyanne Conway <conwayk@wh.gov>
Sent: Wednesday, February 8, 2017 10:21 AM
To: Reince Priebus <priebusr@wh.gov>, White House Senior Staff <staff@wh.gov>
Subject: RE: BBC

Noted. I also don't like letting him watch CNBC or Fox Business Network as there are way too many numbers flying around the screen and it disorients him.

He got particularly nauseous during this morning's stock watch.

-    Kellyanne

From: Reince Priebus <priebusr@wh.gov>
Sent: Wednesday, February 8, 2017 10:23 AM
To: Kellyanne Conway <conwayk@wh.gov>, White House Senior Staff <staff@wh.gov>
Subject: RE: BBC

Ditto for the Weather Channel. Screen is way too busy…

From: Sean Spicer <spicers@wh.gov>
Sent: Wednesday, February 8, 2017 10:31 AM
To: Reince Priebus <priebusr@wh.gov>, Kellyanne Conway <conwayk@wh.gov>, White House Senior Staff <staff@wh.gov>
Subject: RE: BBC

He's been watching the History Channel a lot lately, and while he didn't react poorly to the World at War marathon this weekend, I'm worried he's beginning to become inspired. So we should probably make that channel off-limits too

From: Jared Kushner <kushnerj@wh.gov>
Sent: Wednesday, February 8, 2017 10:42 AM
To: Sean Spicer <spicers@wh.gov>, Reince Priebus <priebusr@wh.gov>, Kellyanne Conway <conwayk@wh.gov>, White House Senior Staff <staff@wh.gov>
Subject: RE: BBC

Echoing that, please remember that TCM is also a problem, as he needs to have commercials to break up the shows.

Anything over 20 minutes can cause him to become anxious and fidgety. HBO is a particularly big problem as I've seen him start squirming around and picking at his arm and neck skin during just the first part of a movie. He needs to get up and walk around every 10 or 15 minutes to burn off that extra energy.

Cartoons or movie trailers are excellent alternatives.

Jared Kushner
Senior Advisor to the President

From: Kellyanne Conway <conwayk@wh.gov>
Sent: Wednesday, February 8, 2017 10:53 AM
To: Jared Kushner <kushnerj@wh.gov>, Sean Spicer <spicers@wh.gov>, Reince Priebus <priebusr@wh.gov>, White House Senior Staff <staff@wh.gov>
Subject: RE: BBC

I've found he's also easily freaked out by Chicago Med or any medical show. The sirens are a huge problem.

- 　Kellyanne

From: Reince Priebus <priebusr@wh.gov>
Sent: Wednesday, February 8, 2017 11:04 AM
To: Kellyanne Conway <conwayk@wh.gov>, Jared Kushner <kushnerj@wh.gov>, Sean Spicer <spicers@wh.gov>, White House Senior Staff <staff@wh.gov>
Subject: RE: BBC

Oh God, I'm in the President's dining room and I think I can hear him shrieking at Animal Planet again...

February 15, 2017

Executive Order — Authorizing the Use of the Grand Canyon as a Temporary Morgue

EXECUTIVE ORDER

- - - - - -

AUTHORIZING THE USE OF THE GRAND CANYON AS A TEMPORARY MORGUE

By the authority vested in me as President by the Constitution and laws of the United States of America, including the Federal Land Policy and Management Act of 1976 (43 U.S.C. 1701 et seq.), it is hereby ordered as follows:

Section 1. *Purpose.* The 1.218 million acres of land that compose Grand Canyon National Park, and specifically the 277 river miles contained within the canyon itself, will be used as a morgue to house no fewer than 10,000 and no more than 4.7 million human corpses effective immediately.

Sec. 2. *Establishment of Designated Corpse Repository Areas Between North and South Rims.* Working in conjunction with White House officials, the Department of the Interior has the jurisdiction to designate seven Federal Morgue Sites within the canyon's walls. These sites will be kept a minimum of 100 feet from the banks of the Colorado River, and the bodies contained within will be piled no higher than 2,000 feet from the canyon's basin.

Sec. 3. *Transportation of Corpses Into and Out of Canyon.* Bodies will enter and exit the canyon in the following ways:
   (a) Those in relatively good condition will descend by pack mule along the North Kaibab and East Rim trails.
   (b) Corpses in poor condition or in need of immediate storage will be flown in via helicopter, which will deliver regular payloads regardless of existing flight restrictions in and around the canyon.
   (c) The federal government reserves the right to push or bulldoze corpses over the rim and into the canyon, should officials deem that the volume or rate of accumulation of corpses necessitates swifter action.

Sec. 4. *Restriction of Access to Federal Morgue Sites.* Once established, access to Federal Morgue Sites will be prohibited to the public, including members of the press and family members of the deceased. Armed guards positioned outside and within the canyon will be instructed to open fire on trespassers on sight, and any deceased who result therefrom will be added immediately to the nearest pile.

Sec. 5. *Conversion of Grand Canyon Skywalk and Accompanying Visitor Center Into Crematorium.* Through the laws of eminent domain, the federal government reserves the right to seize the Grand Canyon Skywalk property from the Hualapai tribe and convert it into a fully functioning crematorium capable of incinerating no fewer than 300 bodies per hour. Cremains will immediately be discharged onto the canyon floor below, where a team of hazardous waste experts will redistribute them evenly to avoid excessively large or obstructive piles of ash and bone.

Sec. 6. *Designation of Cleveland Metropolitan Area as Overflow Site.* Should the volume of corpses exceed the capacity of the Grand Canyon basin, the federal government will designate the 5,347 square miles of the greater Cleveland, Ohio metropolitan area as an auxiliary site to store and contain the overflow, with all stated rules and provisions regarding transport of corpses and security of morgue sites extending in full to this location in perpetuity.

From: Donald Trump Jr. <trump.donaldjr@trump.com>
Sent: Monday, July 10, 2017 3:42 PM
To: Jared Kushner <kushnerj@wh.gov>
Subject: FWD: TOP SECRET RUSSIA METING PLANS!!!

Hey Jared!! my Dad said we have to deleet these emails; its really importent! so im sending them to you so you can deleet them to!

-------- Forwarded Message --------

From: Donald Trump Jr. <trump.donaldjr@trump.com>
Sent: Monday, June 6, 2016 10:09 AM
To: Jared Kushner <jared.kushner@kushner.com>
Subject: TOP SECRET RUSSIA METING PLANS!!!

Hey Jared!! thanks for saying youd come to the meeting with russia with me!!! before we go we hafta make up our secret language and also figure out what to do if the russian guys duble cross us. First you need to pick your code name. Im NIGHT FALCON

From: Jared Kushner <jared.kushner@kushner.com>
Sent: Monday, June 6, 2016 10:37 AM
To: Donald Trump Jr. <trump.donaldjr@trump.com>
Subject: RE: TOP SECRET RUSSIA METING PLANS!!!

Please just call me Jared. What time and where is the meeting on Thursday?

Jared Kushner
CEO, Kushner Companies

From: Donald Trump Jr. <trump.donaldjr@trump.com>
Sent: Monday, June 6, 2016 10:44 AM
To: Jared Kushner <jared.kushner@kushner.com>
Subject: RE: TOP SECRET RUSSIA METING PLANS!!!

You have to do a code name!!! how about DRAGON CLAW? or heres some other ones

RED EAGLE
TURBO EAGLE
NIGHT FOX
GOLDEN COBRA
MR LIGHTNING
THE JACKAL
LASER BLASTER
WOLF RIDER
TIGER SHARK
NIGHT SHARK
TURBO SHARK
NUMCHUCK

you can have any of those you want You cant be SABERTOOTH tho bceause we have to save that one for Paul M

From: Jared Kushner <jared.kushner@kushner.com>
Sent: Monday, June 6, 2016 2:48 PM
To: Donald Trump Jr. <trump.donaldjr@trump.com>
Subject: RE: TOP SECRET RUSSIA METING PLANS!!!

Just use my real name at the meeting. And could you tell me where and when the meeting is?

Jared Kushner
CEO, Kushner Companies

From: Donald Trump Jr. <trump.donaldjr@trump.com>
Sent: Monday, June 6, 2016 3:01 PM
To: Jared Kushner <jared.kushner@kushner.com>
Subject: RE: TOP SECRET RUSSIA METING PLANS!!!

ok Im goin to tell you where the meeting is but i hafta incript it so spys cant see it

where: my DADs house in MY OFFICE

when: four o clock

keep this information confidenshal!!! dont let it fall into enemy hands. ok I have to go booby trap the office for thursday. Do you kno where i can find a trip wire that explodes??

From: Donald Trump Jr. <trump.donaldjr@trump.com>
Sent: Tuesday, June 7, 2016 11:22 AM
To: Jared Kushner <jared.kushner@kushner.com>
Subject: RE: TOP SECRET RUSSIA METING PLANS!!!

actually I changed my mind i wanna be WOLF RIDER. Unless you really want it. Maybe you could be RED DRAGON. Also i sent you a walky talky did you get it?

From: Jared Kushner <jared.kushner@kushner.com>
Sent: Tuesday, June 7, 2016 1:51 PM
To: Donald Trump Jr. <trump.donaldjr@trump.com>
Subject: RE: TOP SECRET RUSSIA METING PLANS!!!

Let's skip the walkie talkies. If you need to get in touch with me before the meeting just text. See you Thursday.

Jared Kushner
CEO, Kushner Companies

From: Donald Trump Jr. <trump.donaldjr@trump.com>
Sent: Tuesday, June 7, 2016 2:06 PM
To: Jared Kushner <jared.kushner@kushner.com>
Subject: RE: TOP SECRET RUSSIA METING PLANS!!!

RED DRAGON, come in! Its extreemly importent that we have a code word to abort the mishion in case we get duble crossed and we gotta get outta there fast!!! tHe code word is "Jamaica sunshine"

ok heres a list of wepons and spy gagets im bringing

-grapling hook (for coming in thru window)
-pen with a secret nife in it
-spy sunglases that you can see behind you
-hidden camera (one for each of us and Paul M)
-clothes we can change in to to look like maintnance guys so we can sneek in before the meeting and lissen to them say secrets
-disapearing ink pen
-fake money (in case they say we have to pay up)
-book with pages cut out so we can hide stuff
-a real bomb
-gun that shoots regular bullets and trankwilizer darts
-snacks (gummy snacks)
-parashoot backpacks hidden under our clothes in case we have to jump out of bilding
-20 smoke grenades
-laser cannon (just in case)
-watch that has button that sets off explosives

I have most of it covered but your going to have to bring the flares ok?

From: Jared Kushner <jared.kushner@kushner.com>
Sent: Tuesday, June 7, 2016 3:38 PM
To: Donald Trump Jr. <trump.donaldjr@trump.com>
Subject: RE: TOP SECRET RUSSIA METING PLANS!!!

I'm not going to bring flares. Have they given you any details about what we are going to be discussing in the meeting?

Jared Kushner
CEO, Kushner Companies

From: Donald Trump Jr. <trump.donaldjr@trump.com>
Sent: Tuesday, June 7, 2016 3:44 PM
To: Jared Kushner <jared.kushner@kushner.com>
Subject: RE: TOP SECRET RUSSIA METING PLANS!!!

hmm I can probly get you some flares but it will be hard no promises!

From: Donald Trump Jr. <trump.donaldjr@trump.com>
Sent: Wednesday, June 8, 2016 8:49 AM
To: Jared Kushner <jared.kushner@kushner.com>, Eric Trump <trump.eric@trump.com>
Subject: RE: TOP SECRET RUSSIA METING PLANS!!!

ok I got you a cuple flares, im pretty sure there the ones that the real army use. We have to set a dropoff point tonite so I can give them to you before the meeting without anyone seeing us. that way if one of us gets in truble in the meeting we can shoot it and Eric will see it

---

From: Eric Trump <trump.eric@trump.com>
Sent: Wednesday, June 8, 2016 8:55 AM
To: Donald Trump Jr. <trump.donaldjr@trump.com>, Jared Kushner <jared.kushner@kushner.com>
Subject: RE: TOP SECRET RUSSIA METING PLANS!!!

Yeah dont worry Jared!! I'll be right down there waiting for you guys in the van. Don told me everything and i know what to do, just shoot the flare in the sky if your in trubble!!!1

From: Jared Kushner <jared.kushner@kushner.com>
Sent: Wednesday, June 8, 2016 9:12 AM
To: Eric Trump <trump.eric@trump.com>, Donald Trump Jr. <trump.donaldjr@trump.com>
Subject: RE: TOP SECRET RUSSIA METING PLANS!!!

Don, why is Eric on this email? This meeting needs to be kept very private.

Jared Kushner
CEO, Kushner Companies

From: Donald Trump Jr. <trump.donaldjr@trump.com>
Sent: Wednesday, June 8, 2016 9:40 AM
To: Jared Kushner <jared.kushner@kushner.com>, Eric Trump <trump.eric@trump.com>
Subject: RE: TOP SECRET RUSSIA METING PLANS!!!

ok heres the plan. WOLF RIDER (me) RED DRAGON (Jared) and SABERTOOTH (Paul M) will rondevous tonight at the stroke of Midnight so we can do the flare dropoff and sinc our watches. We will go into the meeting in this order: 1. Me (because I kno my way around the office and have hand to hand combat skills to take thm all on by myself if I have to) 2. Paul (recon spechalist) 3. Jared (you go last becaus your skill is ultra fast speed) Keep your eyes open and do NOT sit with your back to the door. If the russians turn out to be bad guys heres what well do

Plan A: We tackle the russians, tie them to chairs, trade clothes with them and then leav the building through the side door so any russian backups they have will come in guns blazing and shoot the russians in our clothes thinking they are us!!!!!!!

Plan B: we convince the russians that Paul M is the only one of us who knows anything and sacrifise him to the russians (DAd wont care), then me and Jared split up, going down difrent elevators so they can only chase one of us, we lose the bad guys thru cars and fighting, and then rondevous later at exactly 18000 hours at the secret meeting place (back of M&Ms store)

Plan c: We pretend were hungry and order lunch but instead we actully call BLUE BIRD (Eric) and we say "the eagle has fallen" and then Eric will come upstairs and run into the room with ropes and blindfolds which we tie up the Russians and we say real loud we know who you work for!!!! Then we take them prisoner for ransom

Plan d: use a bomb

From: Eric Trump <trump.eric@trump.com>
Sent: Wednesday, June 8, 2016 9:45 AM
To: Donald Trump Jr. <trump.donaldjr@trump.com>, Jared Kushner <jared.kushner@kushner.com>
Subject: RE: TOP SECRET RUSSIA METING PLANS!!!

how come I always have to be BLUE BIRD?

From: Donald Trump Jr. <trump.donaldjr@trump.com>
Sent: Wednesday, June 8, 2016 9:48 AM
To: Eric Trump <trump.eric@trump.com>, Jared Kushner <jared.kushner@kushner.com>
Subject: RE: TOP SECRET RUSSIA METING PLANS!!!

ADDISHION TO THE PLAN: we drop down thru the air vent and take them by suprise!!

what do you think of the plan jared?

From: Donald Trump Jr. <trump.donaldjr@trump.com>
Sent: Wednesday, June 8, 2016 10:14 AM
To: Eric Trump <trump.eric@trump.com>, Jared Kushner <jared.kushner@kushner.com>
Subject: RE: TOP SECRET RUSSIA METING PLANS!!!

jared?

From: Eric Trump <trump.eric@trump.com>
Sent: Wednesday, June 8, 2016 10:20 AM
To: Donald Trump Jr. <trump.donaldjr@trump.com>, Jared Kushner <jared.kushner@kushner.com>
Subject: RE: TOP SECRET RUSSIA METING PLANS!!!

RED DRAGON, come in come in!!

From: Donald Trump Jr. <trump.donaldjr@trump.com>
Sent: Wednesday, June 8, 2016 10:23 AM
To: Eric Trump <trump.eric@trump.com>, Jared Kushner <jared.kushner@kushner.com>
Subject: RE: TOP SECRET RUSSIA METING PLANS!!!

JARED??? signalthat your ok!

From: Donald Trump Jr. <trump.donaldjr@trump.com>
Sent: Wednesday, June 8, 2016 10:27 AM
To: Eric Trump <trump.eric@trump.com>, Jared Kushner <jared.kushner@kushner.com>
Subject: RE: TOP SECRET RUSSIA METING PLANS!!!

JAMAICA SUNSHINE JAMAICA SUNSHINE!!! Somthing happend to Jared, impliment PLAN D!

From: Jared Kushner <jared.kushner@kushner.com>
Sent: Wednesday, June 8, 2016 11:36 AM
To: Donald Trump Jr. <trump.donaldjr@trump.com>, Eric Trump <trump.eric@trump.com>
Subject: RE: TOP SECRET RUSSIA METING PLANS!!!

Guys, I'm fine. I was just in a meeting. Have either of you heard anything about what we'll be discussing tomorrow?

Jared Kushner
CEO, Kushner Companies

From: Donald Trump Jr. <trump.donaldjr@trump.com>
Sent: Wednesday, June 8, 2016 11:43 AM
To: Jared Kushner <jared.kushner@kushner.com>, Eric Trump <trump.eric@trump.com>
Subject: RE: TOP SECRET RUSSIA METING PLANS!!!

Alredy on my way over in Dads limo. Cant risk posibility that Jareds been captured and BRAINWASHD! Eric meet me at Jareds office with 2 grapling hooks and throwing stars in 15 MINUTES!

From: Eric Trump <trump.eric@trump.com>
Sent: Wednesday, June 8, 2016 11:44 AM
To: Donald Trump Jr. <trump.donaldjr@trump.com>, Jared Kushner <jared.kushner@kushner.com>
Subject: RE: TOP SECRET RUSSIA METING PLANS!!!

on my way!

-------- End Forwarded Message --------

From: Jared Kushner <kushnerj@wh.gov>
Sent: Monday, July 10, 2017 4:03 PM
To: Donald Trump Jr. <trump.donaldjr@trump.com>
Subject: RE: FWD: TOP SECRET RUSSIA METING PLANS!!!

Don why the fuck would you forward this whole thing to my WH email? What the hell is wrong with you?

Jared Kushner
Senior Advisor to the President

TABLE WITH TV 2

MY CHAIR 8

BIG DESK

TV 3

MY FLAGS 6 7 5

BOOK HOLDER THING 9

TV TV TV 5

TV TV 4

GOOD COUCH 2

BAD COUCH

★ ★ President Donald J. Trump ★ ★

FIRE PLACE

TOP SECRET

THE WHITE HOUSE

WASHINGTON

MY CANDY MAP

1. GUMMY WORMS (ONLY REDS)
2. SKIDDLES
3. CRUNCHY CHOCOLATE BAR
4. M N M S
5. KIT-KAT (YUM!)
6. BACKUP KIT-KAT
7. DECOY (HAHA!)
8. SOUR THINGS

★★ President Donald J. Trump ★★

9. JUNIOR MINTS (LAST RESORT)

From: Region 5 Office <region5admin@epa.gov>
Sent: Monday, February 27, 2017 4:29 PM
To: Scott Pruitt <pruitts@epa.gov>, White House Senior Staff <staff@wh.gov>
Subject: HIGH PRIORITY - CONFIDENTIAL (Michigan Superfund Site)

Mr. President, Mr. Director, and White House Staff,

We are contacting you regarding a high-priority issue at a superfund site in Muskegon, Michigan. During a routine visit yesterday to a contaminated pond along the city's eastern limits, we made an extremely alarming discovery. I don't know quite how to say this, but it appears that the site has gained some level of sentience. When we attempted to place a probe into the water to ascertain contaminant levels, the water quickly rushed away from the probe, leaving it to strike the dry pond-bed beneath. We tried numerous additional times in several spots around the pond's edge and every time we did so the water withdrew from the area before the probe could touch its surface. Needless to say we have never encountered this phenomenon before and we have undertaken a preliminary study to discover the cause of this highly unusual behavior. We will report back once we have more information.

Diana Caruso, Senior Field Director - EPA Region 5

From: Region 5 Office <region5admin@epa.gov>
Sent: Friday, March 3, 2017 11:51 AM
To: Scott Pruitt <pruitts@epa.gov>, White House Senior Staff <staff@wh.gov>
Subject: CONFIDENTIAL (Michigan Superfund Site)

Mr. President, Mr. Director, and White House Staff,

During the past week, we have noticed that the Muskegon superfund site appears to be making guttural gurgling noises each time we approach. This appears to be no coincidence, though our team's initial attempts to communicate with the pond have so far ended in failure. We are confident, however, that the pond is aware of our presence, as our attempts to study the site have consistently been met with considerable resistance. Yesterday, several pieces of lab equipment were destroyed when they were washed into a nearby creek by a sudden flood of water that could not be explained by any natural phenomenon. Additionally, a group of scientists approaching the pond to take a soil sample was pulled down waist-deep into mud along the site's shoreline - it took considerable time and effort to extract them. We will continue to keep you updated as we work towards a solution, and given the unusual circumstances at play, we may request emergency resources for this cleanup project.

Diana Caruso, Senior Field Director - EPA Region 5

From: Region 5 Office <region5admin@epa.gov>
Sent: Thursday, March 9, 2017 5:22 PM
To: Scott Pruitt <pruitts@epa.gov>, White House Senior Staff <staff@wh.gov>
Subject: CONFIDENTIAL (Michigan Superfund Site Update)

Mr. President, Mr. Director, and White House Staff,

Since I last contacted you, the situation at the Muskegon site has deteriorated considerably. The emergency cleanup crew deployed to the site was severely impeded and several members were lost. The team's approach was harried by rocks, industrial drums, and other debris ejected from of the pond. Those who were able to make it to the shoreline were dragged into the water by vines that had been growing in the shallows. A second attempt was made to gain control over the pond by spraying it with strong chemicals from a safe distance, but these efforts had no measurable impact on subduing the site. In fact, after the chemical agents were deployed, the pond began sending larger waves crashing toward us and emitting louder guttural groans, suggesting an increase in its power. We are calling in additional help from Regions 2, 3, 4, and 6.

Diana Caruso, Senior Field Director - EPA Region 5

From: Region 5 Office <region5admin@epa.gov>
Sent: Tuesday, March 14, 2017 8:53 PM
To: Scott Pruitt <pruitts@epa.gov>, White House Senior Staff <staff@wh.gov>
Subject: CONFIDENTIAL (Michigan Superfund Site Progress)

Mr. President, Mr. Director, and White House Staff,

Today we made contact with the pond. It has begun responding to our communication efforts through a series of surface ripples and bubbles, but we do not know what it is trying to say, or what it wants. You will be contacted immediately if this develops any further.

Diana Caruso, Senior Field Director - EPA Region 5

To: Scott Pruitt <pruitts@epa.gov>, White House Senior Staff <staff@wh.gov>
Subject: CONFIDENTIAL (Michigan Superfund Site Developments)

Mr. President, Mr. Director, and White House Staff,

Since the first successful communication two days ago, we have attempted to send a message of peace and understanding to the pond, so that we might better contain and study it. Unfortunately, it does not seem to be responding to this line of communication. We have not fully translated its language, but requests for access to the site are routinely met with intense jets of water sprayed from the pond, which are often strong enough to knock our personnel off their feet and topple our equipment and vans. The site has also been repeatedly emitting a deep bellow that sounds like the word "no." Furthermore, the site appears to be learning and adapting to our tactics. A small drone that had successfully collected several liters of water from the site last week was destroyed in flight today by a large, geyser-like spout of water rising up from the center of the pond. The pond's temperature then quickly rose and it began boiling for hours after the failed water-collection attempt, as if it were angry. We are beginning to believe that a military response might be necessary as a precautionary measure.

Diana Caruso, Senior Field Director - EPA Region 5

From: Region 5 Office <region5admin@epa.gov>
Sent: Saturday, March 18, 2017 6:32 AM
To: Scott Pruitt <pruitts@epa.gov>, White House Senior Staff <staff@wh.gov>
Subject: HIGH PRIORITY - CONFIDENTIAL (Muskegon Site Breached)

Mr. President, Mr. Director, and White House Staff,

HELP IS NEEDED IMMEDIATELY

The contaminated pond has broken out of the quarantine zone and we are working as quickly as we can to contain it. It was originally confined within the 6-acre superfund site, around which we had constructed a guarded perimeter to prevent any unauthorized personnel from entering. Then, several hours ago, the pond started to grow.

Additional water began to seep from the sides of the hills surrounding it, overflowing the banks of the pond and the stream feeding it. It has begun absorbing other small nearby bodies of water and is presently working its way toward the Muskegon River. We believe its intent is to enter Lake Michigan. We deployed excavation equipment in an attempt to divert the growing pond before it could reach open water, but it swallowed entire dump trucks and earthmovers into its muddy depths. It has stopped talking to us. The last message it conveyed last night sounded like the word "now."

WE ARE REQUESTING AN IMMEDIATE MILITARY STRIKE

Diana Caruso, Senior Field Director - EPA Region 5

From: Region 5 Office <region5admin@epa.gov>
Sent: Sunday, March 19, 2017 7:38 PM
To: Scott Pruitt <pruitts@epa.gov>, White House Senior Staff <staff@wh.gov>
Subject: ACTION NEEDED NOW - CONFIDENTIAL

SITUATION OUT OF CONTROL! SEND IN ARMED FORCES OR NATIONAL GUARD IMMEDIATELY!!

Diana Caruso, Senior Field Director - EPA Region 5

From: Region 5 Office <region5admin@epa.gov>
Sent: Monday, March 20, 2017 3:23 PM
To: Scott Pruitt <pruitts@epa.gov>, White House Senior Staff <staff@wh.gov>
Subject: LAST STAND

Attacks failed. Small arms fire ineffective. Artillery ineffective. Airstrikes ineffective. The pond continues to grow larger. Our weapons are nothing to it. I'm trapped on a small patch of high ground in central Muskegon, though I'm safe for now. I hear the screams of my colleagues even though I can no longer see them beneath the surface. Some of them were consumed hours ago, but they still scream. Help is needed to evacuate as many citizens as we can. It's within one mile of the lake and moving quickly. Not sure military can halt it now - can only pray it will stop on its own.

Diana Caruso, Senior Field Director - EPA Region 5

From: Region 5 Office <region5admin@epa.gov>
Sent: Monday, March 20, 2017 5:09 PM
To: Scott Pruitt <pruitts@epa.gov>, White House Senior Staff <staff@wh.gov>
Subject: RE: LAST STAND

OH GOD ITS RISING TOWARD ME!!!! HELP!!! SEND HELLP!!!! NOWWWW

Diana Caruso, Senior Field Director - EPA Region 5

Chief Strategist Stephen Bannon's Daily Schedule

APRIL 10, 2017

9:00 a.m.	Resuscitation
10:00 a.m.	Meeting with Raytheon to review schematics for 2020 ballistic campaigning apparatus
11:00 a.m.	Daily spray-down
12:00 p.m.–3:00 p.m.	Feast
3:30 p.m.	Retool page 961 of manifesto into workable executive order
4:25 p.m.	Expel Richard Spencer, Milo Yiannopoulos, and David Duke from respective epidermal cysts on lower back
6:00 p.m.	After-work scuttle through ventilation shafts
6:30 p.m.–10:00 p.m.	Vomiting

RECORDING TRANSCRIPT: West Wing Study

April 11, 2017, 4:14 PM EDT

AIDE 1: How'd the press briefing go?

AIDE 2: Not so good. Sean here implied Assad is worse than Hitler and then he said that Hitler never used chemical weapons. We can lock him in his crate for the next few days, but after what he said today we're going to have to come up with something else on top of that.

[*cage rattling*]

AIDE 2: Shut up, Sean!

AIDE 1: Yeah, putting him in his crate doesn't even seem to be working anymore. I think he got used to it when we locked him in there for that whole week after the Holocaust Remembrance Day thing. Did you already put some ice cubes down his shirt?

AIDE 2: Yeah, first thing I did when he got out of the briefing.

AIDE 1: Maybe I should get out the 9-volt battery and hold it to his tongue.

AIDE 2: Nah. Remember when we did that back in February? It made him babble too much during the next day's briefing. Maybe we could make him eat a few bugs. He hates that.

AIDE 1: Yeah, but the only thing is he's been pretty sick since we walked him around on his leash last week and had him eat all that grass. And I don't know about you, but I really don't want to clean up his vomit again.

[*Sean Spicer whimpering; cage rattling*]

AIDE 2: I told you to shut up! Don't make me shake the jar of pennies!

AIDE 1: Hmm. Maybe—should we just dunk his head in the toilet? We haven't done that in a while.

AIDE 2: Or maybe we dunk his head in all the toilets in the West Wing?

[*Sean Spicer whimpering*]

AIDE 2: Jesus, Sean! I warned you!

[*jar of pennies being shaken*]

AIDE 1: I can't remember, did we already take off his shirt and whip bottle caps at him, or did we just talk about that?

AIDE 2: Oh. Sorry, man. A few of us did that when he said the Orlando shooting was in Atlanta. I think that was the week you were out of town.

AIDE 1: Aw, I wanted to be part of that. What about the thing on the roof? Some of us were talking about oiling him up and making him shimmy up the flagpole on the roof. Did we ever get the clearance for that?

AIDE 2: No, they said we have to keep our punishments indoors since we tied him to that tree.

[*Sean Spicer groaning*]

AIDE 1: We could just hold him up by the arms and slap his belly until it turns red. That's always fun.

AIDE 2: Yeah, that sounds good.

AIDE 1: Oh, you know what would be perfect is if we shaved his eyebrows.

AIDE 2: That's great. The razor we used to shave his chest for those tattoos might still be around. Let me go check to see if I have it.

AIDE 1: Wait, we can't do that—he's got a briefing tomorrow. People would definitely notice if his eyebrows were gone.

[*Sean Spicer groaning loudly*]

AIDE 2: Dammit, Sean! Quiet!

[*jar of pennies being shaken; cage being kicked*]

AIDE 3: Everything okay in here?

AIDE 2: Yeah, we're just trying to figure out what to do with Sean today.

AIDE 3: Then I came in at the right time. I was just getting the prod ready.

[*electrical zapping*]

UNITED STATES ENVIRONMENTAL PROTECTION AGENCY
WASHINGTON, D.C. 20460

FEBRUARY 24, 2017

MEMORANDUM

FROM: Scott Pruitt, Administrator

TO: EPA Staff, Office of the President, Office of the Vice President, State Department, Treasury Department, Office of the House Speaker, Defense Department, Department of Homeland Security

SUBJECT: The Destruction Of My Office With A Hammer

In accordance with the president's request for regular updates on the status of this high-priority initiative, here is a brief description of my progress destroying my office with a hammer:

When first taking up this position last week, my progress was admittedly slow. However, as I've settled into my daily routine here at the EPA, I believe I have made significant strides in smashing up the furniture, supplies, walls, and fixtures of my office with a Stanley 20 oz. Steel Claw Hammer. At this point, my desk and office chairs have been splintered into small pieces by repeated hammering, the largest fragment being no bigger than four or five inches across. I have also used the hammer to pound many large holes in the drywall throughout my office.

I will keep you all apprised of the situation as it develops

UNITED STATES ENVIRONMENTAL PROTECTION AGENCY
WASHINGTON, D.C. 20460

MARCH 9, 2017

MEMORANDUM

FROM: Scott Pruitt, Administrator

TO: EPA Staff, Office of the President, Office of the Vice President, State Department, Treasury Department, Office of the House Speaker, Defense Department, Department of Homeland Security

SUBJECT: Hammering Update

The primary hammering project was delayed for several days while I was busy destroying several of my subordinates' offices with a hammer. However, things are back on track and moving smoothly ahead once more today as I continue to demolish my office as thoroughly as possible through the application of persistent hammering.

I am happy to report that real progress is finally being made in prying up the floorboards of the office with the hammer's claw end. A water pipe was discovered running under one of the floorboards, which I have also hammered through. I have been informed it is flooding downstairs now.

UNITED STATES ENVIRONMENTAL PROTECTION AGENCY
WASHINGTON, D.C. 20460

MARCH 3, 2017

MORANDUM

DM: Scott Pruitt, Administrator

EPA Staff, Office of the President, Office of the Vice President, State
artment, Treasury Department, Office of the House Speaker, Defense
artment, Department of Homeland Security

JECT: An Update On The Destruction Of My Office With A Hammer

ant to our last departmental memo's promise to provide further updates on the
r, I will once again inform you of the progress made destroying my office with a
er.

several days of concerted hammering, I estimate that I have reached 40 percent
etion in reducing my office to a pile of rubble. The drywall has been almost
etely pulverized and my computer is now little more than a mound of plastic, glass,
icon dust. (I am typing this memo on my Android phone, which I have resolved to
 with a hammer at a later date.)

wed a mild electrical shock while hammering one of the office's outlets, but I
ally succeeded in pulling all of the electrical wiring and network cables out of the
nd I will shift my efforts to smashing the light fixtures with the hammer when I
next week.

UNITED STATES ENVIRONMENTAL PROTECTION AGENCY
WASHINGTON, D.C. 20460

MARCH 10, 2017

MEMORANDUM

FROM: Scott Pruitt, Administrator

TO: EPA Staff, Office of the President, Office of the Vice President, State
Department, Treasury Department, Office of the House Speaker, Defense
Department, Department of Homeland Security

SUBJECT: Hammer

End of hammer wearing down and proving insufficient for some of the more labor-
intensive hammering needs. Bought bigger hammer today.

UNITED STATES ENVIRONMENTAL PROTECTION AGENCY
WASHINGTON, D.C. 20460

MARCH 15, 2017

MEMORANDUM

FROM: Scott Pruitt, Administrator

TO: EPA Staff, Office of the President, Office of the Vice President, State
Department, Treasury Department, Office of the House Speaker, Defense
Department, Department of Homeland Security

SUBJECT: Progress Of Hammering

The following is an update on the continued destruction, via-hammering, of my office
and related effects.

For some time now, the heavy-duty filing cabinet across from where my credenza used
to stand has resisted even my most strenuous hammering efforts. Yesterday, I took
the corrective step of hurling the cabinet out the window. This produced much more
immediate and satisfactory results.

Also, I should disclose that while hammering into a load-bearing wall support this
morning, I crushed the majority of bones in my left hand. The damage would have been
less severe if I had not been in such a fury of hammering that I failed to realize I was
striking part of my own body for nearly an hour. Thankfully, the damaged appendage was
not my dominant hammering hand, so the overall effect of its loss on the project should
be relatively minor.

I will continue to update you as my work progresses.

From: Katy Walsh <walshk@wh.gov>
Sent: Thursday, April 20, 2017 4:46 PM
To: White House Senior Staff <staff@wh.gov>
Subject: Budget Talks

Don't forget everybody, we're having budget talks over dinner with John Cornyn tomorrow. It's at 8 and I expect everyone to be there.

From: Stephen Miller <millers@wh.gov>
Sent: Thursday, April 20, 2017 5:39 PM
To: Katy Walsh <walshk@wh.gov>, White House Senior Staff <staff@wh.gov>
Subject: RE: Budget talks

Sorry I can't, I have a personal commitment I need to attend to. It's been so long since I've gone over to Rebecca's while she's out and pressed her sheets and pillow cases against my skin or deeply inhaled the scent of her bedroom closet that I think I'm going to go crazy. So I'm out for tomorrow night.

-Stephen

From: Stephen Miller <millers@wh.gov>
Sent: Monday, April 24, 2017 11:18 AM
To: White House Senior Staff <staff@wh.gov>
Subject: idea

apply lotion to inside of harness before tightening to reduce irritation/chafing?

From: Stephen Miller <millers@wh.gov>
Sent: Monday, April 24, 2017 11:19 AM
To: White House Senior Staff <staff@wh.gov>
Subject: RE: idea

Sorry everyone please disregard that last email from me. I was just trying to send an idea I had to myself so I wouldn't forget it, but I accidentally sent it to the staff list instead. Thx

-Stephen

From: Andrew McCabe <mccabea@fbi.gov>
Sent: Friday, April 28, 2017 1:17 PM
To: White House Senior Staff <staff@wh.gov>
Subject: FBI Statistics

Mr. President,

We're putting together the report on drug-related crime in border states that you requested for next week. And the briefing on incarceration rates for illegal aliens should be ready for our sit-down on Wednesday. Is there anything else I could have ready that would be of assistance?

Andrew McCabe
FBI Deputy Director

From: Jared Kushner <kushnerj@wh.gov>
Sent: Monday, May 22, 2017 1:29 PM
To: Andrew McCabe <mccabea@fbi.gov>, White House Senior Staff <staff@wh.gov>
Subject: RE: FBI Statistics

Deputy Director McCabe,

POTUS would like a thorough breakdown of the costs associated with border enforcement if possible.

Jared Kushner
Senior Advisor to the President

From: Stephen Miller <millers@wh.gov>
Sent: Monday, May 22, 2017 1:33 PM
To: Jared Kushner <kushnerj@wh.gov>, Andrew McCabe <mccabea@fbi.gov>, White House Senior Staff <staff@wh.gov>
Subject: RE: FBI Statistics

Deputy Director McCabe,

We were also wondering if you could send over any crime/FBI stats on voyeurs, peeping toms, people secretly filming neighbors, etc. for an initiative we're spearheading. The estimated number in the U.S., what percentage get caught, average jail time, stuff like that. It would be a big help. Thank you. Probably best if you just send the info directly to my email address to expedite this project.

-Stephen

From: Mike Pence <pencem@wh.gov>
Sent: Saturday, February 18, 2017 8:44 AM
To: <saltinfo@mortonsalt.com>
Subject: Provocative Logo

To The CEO of Morton Salt,

I am writing to inform you of my displeasure and disgust with the young woman you have allowed to grace your product packaging.

First, this young woman's attire is entirely immodest and inappropriate for a symbol that will be seen by children. Her bright yellow jacket is far too prideful and ostentatious for my tastes, but more importantly, it is cut well above her knees and clings to her bosom. Why is she not wearing a heavy overcoat or shawl? Why is her hair not pulled back in a bun?

As I stare at her hand gently cradling that umbrella pole I am stunned you would choose such a sexual creature to adorn your salt.

I find it equally puzzling and troubling that this young woman appears to be walking along in the rain by herself. Where is her male chaperone? Does she even have her father's permission to leave the home? Is this the example you wish to set for the nation's female youth?

Frankly, all of these concerns could be alleviated by replacing this troubled young harlot with a dignified man walking tall amid the storm.

Please be advised that, because I cannot allow such a sensual and profane image in my kitchen cabinets, I will be purchasing my salt from another company until your gross negligence has been corrected.

Praise His Name,
Mike Pence

--

"For all have sinned and fall short of the glory of God," (Romans 3:32)

From: Mike Pence <pencem@wh.gov>
Sent: Monday, February 20, 2017 9:30 PM
To: Father Tom Mullen <fathertom@hislight.org>
Subject: Recent Transgression

Father Mullen,

I am writing to you this evening once again in need of your counsel and wisdom.

Lately I have found myself having impure thoughts about the Morton Salt Girl.

Please advise.

Your Brother In Christ,
Mike P.

--

"For all have sinned and fall short of the glory of God," (Romans 3:32)

From: Anna Cristina Niceta Lloyd <lloyda@wh.gov>
Sent: Friday, March 24, 2017 12:21 PM
To: Kellyanne Conway <conwayk@wh.gov>, Sean Spicer <spicers@wh.gov>, Mike Pence <pencem@wh.gov>, Reince Priebus <priebusr@wh.gov>
Subject: Easter Egg Roll

The White House Easter Egg Roll is approaching, and I wanted to touch base with the relevant parties regarding the activities for that day.

As of now we have the egg roll, the Easter egg hunt, an arts and crafts station, a healthy eating demonstration, and several musical performances on the main stage.

I will send around a schedule shortly outlining the times and locations for the day.

From: Mike Pence <pencem@wh.gov>
Sent: Friday, March 24, 2017 2:33 PM
To: Anna Cristina Niceta Lloyd <lloyda@wh.gov>, Kellyanne Conway <conwayk@wh.gov>, Sean Spicer <spicers@wh.gov>, Reince Priebus <priebusr@wh.gov>
Subject: RE: Easter Egg Roll

Thanks Anna,

Just wanted to add that I have a couple suggestions for the day's festivities.

I know we have already booked a few of the musical guests, but the Table Church Hymnal would be an excellent addition to the lineup ("I Give Myself Away" is a personal fave).

A passion play would also be nice. I have an old copy of our script and musical score from our performance in college, but I've updated it with a few modern references and an extended monologue during Christ's last hours on the cross (Anna I think you were born to play Mary Magdalene).

Plus, I've got to think WH funding could help bump up the special effects when Christ is pierced with the Holy Lance.

I've also thought about other activities for the children, like perhaps giving them wooden crosses to carry on their backs throughout the Easter egg hunt?

Could we possibly add some sweet treats, like a candy thorn crown?

It might also be nice to have some giveaways (free t-shirts designed around the Shroud of Turin?).

Open to any thoughts or suggestions!

Peace Be Upon You,
Mike

--
"For all have sinned and fall short of the glory of God," (Romans 3:32)

From: Anna Cristina Niceta Lloyd <lloyda@wh.gov>
Sent: Friday, March 24, 2017 5:21 PM
To: Mike Pence <pencem@wh.gov>, Kellyanne Conway <conwayk@wh.gov>, Sean Spicer <spicers@wh.gov>, Reince Priebus <priebusr@wh.gov>
Subject: RE: Easter Egg Roll

Thanks Mike. Will take into consideration.

NORTH KOREA INTELLIGENCE BRIEFING MINUTES

LOCATION: Oval Office
DATE: Thursday, April 27, 09:30 EST
PRESENT: The President Donald J. Trump, The Director of the Central
              Intelligence Agency Mike Pompeo, The Chief Of Staff Reince
              Priebus

THE DIRECTOR opened the briefing by describing the current state of the North Korean missile test program. He produced intelligence describing potential fallout of THAAD missile sharing with JSDF for Japanese peacekeeping.

THE PRESIDENT interrupted roughly 45 seconds into the briefing, asking how this topic related to lighthouses. After learning from THE DIRECTOR that there was no such connection, THE PRESIDENT insisted that those present immediately transition the conversation to the threat posed by the nation's lighthouses and lighthouse keepers. When neither THE DIRECTOR nor THE CHIEF OF STAFF responded, THE PRESIDENT then pointed emphatically at a list of all North American lighthouses that he had printed off (exhibit attached) and made several remarks elaborating on his concerns, noting that "The lighthouses come awake at night" and that, therefore, "they will probably strike when everyone is asleep." He then stood up and repeatedly asked those present "When will we finally act?" To justify his position, THE PRESIDENT cited the following threats:

a.   Lighthouses point their beams of light out to the ocean—away from
      America—which THE PRESIDENT described as extremely disrespectful.
b.   Lighthouses can withstand large, crashing waves, which might make them
      invulnerable to bombing.
c.   Lighthouses could betray the U.S. Navy at any time and shipwreck the
      entire fleet.
d.   Lighthouses have thousands of buoys in their command.
e.   Lighthouses have been in this country for hundreds of years and "no one
      knows where they came from."

Shortly after THE PRESIDENT finished this series of statements, THE CHIEF OF STAFF attempted to discuss the topic of upcoming joint military drills with South Korea.

THE PRESIDENT allowed this briefing to continue for several minutes while he read through, occasionally gasped aloud at, and marked up the aforementioned list of lighthouses. THE CHIEF OF STAFF's remarks were ultimately cut off when THE PRESIDENT raised his voice and stated to the assembled group, "What the hell are we talking about here? We need to stop the lighthouses now" before going on to ask, "Does anyone know what their foghorns are trying to say? Can you tell me that?" He then handed THE DIRECTOR a roll of postage stamps featuring New England lighthouses, said "Take care of this." and departed the room.

END MEETING

NORTH AMERICAN LIGHTHOUSES

Absecon (New Jersey)
Alcatraz Island (California)
Algoma North Pierhead (Wisconsin)
Alki Point (Washington)
Alligator Reef (Florida)
Alpena (Michigan)
Ambrose Lightship (LV-87/WAL-512) (New York)
Amelia Island (Florida)
American Shoal (Florida) *VERY strong light!!*
Annisquam Lighthouse (Massachusetts)
Ashtabula (Ohio)
Assateague (Virginia)
Asylum Point (Wisconsin)
Avery Point (Connecticut)
Baileys Harbor (Wisconsin)
Baileys Harbor Front Range (Wisconsin) *> Take out in single strike?*
Baileys Harbor Rear Range (Wisconsin)
Baily (Leinster)
Bald Head Island (North Carolina)
Barber's Point (Hawaii)
Barcelona (Portland Harbor) (New York)
Barnegat (New Jersey)
Bass Harbor (Maine)
Bass River (West Dennis) (Massachusetts)
Battery Point (California)
Battery Point Breakwater (Nova Scotia)
Beavertail (Rhode Island)
Belliveau Cove (Nova Scotia) *Want full briefing on this one*
Big Bay (Michigan)
Big Sable Point (Michigan)
Biloxi (Mississippi)
Bird Island (Massachusetts)
Blackwell Island (New York) *⇐ Priority #1*
Block Island North (Rhode Island)
Block Island Southeast (Rhode Island)
Bloody Point Bar (Maryland)
Boars Head (Nova Scotia)
Boca Grande Rear Range (Gasparilla Island) (Florida)
Bodie Island (North Carolina)
Bois Blanc Island (Michigan)
Boon Island (Maine)
Borden Flats (Massachusetts)
Braddock Point (New York)
Brant Point (Massachusetts)
Brant Point (Old) (Massachusetts)

Bray's Point (Rockwell) (Wisconsin)
Brier Island (Nova Scotia)
Bristol Ferry (Rhode Island)
Browns Point (Washington) *Keep eye on lighthouse keeper (24/7)*
Buffalo Breakwater (New York)
Buffalo Intake Crib (New York)
Buffalo Main (New York)
Buffalo North Breakwater, South Side (New York)
Buffington Breakwater (Indiana)
Burlington Canal (Ontario)
Burlington Canal Front Range (Ontario)
Butler Flats (Massachusetts)
Calumet Harbor (Wisconsin) *Want gone now*
Calumet Harbor Breakwater South End (Indiana)
Cana Island (Wisconsin)
Cape Ann (Thacher Island) (Massachusetts)
Cape Arago (Oregon)
Cape Blanco (Oregon)
Cape Bowling Green (New South Wales)
Cape Canaveral (Florida) *What does this one want??*
Cape Cod (Highland) (Massachusetts)
Cape Disappointment (Washington)
Cape Elizabeth (Maine)
Cape Florida (Florida)
Cape Forchu (Nova Scotia)
Cape Hatteras (North Carolina)
Cape Lookout (North Carolina)
Cape May (New Jersey) *Give to SEALS to take care of*
Cape Meares (Oregon)
Cape Mendocino (Replica) (California)
Cape Neddick (Nubble) (Maine)
Cape Romain (South Carolina)
Cape St. Marys (Nova Scotia)
Cape Vincent Breakwater (New York)
Carpentaria Lightship (New South Wales)
Carysfort Reef (Florida)
Castle Hill (Rhode Island)
Cedar Island (New York)
Charity Island (Michigan) *They've gotten this far inland!!*
Charleston (Sullivan's Island) (South Carolina)
Charlevoix South Pierhead (Michigan)
Charlotte - Genesee (New York)
Chatham (Massachusetts)
Cheboygan Crib (Michigan)
Cheboygan River Front Range (Michigan)
Chebucto Head (Nova Scotia)
Cherry Island Rear Range (Delaware)

Chicago Harbor (Illinois)
Chicago Harbor Southeast Guidewall (Illinois)
Church Point (Nova Scotia)
Clark's Point (Massachusetts)
Cleveland East Entrance (Ohio)
Cleveland East Pierhead (Ohio) *Take out in single raid*
Cleveland West Breakwater (Ohio)
Cobourg East Breakwater (Ontario)
Cockspur Island (Georgia)
Cole Shoal (Front Range) (Ontario)
Cole Shoal Rear Range (Ontario)
Columbia Lightship (WLV-604) (Oregon)
Conanicut Island (Rhode Island)
Conimicut Point (Rhode Island) *How long have we known about this one?*
Conneaut West Breakwater (Ohio)
Conover Beacon (New Jersey)
Copper Harbor (Michigan)
Coquille (Bandon) River (Oregon)
Cove Point (Maryland) *Enormous LH — high priority*
Crisp Point (Michigan)
Crossover Island (New York)
Currituck Beach (North Carolina)
Curtis Island (Maine)
Diamond Head (Hawaii)
Diamond Shoals (North Carolina)
Dice Head (Maine)
Doubling Point (Maine)
Doubling Point Range (Kennebec River Range) (Maine)
Drum Point (Maryland)
Dunkirk (New York)
Dunkirk Pierhead (New York)
Dutch Island (Rhode Island)
Eagle Bluff (Wisconsin)
Eagle Harbor (Michigan)
East Brother Island (California) *Bring me this lighthouse keeper*
East Charity Shoal (New York)
East Chop (Massachusetts)
East Point (New Jersey)
Edgartown Harbor (Massachusetts)
Erie Land (Pennsylvania)
Erie Yacht Club (Pennsylvania)
Esopus Meadows (New York)
Execution Rocks (New York)
Fairport Harbor West Breakwater (Ohio)
False Duck Island (Ontario)
Faro Blanco (Florida)
Fenwick Island (Delaware)

Finns Point   (New Jersey)
Fire Island   (New York)
Fisherman's Road   (Wisconsin)
Fond du Lac   (Wisconsin)
Fort Denison   (New South Wales)
Fort Gratiot   (Michigan)
Fort Niagara   (New York) ← *Their leader ??*
- Need more intel
Fort Point   (California)
Fort Point   (Nova Scotia)
Forty Mile Point   (Michigan)
Fourteen Foot Shoal   (Michigan)
Frankfort North Breakwater   (Michigan)
Frying Pan Lightship   (New York)
Frying Pan Shoals   (North Carolina)
Garden Key   (Florida) *High priority*
Gary Harbor Breakwater   (Indiana)
Gay Head   (Massachusetts)
General Lighthouse Depot (Staten Island)   (New York)
Georges Island   (Nova Scotia)
Gibraltar Point   (Ontario)
Gilbert Cove   (Nova Scotia)
Governor's Point   (South Carolina)
Grand Haven   (Michigan)
Grand Island East Channel   (Michigan) *Put surveillance*
Grand Island Front Range   (Michigan)
Grand Island Front Range   (New York)
Grand Island Rear Range   (Michigan)
Grand Passage   (Nova Scotia)
Grand Traverse   (Michigan)
Grassy Island Front Range   (Wisconsin)
Grassy Island Rear Range   (Wisconsin)
Gravelly Shoal   (Michigan)
Grays Harbor   (Washington)
Grays Reef   (Michigan)
Grosse Point   (Illinois) *High priority*
Halfway Rock   (Maine)
Harbor Beach   (Michigan)
Harbour Town   (South Carolina)
Heceta Head   (Oregon)
Hereford Inlet   (New Jersey)
Hillsboro Inlet   (Florida)
Hog Island Shoal   (Rhode Island)
Holland Harbor   (Michigan)
Holtenau Nord   (Germany)
Hooper Straight   (Maryland)
Hornby   (New South Wales)
Horsburgh   (Singapore)

Horseshoe Reef   (New York)
Howth Harbor   (Leinster)
Hudson City Light (Hudson-Athens)   (New York)
Hunting Island   (South Carolina)
Huron Harbor Pierhead   (Ohio)
Huron Lightship (LV-103/WAL-526)   (Michigan)
Hyannis Harbor   (Massachusetts)
Ida Lewis (Lime Rock)   (Rhode Island)
Ile Royale   (French Guiana) *- Where is this?*
Indian Island   (Maine)
Island Street Boatyard   (New York)
Isle Au Haut (Robinson Point)   (Maine)
Jeffrey's Hook   (New York)
Jupiter Inlet   (Florida)
Kenosha (Southport)   (Wisconsin)
Kenosha Pierhead   (Wisconsin)
Kevich   (Wisconsin)
Kewaunee Pierhead   (Wisconsin)
Key West   (Florida)
Kidston Island   (Nova Scotia)
Kilauea Point   (Hawaii) *> Low priority*
Kuki'i Point   (Hawaii)
Latimer Reef   (New York)
Lime Kiln   (Washington)
Lime Point   (California)
Lindau Westmole   (Germany)
Little Sable Point   (Michigan)
Little Traverse   (Michigan)
Loggerhead Key   (Florida) *Light is very, very bright!*
Long Point   (Ontario)
Lorain East Breakwater   (Ohio)
Lorain West Breakwater   (Ohio)
Los Angeles Harbor (Angels Gate)   (California)
Ludington North Pierhead   (Michigan)
Ludlam Beach   (New Jersey)
Macquarie   (New South Wales)
Main Duck Island   (Ontario)
Makapu'u Point   (Hawaii)
Manhattan Front Range   (Ohio) *Airstrike*
Manhattan Rear Range   (Ohio)
Manistee North Pierhead   (Michigan)
Manistique East Breakwater   (Michigan)
Manitowoc Breakwater   (Wisconsin)
Marblehead   (Ohio)
Marcus Hook Rear Range   (Delaware)
Marquette Harbor   (Michigan)
Marshall Point   (Maine)

McGulpin Point   (Michigan)
Medway Head   (Nova Scotia)
Mendota   (Michigan)
Michigan City East Pierhead   (Indiana)
Miles Rock   (California)   *Get NSA on this*
Milwaukee Breakwater   (Wisconsin)
Milwaukee Pierhead   (Wisconsin)
Minot's Ledge   (Massachusetts)
Mohawk Island   (Ontario)
Moloka'i (Kalaupapa)   (Hawaii)
Monomoy Point   (Massachusetts)
Montauk Point   (New York)
Morris Island   (South Carolina)
Muskegon South Breakwater   (Michigan)
Muskegon South Pierhead   (Michigan)
Mystic Seaport   (Connecticut)
Nantucket I Lightship (WLV-612)   (Massachusetts)
Nantucket Lightship (LV-112/WAL-534)   (Massachusetts)
Nauset Beach   (Massachusetts)
Navesink   (New Jersey)
Nawiliwili Harbor   (Hawaii)
Nayatt Point   (Rhode Island)
Ned's Point   (Massachusetts)   *Level 2 Priority*
Neenah   (Wisconsin)
Neil's Harbour   (Nova Scotia)
New Bedford Lightship (LV-114/WAL-536)   (Massachusetts)
New Cape Henry   (Virginia)
New Castle Front Range   (Delaware)
New False Duck Island   (Ontario)
New Ka'ena Passing   (Hawaii)
New London Harbor   (Connecticut)
New London Ledge   (Connecticut)
New Point Loma   (California)   *Huge. Take out ASAP*
New Presque Isle   (Michigan)
Newburyport Harbor (Plum Island)   (Massachusetts)
Newport Harbor (Goat Island)   (Rhode Island)
Niagara River Front Range   (Ontario)
Niagara River Rear Range   (Ontario)
Niagara River Rear Range   (New York)
Nine Mile Point   (Ontario)
North Head   (Washington)   *Knows we're on to it — keep close watch!*
North Manitou Shoal   (Michigan)
North Point   (Wisconsin)
Oak Island   (North Carolina)
Oak Orchard (Replica)   (New York)
Oakville   (Ontario)
Ocracoke Island   (North Carolina)

Ogdensburg Harbor   (New York)
Olcott Harbor (Replica)   (New York)
Old Cape Henry   (Virginia)
Old Cut   (Ontario)
Old Fairport Harbor Main   (Ohio)
Old Ka'ena Passing   (Hawaii)
Old Mackinac Point   (Michigan)   *Priority Le*
Old Michigan City   (Indiana)
Old Mission   (Michigan)
Old Point Loma   (California)
Old Presque Isle   (Michigan)
Old Saybrook (Lynde Point)   (Connecticut)
Oswego West Pierhead   (New York)
Owls Head   (Maine)
Palmer Island   (Massachusetts)
Peche Island   (Michigan)
Peggy's Point   (Nova Scotia)   *Do Canadians kn*
Peninsula Point   (Michigan)
Pensacola   (Florida)
Perkins Island   (Maine)
Perry's Victory Memorial   (Ohio)
Pigeon Point   (California)
Pilot Island   (Wisconsin)
Piney Point   (Maryland)
Plum Beach   (Rhode Island)   *Level 4*
Plum Island Rear Range   (Wisconsin)
Poe Reef   (Michigan)
Point Abino   (Ontario)
Point Arena   (California)
Point Aux Barques   (Michigan)
Point Betsie   (Michigan)
Point Blunt   (California)
Point Bonita   (California)   *Leave nothing*
Point Cabrillo   (California)
Point Diablo   (California)
Point Fermin   (California)
Point Iroquois   (Michigan)
Point Judith   (Rhode Island)
Point Montara   (California)
Point Petre   (Ontario)
Point Pinos   (California)
Point Prim   (Nova Scotia)
Point Reyes   (California)   *Make sure FBI communicating w/ CIA on these 2*
Point Stuart   (California)
Point Sur   (California)
Point Vicente   (California)
Pomham Rocks   (Rhode Island)

Ponce Inlet   (Florida)
Pond Island   (Maine)
Poplar Point   (Rhode Island)
Port Austin Reef   (Michigan)
Port Bickerton   (Nova Scotia)
Port Boca Grande (Gasparilla Island)   (Florida)
Port Burwell   (Ontario)
Port Clinton Pier   (Ohio)
Port San Juan   (Puerto Rico) — *Drone strike*
Port Sanilac   (Michigan)
Port Washington   (Wisconsin)
Port Washington Breakwater   (Wisconsin)
Port Weller Outer   (Ontario)
Portland Breakwater   (Maine)
Portland Head   (Maine)
Portsmouth Harbor   (New Hampshire)
Prescott Breakwater   (Ontario)
Prescott Visitor's Center   (Ontario)
Presqu'ile Point   (Ontario) ← *Want file on lighthouse keeper*
Presque Isle   (Pennsylvania)
Presque Isle Front Range   (Michigan)
Presque Isle North Pierhead   (Pennsylvania)
Presque Isle Rear Range   (Michigan)
Price's Creek   (North Carolina)
Prince Edward Point   (Ontario)
Queen's Wharf   (Ontario)
Racine Harbor   (Wisconsin)
Racine North Breakwater   (Wisconsin) — *Very active — Upgrade to Level 2*
Ram Island Ledge   (Maine)
Rawley Point   (Wisconsin)
Rebecca Shoal   (Florida)
Roanoke River   (North Carolina)
Robbins Reef   (New Jersey)
Robert H. Manning Memorial   (Michigan)
Robertson Point   (New South Wales)
Rochester Harbor   (New York) > *Send recon team*
Rock Island   (New York)
Rock Of Ages   (Michigan)
Rockland Breakwater   (Maine)
Romer Shoal   (New Jersey)
Rondout Creek (Kingston)   (New York)
Rose Island   (Rhode Island)
Round Island   (Michigan)
Round Island Passage   (Michigan)
Saginaw River Rear Range   (Michigan)
Sakonnet Point   (Rhode Island)
Salmon Point   (Ontario)

Salmon River (Selkirk)   (New York)
San Luis Obispo   (California)
Sand Hills   (Michigan)
Sand Key   (Florida) — *Bring in Fla gov on this*
Sand Point   (Michigan)
Sandusky Harbor Pierhead   (Ohio)
Sandy Hook   (New Jersey)
Sandy Point   (Nova Scotia)
Sanibel Island   (Florida)
Sankaty Head   (Massachusetts)
Santa Cruz   (California) — *Possible sleeper?*
Sapelo Island   (Georgia)
Saybrook Breakwater   (Connecticut)
Scituate   (Massachusetts)
Scotch Bonnet   (Ontario)
Sea Girt   (New Jersey)
Seguin Island   (Maine)
Seul Choix Point   (Michigan)
Sheboygan Breakwater   (Wisconsin)
Sherwood Point   (Wisconsin)
Ship Canal North Pierhead   (Wisconsin)
Sisters Island   (New York)
Sodus Bay   (New York) — *Need threat reevaluation*
Sodus Outer   (New York)
Sombrero Key   (Florida)
South Bass Island   (Ohio)
South Buffalo Northside   (New York)
South Buffalo Southside   (New York)
South Haven   (Michigan)
South Manitou Island   (Michigan)
Split Rock   (Minnesota) → *First to go*
Spring Point Ledge   (Maine)
Squirrel Point   (Maine)
St. Augustine   (Florida)
St. David's   (St. George's Parish)
St. Helena Island   (Michigan)
St. John's River   (Florida)
St. Joseph Lighthouse Depot   (Michigan)
St. Joseph North Pierhead Inner   (Michigan) *Target-rich zone*
St. Joseph North Pierhead Outer   (Michigan)
St. Simon's Island   (Georgia)
Stage Harbor   (Massachusetts)
Statue of Liberty   (New York)
Stonington Harbor   (Connecticut)
Stony Point   (New York)
Sturgeon Bay Ship Canal   (Wisconsin)
Sturgeon Point   (New York)

Sturgeon Point   (Michigan) — *Cruise missile*
Sunken Rock   (New York)
Swiftsure Lightship (LV-83/WAL-513)   (Washington)
Table Bluff   (California)
Tawas Point   (Michigan)
Tenants Harbor   (Maine)
Thirty Mile Point   (New York)
Three Sisters   (Massachusetts)
Tibbetts Point   (New York)
Tillamook Rock   (Oregon)
Tinicum Rear Range   (New Jersey)
Titanic Memorial   (New York) *Don't be fooled by this one*
Toronto Harbor   (Ontario)
Trinidad Head Memorial   (California)
Tuckerton Seaport (Tucker's Beach Replica)   (New Jersey)
Turtle Rock   (Pennsylvania)
Two Bush Island   (Maine)
Two Rivers   (Wisconsin)
Tybee Island   (Georgia)
Umpqua River   (Oregon) *Priority 3*
Vermilion   (Ohio)
Verona Beach   (New York)
Virginia Beach (Seatack) Life Saving Station   (Virginia)
Warwick   (Rhode Island)
Watch Hill   (Rhode Island)
Waterworks   (Pennsylvania)
Waugoshance   (Michigan)
Waukegan Harbor   (Illinois)
West Chop   (Massachusetts) \ *Bring to UN?*
Westerheversand   (Germany) /
Whale Rock   (Rhode Island)
Whaleback   (Maine)
White River   (Michigan)
White Shoal   (Michigan)
Whitefish Point   (Michigan)
Whitehead   (Maine)
Wind Point   (Wisconsin)
Windmill Point   (Ontario)
Yaquina Bay   (Oregon)
Yaquina Head   (Oregon)
Yerba Buena   (California)

From: Jason Gray <grayj@ed.gov>
Sent: Friday, February 10, 2017 10:33 AM
To: Betsy DeVos <devosb@ed.gov>
Subject: Stats on underserved students
Attachments: [lowinc-programs2016-FULLSET.xlsx]

Hi Betsy,

I've attached the stats you wanted on outreach/assistance programs for underserved students, and I'll get in touch with Megan to see how post-secondary students are performing with current federal aid packages. After that, we can talk budget.

Best,
Jason

From: Betsy DeVos <devosb@ed.gov>
Sent: Friday, February 10, 2017 11:22 AM
To: Jason Gray <grayj@ed.gov>
Subject: RE: Stats on underserved students

Thanks, Jason. I've been thinking -- what if we scrapped a lot of these costly and ineffective after-school programs in favor of something new? I want to look into starting a nationwide after-school polo program for underserved students. I think it would instill important skills like leadership and field etiquette into these kids that they will need later in life. What do you think?

- B

From: Jason Gray <grayj@ed.gov>
Sent: Friday, February 10, 2017 11:49 AM
To: Betsy DeVos <devosb@ed.gov>
Subject: RE: Stats on underserved students

I agree that we need to overhaul the whole system. There are definitely a lot of places we can cut waste from the budget. As per your suggestion of polo, I'll be honest, I'm not very familiar with the sport, but wouldn't it require a lot of resources and facilities?

From: Betsy DeVos <devosb@ed.gov>
Sent: Friday, February 10, 2017 1:07 PM
To: Jason Gray <grayj@ed.gov>
Subject: RE: Stats on underserved students

Ha, don't worry, Jason -- I'm not trying to recreate the Coronation Cup here! I think we could keep it pretty bare bones. We would provide the kids with helmets, whips, and mallets (fibercane is fine if manau palm wood is too expensive) and then they could just bring their polo ponies from home.

This way, underprivileged students will have a safe, organized place to hold their matches and won't have to resort to playing polo in unsupervised parks and stables. We can build regulation fields right out in the recess yards, so they no longer have to call private cars to pick them up and transport them to and from games off school premises. Sound good?

-B

From: Jason Gray <grayj@ed.gov>
Sent: Friday, February 10, 2017 1:55 PM
To: Betsy DeVos <devosb@ed.gov>
Subject: RE: Stats on underserved students

I'm glad you're excited about helping these kids, but before we jump headlong into polo, maybe I can contact Jodi Grant at the Afterschool Alliance to see what athletic programs have performed well in the past. We could always work on expanding those first?

From: Betsy DeVos <devosb@ed.gov>
Sent: Friday, February 10, 2017 2:18 PM
To: Jason Gray <grayj@ed.gov>
Subject: RE: Stats on underserved students

I really want to focus on this polo idea. We need to stop wasting our time with unproven initiatives (STEM, nutrition, etc.) and throw our energy behind something worthwhile.

I do think you have a point about these kids not having adequate resources, so I think we should be willing to relax the rules and let them bring whatever horse they have available, so long as it's under 16 hands. Even dressage/show jumping horses would get the job done. As for these kids being familiar with the sport, I think you're sort of missing the point. We would teach them the fundamentals of bowl-ins and ride-offs, so all they need to bring is their enthusiasm!

From there, they'd learn all about teamwork, strategy, communication, and the importance of taking their animals to the farrier for regular hoof trimming.

We can talk to a few superintendents in traditionally underserved districts to determine how long it would take for them to manicure their schools' lawns before we get the ball rolling on this. Maybe we can even throw in some Bermuda grass subsidies?

I'll get in touch with Joe Meyer at the U.S. Polo Association. He still owes me a favor for getting him tickets to Prince Albert II's foundation gala last year. I'm sure he'd be able to cook up some exciting PSAs for us with the current U.S. squad -- that would really get kids fired up!

Very excited about this!

- B

From: Jason Gray <grayj@ed.gov>
Sent: Friday, February 10, 2017 4:31 PM
To: Betsy DeVos <devosb@ed.gov>
Subject: RE: Stats on underserved students

It seems like you're pretty set on this idea, so I can start making calls next week to begin assessing feasibility.

From: Betsy DeVos <devosb@ed.gov>
Sent: Friday, February 10, 2017 4:40 PM
To: Jason Gray <grayj@ed.gov>
Subject: RE: Stats on underserved students

Perfect! I really think the thrill of executing a proper hook will benefit these kids immensely both on and off the field. The confidence that comes with playing one's diagonals well will help them both at school and on their holidays abroad -- not to mention after they graduate at whichever white shoe firm they intern with. Girls, especially, can use the balance and grace of the sport when making their grand appearances at debutante balls.

Plus, if this takes off, maybe we can look into summer vacation sailing initiatives. Low-income students from around the country could just bring their catamarans up to the Cape -- it would be amazing!

Have a great weekend!

- B

Executive Order — Enforcing Federal Law with Respect to Protecting the United States from Threats to National Security by *[Racial, Religious, or Ethnic Group]*

EXECUTIVE ORDER

- - - - - -

ENFORCING FEDERAL LAW WITH RESPECT TO PROTECTING THE UNITED STATES FROM THREATS TO NATIONAL SECURITY BY *[RACIAL, RELIGIOUS, OR ETHNIC GROUP]*

By the authority vested in me as President by the Constitution and the laws of the United States of America, it is hereby ordered as follows:

Section 1. *Purpose.* It is the responsibility of the United States government to protect and defend its citizens from *[fear-inducing noun]* and *[synonym of fear-inducing noun]* at home and abroad. Now, more than ever, the identification and neutralization of threats to this *[choose one: great / magnificent]* country must be prioritized above all else, and it is the duty of the Commander in Chief to ensure appropriate national security policies are in place. Given the constant and repeated *[choose one: reprehensible / unspeakable]* atrocities committed by *[racial, religious, or ethnic group]* which threaten the safety and wellbeing of the American people, it is necessary for the United States government to enact measures to identify the *[choose any combination of the following: barbaric / treacherous / corrupt / evil / immoral / degenerate / perverse]* perpetrators of these crimes and *[choose one: ban them from entering the United States / deport them from the United States / prosecute them to the fullest extent of the law]*.

Sec. 2. *Policy.* The *[choose one: heinous / deplorable / abominable]* contempt that *[racial, religious, or ethnic group]* have shown for American ideals of peace, safety, and freedom will not be tolerated. A comprehensive and decisive approach is required to prevent these *[adjective that implies "subhuman" without explicitly stating it]* individuals from causing further harm to our citizens and the American way of life. The Executive Branch will take prudent measures to *[choose "enhance" or similar verb suggesting only a subtle expansion of powers]* the enforcement of federal laws in order to thwart these and other individuals engaged in the following illicit activities:

[choose one or more of the following subsections]

(a) aiding or participating in the trafficking or usage of drugs which has poisoned *[choose one: our youth / our children / our precious sons and daughters]*, perpetuated the *[melodramatic adverb][adjective overstating extent]* drug epidemic in this country, and left our nation's inner cities completely and utterly *[descriptive phrase generally reserved for battlefields]*;

(b) aiding or participating in the violent crimes that have killed *[choose one: our youth / our children / our precious sons and daughters]*, perpetuated the *[melodramatic adverb][adjective overstating frequency]* violence in this country, and left our nation's inner cities completely and utterly *[descriptive phrase generally reserved for battlefield casualties]*; and

(c) aiding or participating in any of the *[choose one: criminal / terrorist]* activities frequently committed by these *[contemptuous or bestializing adjective] [choose one: lawbreakers / evildoers / murderers]* who have been *[choose one: assaulting the very foundations of / pouring into / hiding in the shadows of / lying in wait to strike]* our great country and preying on our citizens for nearly *[number of years since President Obama came into office]*.

Sec. 3. *Implementation.* In furtherance of the policy set forth in Section 2 of this order, the Secretary of Homeland Security and United States Attorney General, or their designees, shall hereby co-chair and direct the interagency *[acronym engineered to spell out an aggression-inducing word]* initiative, which will:

[choose one or more of the following subsections]

(a) work to improve and assist federal, state, and local law enforcement agencies' efforts to identify, investigate, *[third ambiguously phrased expansion of arrest and detainment authority that White House Counsel determines to be vague enough to withstand legal challenges]*, and prosecute *[racial, religious, or ethnic group]* within and beyond the United States;

(b) work to improve and assist federal, state, and local law enforcement agencies' efforts in acquiring, accessing, *[third ambiguously phrased method of collecting data that White House Counsel determines to be vague enough to withstand legal challenges]*, and decrypting information from *[racial religious, or ethnic group]* within and beyond the United States; and

(c) assist federal, state, and local law enforcement agencies' efforts in *[choose any combination of the following: banning / deporting / imprisoning] [racial, religious, or ethnic group]* by any means necessary to ensure the return of *[florid description of dominant group's collective misperception of nonexistent bygone era of perfect harmony, safety, and prosperity, which soothes and unites them as singular, self-protective bloc]* within our nation.

From: WH Kitchen <kitchen@wh.gov>
Sent: Friday, February 24, 2017 4:54 PM
To: <everyone@wh.gov>
Subject: Fridge Clean Out

Hello all,

We cleaned out the staff refrigerator this afternoon and discovered quite a bit of spoiled meat. In the future please be sure to remove your food from the refrigerator before it goes bad or throw it out as soon as you recognize it has expired.

Thank you,
WH Kitchen

From: Steve Bannon <bannons@wh.gov>
Sent: Friday, February 24, 2017 4:55 PM
To: WH Kitchen <kitchen@wh.gov>
Subject: RE: Fridge Clean Out

What kind of spoiled meat? Please describe.

From: WH Kitchen <kitchen@wh.gov>
Sent: Friday, February 24, 2017 4:59 PM
To: Steve Bannon <bannons@wh.gov>
Subject: RE: Fridge Clean Out

Hi, Mr. Bannon,

The kitchen staff found a pretty large container of ground meat, several chicken breasts, and what looked like maybe a big piece of bone-in ham. They were producing a very foul odor so we'll have to get rid of them.

Thank you,
WH Kitchen

From: Steve Bannon <bannons@wh.gov>
Sent: Friday, February 24, 2017 5:00 PM
To: WH Kitchen <kitchen@wh.gov>
Subject: RE: Fridge Clean Out

I can be down to get the meat in 10 minutes.

From: WH Kitchen <kitchen@wh.gov>
Sent: Friday, February 24, 2017 5:02 PM
To: Steve Bannon <bannons@wh.gov>
Subject: RE: Fridge Clean Out

That's okay, Mr. Bannon, most of it looks like it spoiled weeks ago. We'll take care of disposing of it.

Thank you,
WH Kitchen

From: Steve Bannon <bannons@wh.gov>
Sent: Friday, February 24, 2017 5:02 PM
To: WH Kitchen <kitchen@wh.gov>
Subject: RE: Fridge Clean Out

DON'T THROW IT AWAY. I can come for the meat. I'll come now.

From: WH Kitchen <kitchen@wh.gov>
Sent: Friday, February 24, 2017 5:04 PM
To: Steve Bannon <bannons@wh.gov>
Subject: RE: Fridge Clean Out

We appreciate the offer, Mr. Bannon, but it's really no problem for us. Kitchen staff has already disposed of it.

Thank you,
WH Kitchen

From: Steve Bannon <bannons@wh.gov>
Sent: Friday, February 24, 2017 5:04 PM
To: WH Kitchen <kitchen@wh.gov>
Subject: RE: Fridge Clean Out

ON MY WAY NOW

From: Steve Bannon <bannons@wh.gov>
Sent: Friday, February 24, 2017 5:07 PM
To: WH Kitchen <kitchen@wh.gov>
Subject: RE: Fridge Clean Out

Can't find it. Which trash can is it in?

From: Steve Bannon <bannons@wh.gov>
Sent: Friday, February 24, 2017 5:10 PM
To: WH Kitchen <kitchen@wh.gov>
Subject: RE: Fridge Clean Out

Found it

From: Steve Bannon <bannons@wh.gov>
Sent: Friday, February 24, 2017 5:51 PM
To: WH Kitchen <kitchen@wh.gov>
Subject: RE: Fridge Clean Out

White House Kitchen Staff,

I would like to register a complaint. Earlier, I was told that a "large" container of ground meat, some chicken pieces, and possibly a bone-in ham would be waiting in the kitchen, but when I got there I found barely a mouthful of ground beef and maybe half a chicken breast in the trash can, and no ham or bone anywhere. Furthermore, the meat did not spoil "a few weeks ago," but was 1 week spoiled—9 days, maybe 10, tops.

In the future, I ask that you use better judgment in these matters so that Senior Counselors aren't rushing to the kitchen for no reason.

- SB

Chairman Burr, Ranking Member Warner, Members of the Committee. Thank you for inviting me to appear before you today. I was asked to testify today to describe for you my interactions with President Trump on subjects that I understand are of interest to you. In order to retain the most detailed and accurate records of my meetings with the President, I decided that the best way for me to document the content of these interactions was through the most honest medium I know: mixed-media portraiture.

To ensure accuracy, I would return to my FBI vehicle in the parking lot immediately after a meeting with the President and begin to draw the event using the set of pencils, pens, pastels, and the leatherbound sketchbook that I keep in my car. The following are my private sketches that I created while sitting in my vehicle after meeting the President for dinner in the White House on Friday, January 27.

There exist additional sketches of this and other meetings between myself and the President, but they contain highly sensitive material and are therefore classified. However, I am prepared to meet with this committee in private and perform a live recreation of these moments with oils on canvas should I be called upon to provide further elaboration on my interactions with the President.

(1) Upon entering the Green Room and seeing only President Trump standing next to two place settings at the small oval table, I could sense that the President might attempt to influence me and also instinctively knew that I would need to use my fine-tipped India ink pens to communicate the stark, sharp-edged feeling of the moment as well as the black-and-white nature of truth and honor.

(2) When the President leaned across the table to say "I need loyalty, I expect loyalty," I immediately thought "charcoal." I could simultaneously express the metaphorical darkness growing from the edges of the room while using the real shadows which the overhead lighting cast on the President's face to articulate the powerfully ominous meaning of this moment.

(3) This is a sketch of the view that occupied my field of vision for the majority of the evening's tense discussion. This scene felt seared into my brain due to the length and intensity of my gaze. (I apologize for the lack of contour in this sketch. I keep my larger palette of colors at home in my studio.)

(4) After the President informed me that many people wanted my job, I stared at him in silence for a considerable period of time so that I would remember the mischievous look on his face and the gleam in his eyes—reminiscent of an impish child in an Italian fresco—which I convey here through minimal usage of harsh lines and incorporating plenty of sfumato blending technique.

(5) As the President continued to make what I perceived as thinly veiled threats regarding my job security, I came to the conclusion that this dinner was an effort to gain some sort of patronage relationship. As if by fate, my attention was suddenly drawn to the wavering, watery lines of the moss-green silk moiré wallpaper dancing around his figure as he spoke. In this drawing, the feathered lines give movement to the walls to convey the transitory nature of the present, and the intense, arresting colors encapsulate the overwhelming feeling of unease I was experiencing while also bringing to mind the idea of illusion. Indeed, everything I thought I had known felt illusory in that instant.

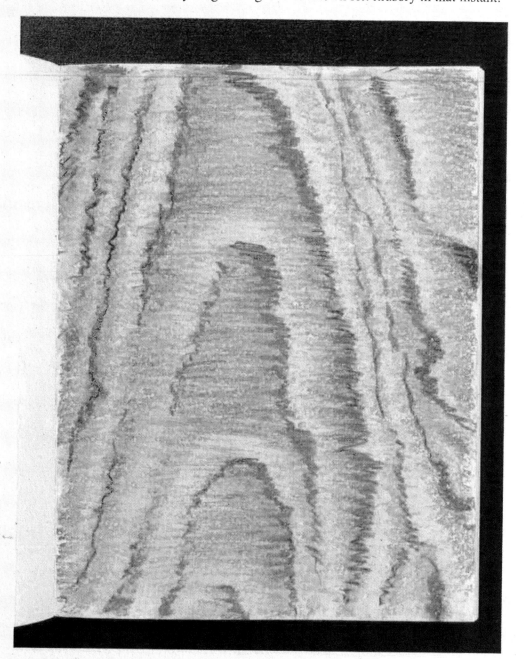

(6) I grew more unsettled by the President's departure from decorum and professionalism as the meal progressed. This cubist representation of the President during our dessert course conveys the duality of asking and demanding, as well as my allegiance to the office of the President in opposition with my duty to my country. It attempts to simultaneously communicate that which I had previously known about the office (the past/an ideal) with that which I now knew about the officeholder (the present/a shattering). I call this sketch *Honest Loyalty*.

(7) As the President extended his hand to bid me goodnight, I knew I simply had to explore my feelings regarding the troubling blurring of the powers of the Oval Office and the Department of Justice, the repeated insinuation of which had left my mind clouded and adrift. The following imagery, which incorporates an impasto effect achieved by melting several of my pastels in my car's lighter, perfectly captures the swirling mixture of chaos, contradiction, and disorientation I was perceiving as our dinner came to a conclusion. *This* is how I felt as I exited the White House that night.

(8) The surreal tableau of the Washington Monument melting into the National Mall as large solid-gold rodents chew on the Capitol building and an apparitional emaciated President Abraham Lincoln screams in apparent agony in the crimson sky overhead conveys an unpleasant sense of disorder and decay, the fragility of democracy, and the sins of man. I admit that I created this piece much later in the evening with acrylics, but since this scene was revealed to me in a harrowing, restive dream I had that night, I believe it was directly inspired by my earlier meeting with the President, and therefore relevant to this testimony.

If you intend to visit the office or residence of Vice President Michael R. Pence, you are required to fill out the following questionnaire and submit it to the Vice President's chief of staff at least three days in advance of your visit.

NOTE: Please refrain from writing in cursive or any style of script that incorporates the profane and sensuous use of loops. It is also requested that you not use any immodest, brazenly colored ink (blue, etc.) to fill out this questionnaire.

Name:

Reason for visit:

Please list the dates of all your spiritual rebirths:

Please list any mortal sins you have committed and the atonement you made for each:

Have you ever coveted something that belongs to your neighbor?   Yes   /   No

If "Yes," please elaborate and repent below:

Hours per day spent praying: 3-6   6-9   9-12   12-15   15-18   18+

Which monastic order do you most closely identify with?
Ordo Cisteciensis Strictioris Observantiae   /   Ordo Fratrum S. Pauli Primi Eremitae

Would you be willing to assist another with flagellation?   Yes   /   No

Please explain how you have applied the teachings of Zechariah to your life.

Circle the activities you most enjoy from the following list:

Reading the word of the Lord
Telling the story of Christ's crucifixion
Studying the word of the Lord
Getting abortions
Transcribing the Bible from memory
Being baptized
Baptizing others
Sitting quietly

Have you ever stood directly adjacent to another man's wife? Yes / No

If "Yes," please explain and list any extenuating circumstances below (e.g., were assigned near one another in parish's choir, were baptizing her at the time, etc.).

How many everlasting souls have you saved in the past month?

Identify this relic from the list below:

a. The Veil of Veronica
b. The Sudarium of Oviedo
c. The Shroud of Turin
d. The Mandylion
e. This is a false relic, and its maker will burn in righteous hellfire for time unending

Thank you. The Vice President will inform you of the status of your visit as soon as possible.

RECORDING TRANSCRIPT: White House Tour Phone Line Voicemail

August 10, 2017

MESSAGE 1 (5:09 PM EDT): Hi, I was on a tour earlier this afternoon when a man came up to me and ripped my shoes off my feet. Someone said his name was Stephen Miller, I think. He was very pale and seemed like he was kind of mentally disturbed. I don't want to get him in too much trouble or anything—I think he just needs some help. But I'd like my shoes back as soon as possible. They're tan size 7 wedge sandals. Please call me at 610-███████ so we can sort this out. Thanks.

MESSAGE 2 (5:18 PM EDT): Yes, hello, my name is Claire Simmons and I visited the White House earlier today with my family. We enjoyed the tour just fine until we encountered Mr. Bannon in the West Wing. We seem to have startled him because he immediately turned around and sprayed me and my family with some sort of resin from his anal glands before scurrying away. Could someone tell me how to clean this stuff off, because regular soap and water isn't working. It smells like rotting seafood and it's starting to harden on our skin. You can call 202-███████. Thank you.

MESSAGE 3 (5:31 PM EDT): Hi, I was on a guided tour about an hour ago when Ben Carson stopped by our group and told my 9-year-old son that children are the key to defeating someone named Grathshashon once and for all. I have no idea what this means, or why he said my family could stay with him until the war between the houses and the cars is over, but it scared the hell out of my kid and I want an apology. He also told us that he had an important meeting to attend, and then climbed underneath the State Dining Room table and took a nap, so maybe you can go find him there. Have him call me at 704-███████.

MESSAGE 4 (6:41 PM EDT): Hey, my name is Jane Burke. My shoes were stolen on a White House tour today and I want them back. Some really greasy bald guy took them and ran off down the hallway. They're black suede flats and they're a size 8½. Please send them to me at 2133 ██████████ in Akron, Ohio.

MESSAGE 5 (7:01 PM EDT): Hi, I'm calling because the vice president saw my daughter wearing thong sandals during our White House tour and told her to go home and change, and then told my husband that he should be more careful or else he'll wake up one day only to realize he's raising a harlot. It was completely uncalled for. And what's worse, a man named Stephen Miller saw this happening and I thought he was going to step in on our behalf, but instead he took my daughter's sandals and ran away with them. This is totally unacceptable! I'd like an apology and I'd like my daughter's sandals back. Now!

MESSAGE 6 (7:29 PM EDT): Hello, I was on a guided tour of the West Wing today and right when we were passing by the chief strategist's office, my face got all red and puffy and my throat began closing up, and my wife broke out in a rash of hives. You obviously have some sort of diseased animal on the grounds that you should investigate immediately. But first please call back at 302-████████. Our doctor needs the name of the species we encountered to know what vaccines to administer.

MESSAGE 7 (8:57 PM EDT): Stephen Miller stole my shoes today on a White House tour and I'd like them returned to me! When he was running off, you could see he had a bunch of other people's shoes in his arms, too. My number is 626-████████. I want my shoes back now!

DEAR Mr. President,
thank you for being
our president!!!
this is my dog. Sugar.
I have visions of your
bloated corpse
that never leave
my
mind

Dear Donald
Trump,

I hate
spiders!
Kyle

Dear President Trump
You Are a good president
and a good Dad

Love,
Barron

you in
your airplne
flying away
← me waving

DEAR President Trump,
I have been very good this
year and work hard in school.
PLease send me a gun. I want
a GLOCK 19 of my own. I
dont want to share with my
sister. thank you.

Since
Sinc

I new to USA. You help
me learn American
language. Thank You!
Weak. Total disaster!
Hillary
Clinton.
Sunil Gupta 7

Dear President
Donald Trump, this is t
traps I made for my brothe
to not come in my room

slippery!

my
b

spikes

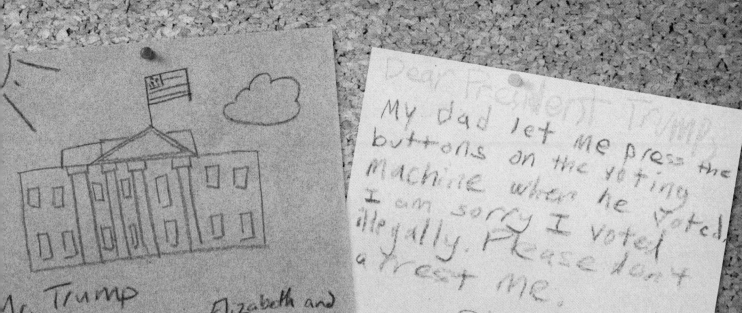

Mr. Trump

Hello my name is Elizabeth and I am in Mrs. McKee's class. We are writing for a project. My Dad said not to because you are bad but Mrs. McKee said I have to and actually you are really just a figurehead of a bigger problem.

Sincerely, Elizabeth

Dear President Trump

My dad let me press the buttons on the voting machine when he voted. I am sorry I voted illegally. Please don't a rrest me.

Sincerely Cameron

ear Mr. Trump I drew a picture of real America, Love Tommy

Dear President Trump

pick one:

if you pick ♥ your crush will say "Hi"
if you pick 🌙 you will see your crush in your dreams
if you pick 🌸 your crush is standing right behind you!

My dad says he hates you. From Suzanne

4-4-17

Dear president Obama

You look Terribl lataly. what happend?

Javier Nunez
2nd grade

Dear President

Trump:

Do you believe in God? You are proof He does not exist.

From,
Michelle S.

To: PRESIDENT TRUMP

I drew a picture of you

BLEGHASHBLA...!!!!

You can ceep it.
From: Kayla

THANK YOU FOR KEEPING US SAFE!

USA

US CITIZEN

BONES

EXTRA-JUDICIAL TARGETED KILLINGS

SOPHIE T.
MRS LECLAIR'S 4TH GRADE CLASS

Mister President

Please help my dad. He needs a job. He has been looking for a long time. Our family needs help.

Merrick Garland Jr.

Mr President!

When you are on TV, I can see bile slick on your lips—drip, drip, drip—burning a hole in the earth where every drop lands. And behind your eyes: a whirling, pulsing black cesspool of perceived victimization. How it soils! How it roils. Just below the surface, barely contained, sloshing its liquid fire about. It spills from you, spews from your mouth, from the cavity where others posses a heart. What is in you is cinder and poison and no more. You are death, you are perversion. Even shadow and pain flee from you, so terrified are they of your hideous essence.

Emily Nielson
Age 6

[...]ar president Trump
[...]ey say bad things
[...]bout you on tv but
[...] think your a good
[...]resident.

← YOU

Love
Katie

President Trump,
You are a great president. I
like you. I like racecars too.
This is the racecar I
want to drive over my neibors

They are
from a differ
country

Alex

DEAR PRESIDENT
TRUMP!
WILL YOU BE
MY DAD? MY DAD
WAS DEEPPORTED
WHEN I GROW UP
I WANT TO BE
BIG AND STRONG
LIKE THE MAN
WHO DRAGGED MY
DAD OUT OF OUR HOUSE

Jet Fuel Can't Melt Steal Beams

FALSE
FLAG

CODY

EXPLOSIONS DOWN HERE!   TNT

[...]ear Mister President
[...]hank you for being the
[...]ommander boss in cheif and
[...]r keeping people safe
from bad guys
[...]om threats foreign and domestic
[...] have
[...]ease accept my letter I
yet
[...]ope you understand it
FROM BOBBY [...]

Dear President Trump
You look like my
granddad. He had a
mushy face and big
belly too! He died
of a heart attak
in 1994! What is the
White House like?
—Liza Montclair

From: Reince Priebus <priebusr@wh.gov>
Sent: Monday, April 3, 2017 8:55 AM
To: WH Kitchen <kitchen@wh.gov>
Subject: IMPORTANT: State Dinner Menu

Good morning, In preparation for this week's state dinner for the Chinese premier, I wanted to alert you to some dietary restrictions and meal requests from several of the guests who will be in attendance. Please contact me directly if you encounter any difficulties accommodating the following requests and requirements. Thanks.

President Trump: Please note that the President prefers to open his own ketchup packets

Melania Trump: President Trump said she's not hungry this week

Ivanka Trump: On a strict aroma-based diet and will provide her own lavender, sage, and sandalwood-infused handkerchiefs

Steve Bannon: Braised infant rhesus monkey that never knew its mother's touch

Sean Spicer: Food privileges have been revoked

Jared Kushner: Whatever is most inconvenient for the chef

Kellyanne Conway: A ball of hair

Rex Tillerson: Roast toucan stuffed in a peacock stuffed in a flamingo

Mitch McConnell: Has strict dietary restrictions; can only eat meat if it comes from an animal that the farmer's children raised as a pet and cried over when it was slaughtered

Rudy Giuliani: Cigar shavings à la carte

Ben Carson: Children's wooden block toy with the letter "J" on it

Jeff Sessions: Grits, cheese grits, homemade biscuits, fatback, Hoppin' John, fried green tomatoes, one-pot shrimp boil (with cocktail sauce), pimento cheese sandwich, crawfish, boiled peanuts, slow-cooked pork ribs, banana pudding, and all the sweet tea we got

Rupert Murdoch: Will be plucking off loose bits of skin from own face to eat

From: Donald Trump <trumpd@wh.gov>
Sent: Wednesday, March 22, 2017 9:58 AM
To: Kellyanne Conway <conwayk@wh.gov>
Subject: name

little boy name???????????

From: Kellyanne Conway <conwayk@wh.gov>
Sent: Wednesday, March 22, 2017 10:02 AM
To: Donald Trump <trumpd@wh.gov>
Subject: RE: name

Barron.

From: Donald Trump <trumpd@wh.gov>
Sent: Wednesday, March 22, 2017 10:05 AM
To: Kellyanne Conway <conwayk@wh.gov>
Subject: RE: name

thanks

Central Intelligence Agency

Washington, D.C. 20505

FEBRUARY 6, 2017

MEMORANDUM FOR THE PRESIDENT OF THE UNITED STATES AND HEADS OF ALL INTELLIGENCE AND DEFENSE AGENCIES

SUBJECT: CNN Organizational Hierarchy And Threat Assessment

As requested by the President and the National Security Council, the Agency has prepared a summary of the information gathered on the hierarchy of the multinational media company CNN. CNN is considered the most prominent actor in a loosely knit coalition of leftist organizations that have adopted the strategy of reporting information pertaining to current events and attempting to pose questions to White House officials, both of which represent extreme threats to the sitting administration.

CNN first emerged in 1980 under the control of the organization's founder and American ideologue Robert Edward "Ted" Turner III. The network gradually rose to prominence and extended its influence by recruiting motivated and highly trained anchors and reporters to carry out its radical agenda of continuously purveying factual information to the public en masse. By the early 1990s, CNN was considered one of the most powerful and influential forces within the highly dangerous media sphere. During that time, they developed an extremist left-wing philosophy that built on the hostile ideologies espoused by older fundamentalist organizations such as NBC and CBS.

Following its rise in the United States, the network has spread to nearly every nation on the globe, extending its influence to almost two billion people. At present, CNN has over 3,000 active recruits carrying out propaganda operations and utilizing a number of dangerous tactics, including fact checks, interviews, and morning talk shows, which together have the ability to devastate the President and this administration, and under certain circumstances, destroy it completely.

With Turner exerting minimal influence over CNNs day-to-day operations, Jeff Zucker is now considered by many to be the group's ideological mastermind and he appears to dictate much of CNN's long-term expansion strategies. These factors have led us to classify Zucker as the highest priority target.

Underneath Zucker, CNN is highly deputized with numerous important players each controlling a faction of the radical media network. The umbrella organization provides resources, training, and expertise to its agents to aid in their missions, but details of specific offensives are the purview of individual anchors and their particular associates. This decentralization allows CNN to stay mobile and varied in its attacks on the U.S. government and ensures that if a single member perishes or is forced out, the power vacuum can be quickly filled by another journalist.

Some leading members, such as Wolf Blitzer, are highly visible but act as little more than figureheads meant to motivate and inspire the true journalists among the network's ranks. The Agency believes the radical media organization's greatest power rests with top anchors like Jake Tapper and prominent commentators like Van Jones, who have proven adept at inflicting harm on the administration and often act independently and with impunity. A more detailed layout of the network's hierarchy and key players follows below.

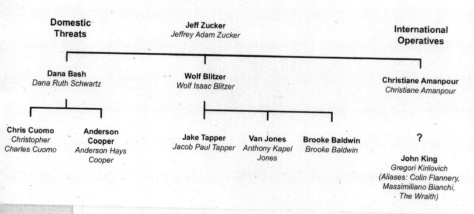

CNN Suspected Organizational Hierarchy

Jeff Zucker
Jeffrey Adam Zucker

Domestic Threats

International Operatives

Dana Bash
Dana Ruth Schwartz

Wolf Blitzer
Wolf Isaac Blitzer

Christiane Amanpour
Christiane Amanpour

Chris Cuomo
Christopher Charles Cuomo

Anderson Cooper
Anderson Hays Cooper

Jake Tapper
Jacob Paul Tapper

Van Jones
Anthony Kapel Jones

Brooke Baldwin
Brooke Baldwin

?

John King
Gregori Kirilovich
(Aliases: Colin Flannery, Massimiliano Bianchi, The Wraith)

Jeff Zucker

FULL NAME: Jeffery Adam Zucker
PLACE OF BIRTH: Homestead, Florida
SEX: Male
HEIGHT: 5' 9"
WEIGHT: Approx. 180 lbs.
HAIR COLOR: Bald
EYE COLOR: Brown
RACE: Jewish
SPECIALIZED SKILLS: Command-and-Control, Analytics, Strategic Thinking

POSITION: President, Operational Director, and Ideological Leader of CNN

KNOWN CRIMES: Organizing funding for hundreds of journalistic pieces targeting President Trump. Conspiring to inform U.S. nationals about the actions undertaken by this administration. Attempting to claim primary credit for the success of The Apprentice.

NOTES: While it may appear Zucker exerts only limited control over CNN, behind the scenes he is known to be ruthless and he will stop at nothing to destroy the administration. He has repeatedly instructed his subordinates to take extraordinary actions, including reporting unflattering quotes President Trump was caught on tape uttering and revealing the personal and professional backgrounds of many of the administration's cabinet nominees. Zucker's removal from power or his complete elimination is the primary goal of our operation as we move forward.

Dana Bash

FULL NAME: Dana Ruth Schwartz
PLACE OF BIRTH: Montvale, New Jersey
SEX: Female
HEIGHT: 5' 2"
WEIGHT: Approx. 120 lbs.
HAIR COLOR: Blonde
EYE COLOR: Hazel
RACE: Jewish
SPECIALIZED SKILLS: Data Manipulation, Brainwashing, Electronics

POSITION: Deputy Operations Chief

KNOWN CRIMES: Deliberately propagating highly damaging information regarding the administration's plans to step up deportations and ban refugees from entering the country. Disseminating the radical beliefs of wanted criminals and known enemies of the American state John McCain and Lindsey Graham. Attempting to harm President Trump directly by asking him several questions during the 2016 election campaign.

NOTES: Bash is currently Zucker's top deputy and considered the originator and ideological force behind many of CNN's most egregious attempts at probing, insightful journalism. Because of the damage she has already caused the administration, we are currently planning several clandestine operations to eliminate the considerable threat she poses.

Wolf Blitzer

FULL NAME: Wolf Isaac Blitzer
PLACE OF BIRTH: Augsburg, Germany
SEX: Male
HEIGHT: 5' 10"
WEIGHT: Approx. 175 lbs.
HAIR COLOR: Gray
EYE COLOR: Blue
RACE: German Jewish
SPECIALIZED SKILLS: Tactical Management, Propaganda

POSITION: Chief Commander of American Political Operations

KNOWN CRIMES: Indoctrinating hundreds of thousands of CNN's followers with disturbing assertions and graphic images of President Trump's inaugural crowd. Making numerous destructive claims that the President's business dealings may present conflicts of interest.

NOTES: The most publicly visible member of CNN, Blitzer often appears in the organization's propaganda videos and occupies a prominent spot as the radical group's primary spokesperson. However, intelligence gathering has revealed he holds little true power, generally acting as a messenger for the journalistic efforts carried out by his subordinates. He is highly vulnerable to being overthrown by Tapper.

Jake Tapper

FULL NAME: Jacob Paul Tapper
PLACE OF BIRTH: New York City, New York
SEX: Male
HEIGHT: 6'
WEIGHT: Approx. 185 lbs.
HAIR COLOR: Brown
EYE COLOR: Brown
RACE: Jewish
SPECIALIZED SKILLS: Surveillance, Interrogation, Precision Strikes

POSITION: Political Assassination Specialist

KNOWN CRIMES: Providing critical support for Hillary Clinton's efforts to destroy the nation, typically by interviewing Trump surrogates and asking them direct questions. Ambushing the President on-air with the outrageous demand that he disavow statements made by KKK leaders in support of his campaign. Repeatedly reminding American people of the things the President has said and done.

NOTES: Tapper has risen rapidly through CNN's hierarchy over the last decade. He is highly proficient at targeting representatives of the administration and brutally forcing them to answer all facets of the questions posed to them. He is highly ambitious and may be angling for a leadership position directly below Zucker, if not seeking to replace him outright. He is a top priority for elimination.

John King

FULL NAME: Gregori Kirilovich
PLACE OF BIRTH: Unknown
SEX: Male
HEIGHT: 6' 1"
WEIGHT: Approx. 190 lbs.
HAIR COLOR: Gray
EYE COLOR: Blue
RACE: Eastern European
SPECIALIZED SKILLS: Infiltration, Firearms Marksmanship, Hand-to-Hand Combat

POSITION: Unknown [Possibly an independent gun-for-hire in the employ of CNN]

KNOWN CRIMES: Smuggling. Assassination of Russian government agent. Racketeering. Arms trafficking. Citing Trump's unfavorable poll numbers on live television.

NOTES: Little is known about Kirilovich (alias "John King") other than that he is an extremely dangerous individual with apparent black-ops training. He has been found carrying out various high-profile journalistic initiatives on behalf of numerous hostile media agencies over the past 25 years, often filling power vacuums and assuming leadership positions following the elimination of high-ranking operatives. If we are able to obtain further information about his background and the atrocities he has committed, he may be vulnerable to blackmail. However, he appears extremely hardened and may not surrender to our will under any circumstance, instead seeking to take down as many of those he perceives as aggressors with him.

OTHER KNOWN ALIASES: Colin Flannery, Massimiliano Bianchi, The Wraith

From: Colleen Barros <barrosc@hhs.gov>
Sent: Friday, March 17, 2017 9:07 AM
To: Tom Price <pricet@hhs.gov>
Subject: "Smoldering" Radius

Secretary Price,

I've been looking over the Theseus paperwork, and I was wondering if we should be at all concerned that the "affected radius" for the Smoldering to Come encompasses the entire Eastern seaboard?

Thanks,
Colleen

From: Tom Price <pricet@hhs.gov>
Sent: Friday, March 17, 2017 2:30 PM
To: Colleen Barros <barrosc@hhs.gov>
Subject: RE: "Smoldering" Radius

I asked one of the gebbeths about the size of the deflagration zone, and apparently it's actually essential to bringing their Corpse Lord into the material realm, so no need to worry!

From: Colleen Barros <barrosc@hhs.gov>
Sent: Friday, March 17, 2017 2:47 PM
To: Tom Price <pricet@hhs.gov>
Subject: "Smoldering" Radius

Oh, okay then. Thanks for clarifying. See you Monday! (I'm taking off early today cause my sis is in town!)

Vice President Michael Pence's Daily Schedule

APRIL 7, 2017

6:00 a.m.	Brisk jog through stations of the cross
6:30 a.m.	Shower and dress in darkness to avoid sinful glimpse of nude body
8:00 a.m.	Hair polishing appt.
10:30 a.m.	Talk shop with Marvin & The Whizz on 98.3 District Radio
11:00 a.m.	Look out window for signs of Rapture
12:00 p.m.	Lunch alone
1:00 p.m.–2:30 p.m.	Select aborted-fetus placard from personal collection to hold up in Silver Spring on Saturday
3:00 p.m.	Meet with Attorney General to discuss reintroduction of stoning to criminal justice system
5:00 p.m.	Swearing-in ceremony to act as weekend president
7:00 p.m.	Look out window for signs of Rapture

Brook Trout — State Fish of New Jersey
- State Fish since 1991
- Typically live in small streams and lakes, and definitely prefer colder and purer water
- "Trout" is a misnomer- it's actually a char!

Rio Grande Cutthroat Trout — State Fish of New Mexico
- Dull yellow or bronze coloring on the back, red-orange coloring on the sides, with a pinkish belly and irregular dorsal specks
- Can grow up to 16 inches long
- Diet includes both aquatic and terrestrial insects
- Southern-most subspecies of cutthroat trout

Brook Trout — State Fish of New York
- More sensitive than many fish to high concentration of acidity and poor oxygenation
- Average life span is between 2 and 6 years

Striped Bass — State Fish of New York (marine)
- Average 2 to 3 feet long, and 10 to 30 lbs.
- Younger fish live in estuaries or coastal sounds before migrating to the Atlantic Ocean

Red Drum — State Fish of North Carolina (salt water)
- Dark reddish color on back, white on belly, with distinctive eyespot on tail
- Can grow to over 3 feet long and weigh over 50 lbs.
- Can live for over 40 years!
- Typically live in estuaries near where they're born; they don't travel much

Southern Appalachian Brook Trout — State Fish of North Carolina (fresh water)
- Males color during spawning season, with an impressive color palette
- Ease of catching makes them popular for sport fishing

Northern Pike — State Fish of North Dakota
- Olive-green with black spots on the back, and fins are often reddish
- Grow between 26 and 22 inches long, weigh 30 to 35 lbs.
- Diet includes frogs and fish -- often including other pike
- Aggressive predators, who hide in weeds patiently waiting to ambush their prey

Fun Fact
Ohio doesn't have a state fish!

White Bass — State Fish of Oklahoma
- Pale silver in color, often with greenish hues
- Grow between 10 and 12 inches long, weigh 1 lb.
- Diet includes zooplankton, small crustaceans, and leptodora
- Female white bass can lay over 500,000 eggs during spawning season

Chinook Salmon — State Fish of Oregon
- Grow to 2 to 3 feet long and weigh 10 to 30 lbs.
- Salmon runs require them to travel hundreds or even thousands of miles

Brook Trout — State Fish of Pennsylvania
- Camouflage selves by changing color of scales
- 10 to 14 principle dorsal rays; 9 to 13 principle anal rays

Striped Bass — State Fish of Rhode Island
- Can live up to 39 years old
- Anadromous
- Predators during juvenile stage include cod, weakfish, bluefish; adults have few predators

Striped Bass — State Fish of South Carolina
- Moderate swimmers, but not fast enough to always catch prey
- Prefer to live in temperatures between 55 and 68 degrees F

Walleye — State Fish of South Dakota
- Named for the reflective pigment covering its own (tapetum lucidum), enabling it to see in turbid water
- They're more active at night due to sensitivity to light

Smallmouth Bass — State Fish of Tennessee (sport fish)
- (replacing largemouth bass)
- Grow to 12 to 20 inches, weighing between 1 and 5 lbs.
- Brownish in color, with darker vertical bands or large spots
- Also known as brownie, brown bass, and smallie

Channel Catfish — State Fish of Tennessee (commercial fish)
- Like to live in quiet, warm calm areas, such as deep pools, weedy areas, lake shores, and even beaver dams
- Have distinct, precise breeding habits

Guadalupe Bass — State Fish of Texas
- Olive-green or temme colored, lighter than most bass species
- Rarely grows larger than 3.5 lbs.
- Exists almost exclusively in central Texas, popular in catch-and-release fishing
- Dwindling populations due to interbreeding with other local bass populations

Bonneville Cutthroat Trout — State Fish of Utah
- Can grow to 22 to 26 inches and weigh up to 10 lbs.
- Reside around tributaries to the Great Salt Lake
- Once lived in Lake Bonneville, an ancient freshwater lake
- Important food source for both Mormon pioneers and their Native predecessors

Brook Trout — State Fish of Vermont (cold water)
- 8 to 10 pelvic rays, 11 to 14 pectoral rays
- Typically, one male fertilizes eggs, but can be more

Walleye — State Fish of Vermont (warm water)
- Large mouth is filled with sharp teeth, and it has more than 1,000 taste buds
- Nocturnal, traveling up 50 miles a night in search of food

Brook Trout — State Fish of Virginia (fresh water)
- Typically breeds once per year, in late summer or early fall
- Achieve breeding maturity at 2 years old

Striped Bass — State Fish of Virginia (salt water)
- Lack of eyelids causes them to go to deeper water during bright daytime
- Females typically larger than males

Steelhead Trout — State Fish of Washington
- Gradient of dark olive to silvery-white coloration
- Example of anadromous rainbow trout
- Diet includes insects, mollusks, crustaceans
- Are known among fish for their ability to adapt to a wide variety of environments

West Virginia Brook Trout — State Fish of West Virginia
- Fairly territorial creatures, and dislike competition for space and food
- Disease, predators, and starvation are key factors affecting lifespan

Cutthroat Trout — State Fish of Wyoming
- Distinct red patches around throat and lower mouth
- Species of cutthroat trout can grow from 6 to 40 inches long
- Weigh between 2 and 17 lbs.
- Eat small crustaceans, aquatic insects, small fish, and fish eggs

But Let's Not Forget Saltwater Fish...

Spotlight On The Gulf Coast
- The Gulf of Mexico is around 600,000 sq. mi.
- About 4,000 miles of shoreline
- 60% of U.S. river water drains into Gulf of Mexico

Fish Of The Gulf — Great Barracuda

Fish Of The Gulf — Bonefish

Fish Of The Gulf — Atlantic Bonito

Fish Of The Gulf — Atlantic Bonito

Fish Of The Gulf — Atlantic Croaker

Fish Of The Gulf — Dolphin Fish

Fish Of The Gulf — Southern Flounder

Fish Of The Gulf — Flying Fish

Fish Of The Gulf — Black Grouper

Fish Of The Gulf — Coney Grouper

Fish Of The Gulf — Goliath Grouper

Fish Of The Gulf — Graysby Grouper

Fish Of The Gulf — Red Hind Grouper

Fish Of The Gulf — Nassau Grouper

Fish Of The Gulf — Tiger Grouper

Fish Of The Gulf — Blue-Striped Grunt

Fish Of The Gulf — White Grunt

Fish Of The Gulf — Hogfish

Fish Of The Gulf — Greater Amberjack

Fish Of The Gulf — Horse-Eye Jack

Fish Of The Gulf — Ladyfish

Fish Of The Gulf — Leatherjacket

Fish Of The Gulf — Lionfish

Fish Of The Gulf — Marlin

Fish Of The Gulf — Atlantic Needlefish

Fish Of The Gulf — Pompano

Fish Of The Gulf — Sailfish

Fish Of The Gulf — American Shad

Fish Of The Gulf — Sheepshead

Fish Of The Gulf — Snook

Fish Of The Gulf — Atlantic Spadefish

Fish Of The Gulf — Stingray

Fish Of The Gulf — Tarpon

Fish Of The Gulf — Tilefish

Fish Of The Gulf — Triggerfish

Fish Of The Gulf — Bluefin Tuna

Spotlight On The Pacific Coast
7,623 miles of coastline (including Hawaii)
Pacific is largest and deepest ocean on the planet
Over 60% of world's fish catch comes from Pacific

Fish Of The Pacific Coast — Spotted Eagle Ray

Fish Of The Pacific Coast — Silky Shark

Fish Of The Pacific Coast — Bull Shark

Fish Of The Pacific Coast — Yellow Longnose Butterflyfish

Fish Of The Pacific Coast — Nurse Shark

Fish Of The Pacific Coast — California Moray Eel

Fish Of The Pacific Coast — King Angelfish

Fish Of The Pacific Coast — Barberfish

Fish Of The Pacific Coast — Ocean Sunfish

Fish Of The Pacific Coast — Bat Ray

Fish Of The Pacific Coast — Lemon Shark

Fish Of The Pacific Coast — Longnose Hawkfish

Fish Of The Pacific Coast — Painted Greenling

Fish Of The Pacific Coast — Thornback Ray

Fish Of The Pacific Coast — Guitarfish

Fish Of The Pacific Coast — Cabezon

Fish Of The Pacific Coast — Gopher Rockfish
Fish Of The Pacific Coast — Copper Rockfish
Fish Of The Pacific Coast — Vermilion Rockfish
Fish Of The Pacific Coast — Torpedo Ray
Fish Of The Pacific Coast — Moorish Idol

Fish Of The Pacific Coast — Wolf Eel
Fish Of The Pacific Coast — Lingcod
Fish Of The Pacific Coast — Quillback Rockfish
Fish Of The Pacific Coast — Sargo
Fish Of The Pacific Coast — Garibaldi

Fish Of The Pacific Coast — Salema
Fish Of The Pacific Coast — Scorpionfish
Fish Of The Pacific Coast — Barracuda
Fish Of The Pacific Coast — Queenfish
Fish Of The Pacific Coast — Spiny Dogfish

Heading Back Inland To Freshwater Fish

Let's Take A Trip Around The Lakes Of America!

Spotlight On The Great Lakes — Lake Superior
Largest freshwater lake in the world (31,700 sq. mi.)
Has over 200 rivers feeding into it
Enough water in Lake Superior to cover N. and S. American continents in nearly 1 foot of water!
Boasts more than 80 different species of fish

Spotlight On The Great Lakes — Lake Michigan
Third-largest Great Lake by surface area (22,404 sq. mi.)
Has an unusual, slow-moving circulatory pattern
Important in many aspects of U.S. trade

Spotlight On The Great Lakes — Lake Huron
Second-largest Great Lake by surface area (23,012 sq. mi.), fifth-largest freshwater lake in world
Over 3,800 miles of shoreline, most of any G. L.
Native fish have been hit hard by invasive species

Spotlight On The Great Lakes — Lake Erie
Fourth-largest Great Lake by surface area (9,910 sq. mi.)
Shortest average water residence time (2.6 years)
Freezes over more than other G. L., but also warmest

Spotlight On The Great Lakes — Lake Ontario
Smallest Great Lake by surface area (7,340 sq. mi.)
Impressive diversity not just of fish, but birds, amphibians, and plants as well
Has been drastically affected by overfishing

Fish Of The Great Lakes — Brook Trout
Fish Of The Great Lakes — Lake Sturgeon
Fish Of The Great Lakes — Lake Trout

Fish Of The Great Lakes — Muskellunge
Fish Of The Great Lakes — Northern Pike
Fish Of The Great Lakes — Pumpkinseed
Fish Of The Great Lakes — Walleye
Fish Of The Great Lakes — Yellow Perch

Fish Of The Great Lakes — Atlantic Salmon
Fish Of The Great Lakes — Brown Trout
Fish Of The Great Lakes — Coho Salmon
Fish Of The Great Lakes — Smelt
Fish Of The Great Lakes — Goby

Fish Of The Great Lakes — Ruffe
Fish Of The Great Lakes — Sea Lamprey
Fish Of The Great Lakes — Alewife
Fish Of The Great Lakes — Sculpin

While The Great Lakes Are Undeniably Great, The Fish Of America's Lesser-Known Lakes Really Show Off The Rich Tapestry Of Fish In The U.S.

Spotlight On Iliamna Lake
Alaska

1,012 sq. mi., average depth of 144 feet
Largest lake in Alaska, connected to Bristol Bay
Rumors of an Iliamna Lake Monster

Fish Of The Iliamna Lake

Northern Pike

Fish Of The Iliamna Lake

Rainbow Trout

Fish Of The Iliamna Lake

Sockeye Salmon

Fish Of The Iliamna Lake

Atlantic Salmon

Fish Of The Iliamna Lake

Coho Salmon

Spotlight On Lake Okeechobee
Florida

Surface area of 734 sq. mi., but unusually shallow—only 9 feet deep
Has dealt with significant hurricanes in its history
Around 60 species of fish

Fish Of Lake Okeechobee

Bluegill

Fish Of Lake Okeechobee

Largemouth Bass

Fish Of Lake Okeechobee

Sunfish

Fish Of Lake Okeechobee

Striped Bass

Fish Of Lake Okeechobee

Carp

Fish Of Lake Okeechobee

American Eel

Fish Of Lake Okeechobee

Alligator Gar

Fish Of Lake Okeechobee

Longnose Gar

Fish Of Lake Okeechobee

Spotted Gar

Fish Of Lake Okeechobee

Oscar Fish

Fish Of Lake Okeechobee

Snook

Spotlight On Lake Champlain
New York/Vermont

Surface area of 514 sq. mi., with average depth of over 60 feet
Its basin collects and drains over half of Vermont's water
Over 80 species of fish

Fish Of Lake Champlain

Yellow Perch

Fish Of Lake Champlain

Sunfish

Fish Of Lake Champlain

Smelt

Fish Of Lake Champlain

Pickerel

Fish Of Lake Champlain

Atlantic Salmon

Fish Of Lake Champlain

Bullhead

Fish Of Lake Champlain

Rainbow Trout

Spotlight On Devils Lake
North Dakota

Largest natural body of water in N.D. (3,810 sq. mi.)
Endorheic basin
Has been drastically affected by overfishing

Fish Of Devils Lake

Brown Trout

Fish Of Devils Lake

Panfish

Fish Of Devils Lake

Northern Pike

Fish Of Devils Lake

Walleye

Fish Of Devils Lake

Crappie

Fish Of Devils Lake

Smallmouth Bass

Spotlight On Lake Cumberland
Kentucky

Ninth-largest reservoir in U.S. (102.4 sq. mi.)
Could cover state of Kentucky in 3 inches of water
Home of many of Kentucky's record-setting fish

Fish Of Lake Cumberland

Rainbow Trout

Fish Of Lake Cumberland

Brown Trout

Fish Of Lake Cumberland

Striped Bass

Fish Of The Great Lakes

Walleye

Fish Of The Great Lakes

Lake Trout

Spotlight On Moosehead Lake
Maine

Largest mountain lake in eastern U.S. (120 sq. mi.)
Its name comes from its shape
Thoreau once waxed poetic about it!

From: Elliot Beliveau <elliot.beliveau@mazarsusa.com>
Sent: Monday, April 3, 2017 9:19 AM
To: Donald Trump <trumpd@wh.gov>
Subject: Personal Accounting Invoice – March 2017

Good morning Donald,

Please find your itemized invoice below for the personal accounting services provided during March. Please note that this month's fees include your personal tax filings for the year 2016.

$1,250 shell company registration charge (61x)	$	76,250.00
General filing and forgery fees	$	9,410.00
"Courtesy donation" to Premier of Cayman Islands	$	25,000.00
Stewardship of Trump Family (all but Tiffany) Trust	$	5,340.00
Replacement gas valve for evidence furnace	$	111.90
Carvel 3D Racecar Signature Cake	$	25.99
Client's Federal and State Tax bill for 2016	$	16.87
Payout to fall guy's family	$	1,850,000.00
TOTAL	**$**	**1,966,154.76**

Regards,

Elliot Beliveau MBA/CMA/CPA
Partner, Private Client Services Director
WeiserMazars LLP
Accounting, Auditing and Assurance

MARCH 23, 2017

MEMORANDUM FOR THE PRESIDENT OF THE UNITED STATES
AND SENIOR WHITE HOUSE STAFF

FROM: REINCE PRIEBUS, ASSISTANT TO THE PRESIDENT
AND CHIEF OF STAFF

SUBJECT: Update On White House's Efforts To Secure Votes In Favor Of American
Health Care Act

At the Speaker's request, the House of Representatives is to vote on the American Health Care Act tomorrow. Presently, there are not enough votes to ensure the bill's passage. Senior members of the White House have been in continuous contact with Republican representatives this week in an attempt to secure votes in favor of the bill. Here is an updated summary of key representatives and what they would require in exchange for a Yea vote:

REPRESENTATIVE	INDUCEMENT
Jason Chaffetz (UT 3)	Demanding a more robust defense strategy to protect him from his constituents
Rob Wittman (VA 1)	OUT - David Koch told him he's not allowed to vote for it no matter what
Jeff Fortenberry (NE 1)	Onboard if Lincoln, Nebraska can get more support for official 2028 Olympics bid
Scott Taylor (VA 2)	Needs pledge from us not to make campaign stop in his district in 2018
Mark Meadows (NC 11)	Will only flip vote if Obamacare fully repealed and replaced with a nationwide infectious disease pandemic
David McKinley (WV 1)	Has a new wood patio out back behind the house he needs help staining
Mark Amodei (NV 2)	OUT - He clearly articulated that any proposed plan needs to improve, rather than destroy, quality of care
Hal Rogers (KY 5)	Wants DoT funding to repair potholes in state's horse tracks
Raul Labrador (ID 1)	IN - Just needs $500,000 cash and he's good to go!
Ken Buck (CO 4)	Wants to see at least 20 fellow Reps in person for his open-mic standup set at Wonderland Ballroom (unclear if we can pull this off)
Rod Blum (IA 1)	Needs our assurance that he can go room-to-room at University of Iowa Children's Hospital and tell families they're losing coverage in person
Andy Biggs (AZ 5)	Ivanka
Billy Long (MO 7)	Only thing he asked for is improvement in the economy and more jobs for his constituents, so he's probably off the table

From: Kellyanne Conway <conwayk@wh.gov>
Sent: Thursday, March 23, 2017 7:41 AM
To: Ainsley Earhardt <aearhardt@fox.com>
Subject: Booking a segment

Hey Ainsley,

Just wanted to check in and see if you had any open spots on Fox & Friends tomorrow. I've got some insight about the new healthcare plan I'd love to share with your viewers. Let me know!

- Kellyanne

From: Ainsley Earhardt <aearhardt@fox.com>
Sent: Thursday, March 23, 2017 8:23 AM
To: Kellyanne Conway <conwayk@wh.gov>
Subject: RE: Booking a segment

Hi Kellyanne,

We already have a number of experts lined up to fill out our healthcare segment, but I'll let you know if something opens up.

Ainsley

From: Kellyanne Conway <conwayk@wh.gov>
Sent: Thursday, March 23, 2017 8:32 AM
To: Ainsley Earhardt <aearhardt@fox.com>
Subject: RE: Booking a segment

Hi Ainsley,

I don't have to talk about healthcare, I can talk about anything! What topics are you covering tomorrow? I can talk about the budget or the Supreme Court or immigration—anything.

I'm not sure if my aides have made this clear to you, but I will physically disappear from the visible spectrum if I do not appear on television every 24 hours, so it would be really great if you could fit me in. I know it would help out your ratings, too! ;)

My fingertips and neck are already starting to become translucent, so please consider it.

- Kellyanne

From: Kellyanne Conway <conwayk@wh.gov>
Sent: Thursday, March 23, 2017 9:58 AM
To: Ainsley Earhardt <aearhardt@fox.com>
Subject: RE: Booking a segment

I'm not sure if you got my last email but I wanted to check in again. Look, the reality here is that I haven't been on anything since Inside Politics yesterday afternoon and light is starting to pass through my body. If I don't get on a morning show first thing tomorrow, I'm pretty sure I will go completely and permanently transparent. I just need a few minutes--90 seconds even--talking in front of some television cameras and lights and I'll be fully visible again. You got that?

If you could just throw to me for a question or two, that's really all I need. Just a short segment--onscreen then off real quick. Okay? I can see my keyboard through my hands as I type this.

- Kellyanne

From: Ainsley Earhardt <aearhardt@fox.com>
Sent: Thursday, March 23, 2017 10:12 AM
To: Kellyanne Conway <conwayk@wh.gov>
Subject: RE: Booking a segment

Hi again Kellyanne,

I'm not sure I totally understand the situation, but like I said, I'll be in touch if we have a spot for you.

Ainsley

From: Kellyanne Conway <conwayk@wh.gov>
Sent: Thursday, March 23, 2017 10:15 AM
To: Ainsley Earhardt <aearhardt@fox.com>
Subject: RE: Booking a segment

Ainsley, someone just tried to sit in this chair while I was still in it!! You have to get me on tomorrow!!! Please, I need this!!

From: Kellyanne Conway <conwayk@wh.gov>
Sent: Thursday, March 23, 2017 10:52 AM
To: Ainsley Earhardt <aearhardt@fox.com>
Subject: RE: Booking a segment

Hey Ainsley, how about this? I have an exclusive scoop on the president's private investments--a totally new revelation that's never been heard before--and I would like to offer your show first access to it!! This is real top of the news cycle stuff!! What do you say?

Of course, I'm also happy to talk about any topic for any amount of time, too. You want me to weigh in on monetary policy, a major weather event, talk about a new springtime fitness routine--it's all good with me. And if you just want to do a video call, that's fine too!

Ainsley, please, I'm almost completely gone from view, so this is probably your last chance to have me on. Honest to God, I'm just a faint outline at this point. Everyone is walking around looking for me even though I keep yelling that I'm right here. Please, Ainsley, please!! This could be the last time I ever communicate with anyone!! Oh, God!

-      Kellyanne

From: Ainsley Earhardt <aearhardt@fox.com>
Sent: Thursday, March 23, 2017 6:26 PM
To: Kellyanne Conway <conwayk@wh.gov>
Subject: RE: Booking a segment

Hi Kellyanne,

We actually just had a spot on tomorrow's show open up. You'd be answering questions about the president's jobs plan. Does that work for you?

Ainsley

From: Kellyanne Conway <conwayk@wh.gov>
Sent: Thursday, March 23, 2017 6:27 PM
To: Ainsley Earhardt <aearhardt@fox.com>
Subject: RE: Booking a segment

Ainsley!!? Can you see this?!?!

They can't see or hear me at all and they took my office!! I am not sure if I exist anymore!! Email me back if you can see this????!!

MARCH 14, 2017

MEMORANDUM FOR   **ALL WHITE HOUSE STAFF**

FROM: **DR. RONNY JACKSON, M.D., U.S.N.,
PHYSICIAN TO THE PRESIDENT**

SUBJECT: **URGENT: INFECTIOUS DISEASE OUTBREAK**

All White House personnel are requested to monitor themselves for signs and symptoms of an as-yet unidentified infectious disease that has been reported in and around the West Wing.

Although the nature and manner of transmission of this illness are still under investigation, the medical team has traced the infection back to several severely mutilated and partially consumed rodent carcasses that were found strewn across the carpet outside Chief Strategist Steve Bannon's office. We must advise against going anywhere near that portion of the first floor.

Medical interventions must be taken immediately if you have experienced any of the following symptoms in the past 24 hours:

- Chills or fever
- Inflamed red eyes
- Diarrhea, nausea, and/or vomiting
- Craving to eat dirt, ice, or paper
- Raised black welts that burn when exposed to sunlight

- Night terrors that persist throughout waking hours
- Caustic or sulfurous skin secretions
- Chronic, uncontrollable screaming
- Lingering feelings of unease around children and reflective surfaces

We are working around the clock to isolate the outbreak and develop a suitable treatment. However, it is imperative that you come to the triage stations that have been erected on the South Lawn before your welts harden, split, and release a cloud of spores. DO NOT scratch at these welts, as broken skin may leave you susceptible to the tularemia and pneumonic plague bacteria we detected within the Chief Strategist's private bathroom quarters last week. Additionally, if you see visions of a winged jackal when you close your eyes, proceed immediately to our lead physician and DO NOT touch anyone.

Leftover surgical masks from February's hoof-and-mouth outbreak are still available in our office, and we strongly encourage everyone to use those through the end of the week.

As a precautionary measure, we're also asking all full-time White House staff to burn their clothing and shave their bodies completely.

Thank you for your compliance.

EXECUTIVE OFFICE OF THE PRESIDENT
WASHINGTON, D.C.

WEST WING EXPENSE REPORT

WEEK OF FEBRUARY 6 – 12, 2017

Date	Staff Member	Description	Amount
2/6	Jared Kushner	Annual Mar-A-Lago membership dues	$ 200,000.00
2/6	Ben Carson	Brain lubricants	$ 800.00
2/6	Steve Bannon	37% Formaldehyde, 500 ml	$ 23.90
2/7	Eric Trump	Caramel toffee square from the sweets shoppe in town	$ 3.00
2/7	Mike Pence	Tithing for US federal government	$ 365,000,000,000.00
2/7	Steve Bannon	Syringe, 20 ml (15)	$ 17.14
2/7	Steve Bannon	Syringe, 60 ml (15)	$ 39.21
2/7	Steve Bannon	Syringe, 100 ml (15)	$ 62.76
2/7	Barron Trump	New business cards	$ 75.00
2/8	Stephen Miller	55-gallon drum petroleum jelly and 86-pack women's pantyhose	$ 301.87
2/8	Ivanka Trump	Unprompted request for $500,000 of taxpayer money	$ 500,000.00
2/9	Steve Bannon	Sklar Henly Vascular Surgery Retractor	$ 712.83
2/9	Steve Bannon	Sklar Zalkind Lung Retractor 3" x 12"	$ 341.14
2/9	Jeff Sessions	Size 4T suit and tie	$ 27.96
2/9	Steve Bannon	Sklar Davidson Scapula Retractor 3" x 3.5"	$ 438.91
2/9	Steve Bannon	Sklar Harrington Splanchnic Retractor 12"	$ 398.45
2/10	Mike Pence	Monthly precautionary gay conversion therapy session	$ 700.00
2/10	Reince Priebus	GoDaddy.com renewal fee for WhiteHouse.gov domain	$ 9.99
2/11	Steve Bannon	Nature's Match Pig Feed - 50 lbs	$ 38.11
2/11	Donald Trump	Replacement for lost nuclear football	$ 13,000.00
2/12	Steve Bannon	Pygmy Hog - Guwahati Zoo of Assam	$ 84,998.00
		TOTAL	$ 365,000,801,988.27

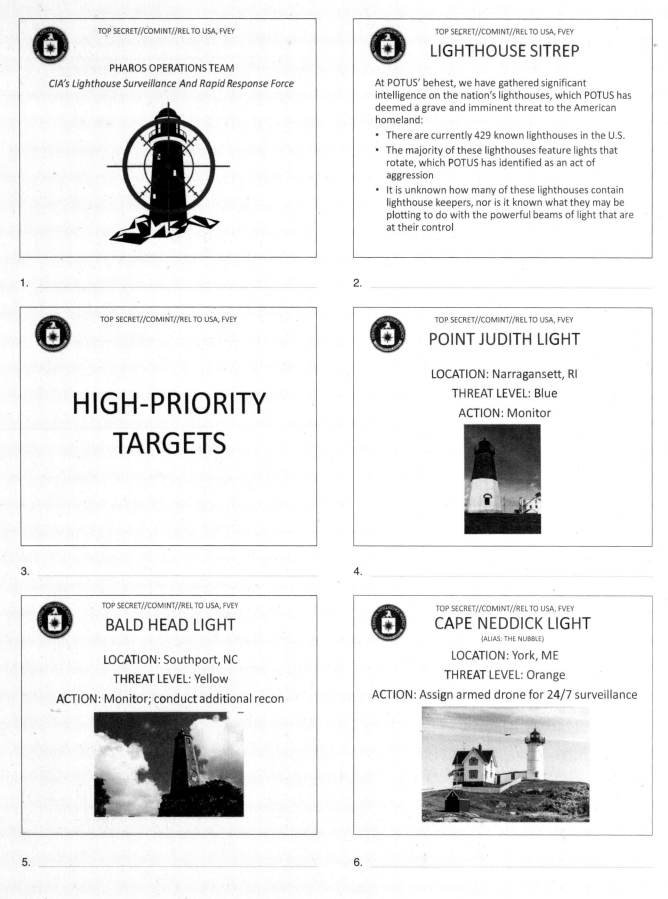

Slide 1

TOP SECRET//COMINT//REL TO USA, FVEY

PHAROS OPERATIONS TEAM

CIA's Lighthouse Surveillance And Rapid Response Force

1.

Slide 2

TOP SECRET//COMINT//REL TO USA, FVEY

LIGHTHOUSE SITREP

At POTUS' behest, we have gathered significant intelligence on the nation's lighthouses, which POTUS has deemed a grave and imminent threat to the American homeland:

- There are currently 429 known lighthouses in the U.S.
- The majority of these lighthouses feature lights that rotate, which POTUS has identified as an act of aggression
- It is unknown how many of these lighthouses contain lighthouse keepers, nor is it known what they may be plotting to do with the powerful beams of light that are at their control

2.

Slide 3

TOP SECRET//COMINT//REL TO USA, FVEY

HIGH-PRIORITY TARGETS

3.

Slide 4

TOP SECRET//COMINT//REL TO USA, FVEY

POINT JUDITH LIGHT

LOCATION: Narragansett, RI
THREAT LEVEL: Blue
ACTION: Monitor

4.

Slide 5

TOP SECRET//COMINT//REL TO USA, FVEY

BALD HEAD LIGHT

LOCATION: Southport, NC
THREAT LEVEL: Yellow
ACTION: Monitor; conduct additional recon

5.

Slide 6

TOP SECRET//COMINT//REL TO USA, FVEY

CAPE NEDDICK LIGHT
(ALIAS: THE NUBBLE)

LOCATION: York, ME
THREAT LEVEL: Orange
ACTION: Assign armed drone for 24/7 surveillance

6.

TOP SECRET//COMINT//REL TO USA, FVEY

MORRIS ISLAND LIGHT

LOCATION: Morris Island, SC

THREAT LEVEL: <u>RED</u> **(EXTREME THREAT)**

ACTION: Disable or destroy

7. _____

TOP SECRET//COMINT//REL TO USA, FVEY

PRESQUE ISLE LIGHT

LOCATION: Erie, PA

THREAT LEVEL: <u>RED</u> **(EXTREME THREAT)**

ACTION: Identified for immediate targeted strike

8. _____

TOP SECRET//COMINT//REL TO USA, FVEY

INVESTIGATIVE OBJECTIVES

- As per POTUS' directive, we have prioritized the investigation of the following lighthouse-related threats:
  - Can a pattern be deciphered from the way their lights rotate around in circles?
  - What would be the result if a lighthouse or lighthouses turned their beams onto the American homeland instead of out to sea?
  - Why are they so tall? And could they get taller?
  - Could we, if necessary, use mirror technology to redirect beams back at lighthouses to use their own power against them?
  - Do lighthouses act in alliance with lobstermen?

9. _____

TOP SECRET//COMINT//REL TO USA, FVEY

INVESTIGATIVE OBJECTIVES

- We are also determining whether striped lighthouses and solid-colored lighthouses might represent rival factions and, if so, whether we could pit them against one another for our own ends.

10. _____

TOP SECRET//COMINT//REL TO USA, FVEY

PHAROS OPERATIONS TEAM

- In conjunction with POTUS, we have devised the following response:
  - 500 MQ-1 Predator drones deployed to patrol nation's seaboards and lakeshores to take out lighthouses if their beams become too powerful
  - 10 ICBMs readied to take out entire Maine coast if deemed necessary
  - Utilize black-ops team to covertly capture Tillamook Rock Light off coast of Oregon and attempt to extract vital information about lighthouse technology and plots against homeland, and if possible, turn lighthouse into mole for U.S. side
  - Through mix of airstrikes, timed charges, and incendiary devices, we estimate we can and will eliminate all lighthouses by mid-2018, as POTUS has requested

11. _____

From: Ryan Zinke <zinker@doi.gov>
Sent: Thursday, March 2, 2017 3:52 PM
To: Donald Trump <trumpd@wh.gov>
Subject: Interior Department Priorities

Mr. President,

In line with your directive to reduce overall size of government, I wanted to reach out with a few initial ideas for reducing redundancies in the Interior Dept. The DOI can certainly stand to roll back a few regulations and downsize some folks, but I think the real opportunity here for eliminating redundancy lies in the nation's Interior itself. To start, I think we can probably scrap at least 60 to 70 percent of the nation's redundant waterways.

I can get this effort up and running immediately with your go ahead.

Thank you,
Ryan

——
Secretary of the Interior

Department of the Interior
1849 C Street, N.W.
Washington, DC 20240
(202) 208-3100

From: Donald Trump <trumpd@wh.gov>
Sent: Friday, March 3, 2017 11:18 AM
To: Ryan Zinke <zinker@wh.gov>
Subject: RE: Interior Department Priorities

Yes. Get rid of as much water as possible

DJT

From: Ryan Zinke <zinker@doi.gov>
Sent: Friday, March 3, 2017 12:02 PM
To: Donald Trump <trumpd@wh.gov>
Subject: RE: Interior Department Priorities

Mr. President,

Thanks for replying so quickly. I was looking through things last night and apparently there's over 250,000 rivers in the country alone- definitely overkill. I think we could eliminate 200,000 rivers over the next two years easy. For example, the Mississippi- it's the biggest one, so I think we start there. You have got the Missouri river and the Illinois river right nearby, so there's no reason to have the Mississippi. If you need water access, you just go to one of those. That saves us over 2,000 miles of water right there.

Some other rivers that can definitely go are the Brazos, Pecos, and Red rivers- probably the Columbia as well. And did you know there's a Canadian River? Runs right through Oklahoma. It's as good as gone, you have my word. I'm also planning to cut anything under 40 miles long, all the waterways in Alaska (badly, badly underutilized), and all Streams. How does that sound?

Thank you,
Ryan

——
Secretary of the Interior

Department of the Interior
1849 C Street, N.W.
Washington, DC 20240
(202) 208-3100

From: Ryan Zinke <zinker@doi.gov>
Sent: Tuesday, March 7, 2017 2:12 PM
To: Donald Trump <trumpd@wh.gov>
Subject: RE: Interior Department Priorities

Mr. President,

Thank you, sir. I will get going on removing the rivers. I am also looking at eliminating redundancies in lakes. For instance it seems absurd to have five Great Lakes. My belief is we can get it down to one Great lake. Personally I think we should keep Lake Superior but I will defer to your judgement.

I've also got my eye on bays. Need more research, but potential cuts there.

Also, we should talk about the issue of water depth- there's a lot of wasted space as water gets deeper that we just don't need. I think there's room to slash some of the really deep water, not only in lakes but in the Gulf as well. Just a thought.

Thank you,
Ryan

———
Secretary of the Interior

Department of the Interior
1849 C Street, N.W.
Washington, DC 20240
(202) 208-3100

From: Donald Trump <trumpd@wh.gov>
Sent: Wednesday, March 8, 2017 10:34 AM
To: Ryan Zinke <zinker@wh.gov>
Subject: RE: Interior Department Priorities

Get rid of puddles too. They need to go

DJT

From: Ryan Zinke <zinker@doi.gov>
Sent: Wednesday, March 8, 2017 12:08 PM
To: Donald Trump <trumpd@wh.gov>
Subject: RE: Interior Department Priorities

Mr. President,

Thank you for your guidance on this matter. Looking forward to getting rid of all this unnecessary water from our country.

There is one more thing I'd like to run by you, sir. The more research we've done into the nation's water, the more that wetlands keep coming up. I believe they're a waste. Everything should either be land or water, not both- wetlands can't keep having it both ways. Personally I vote for land- there's clearly already enough water, but I wanted to hear your thoughts.

Thank you,
Ryan

———
Secretary of the Interior

Department of the Interior
1849 C Street, N.W.
Washington, DC 20240
(202) 208-3100

From: Donald Trump <trumpd@wh.gov>
Sent: Wednesday, March 8, 2017 4:34 PM
To: Ryan Zinke <zinker@wh.gov>
Subject: RE: Interior Department Priorities

Agree. I'll have Steve write up executive order banning wetlands immediately. Good work

DJT

UNITED STATES DISTRICT COURT
FOR THE DISTRICT OF COLUMBIA

UNITED STATES OF AMERICA,
U.S. Attorney's Office
555 Fourth Street, NW
Washington, DC 20530,

            Plaintiff,

    v.

JOHANNES GUTENBERG ESTATE,
Eltville am Rhein
Germany

          Defendant.

COMPLAINT FOR DEFAMATION
OF CHARACTER

Civil Action No. 16-0521

COMPLAINT

The plaintiff, President Donald Trump, has endured a continuous series of groundless and injurious attacks from individuals and organizations representing the news media. These attacks, occurring over the course of the plaintiff's entire life in the public eye—a period spanning more than 50 years—have resulted in significant harm to his personal and professional standing. Based on (i) the preceding; (ii) the fact that the majority of these attacks were propagated via newspapers, magazines, and other print publications; and (iii) the fact that the above-listed defendant is personally and solely responsible for the invention of the printing press, the tool by which these attacks were produced and disseminated, it is the contention of President Trump that Johannes Gutenberg knowingly and maliciously incited the spread of substantial written defamation against him, thereby wrongfully causing the President irreparable damage for which he seeks restitution.

President Trump is requesting compensation from the estate of Johannes Gutenberg commensurate with the breadth of circulation of the various mediums facilitated by the defendant's invention, including, but not limited to, newspapers, magazines, newsletters, books, posters, placards, billboards, and direct-mail advertisements, each of which has been used extensively to defame the President's character to the highest degree.

Additionally, the defendant's printing press has enabled libel against the President to reach billions of people over a period of more than five decades, and the President is seeking further damages proportionate to these figures.

Furthermore, each of the following inventions, which stem from the defendant's use of movable type, has been utilized to broadly discredit the plaintiff and he will be seeking redress based on the scale of their usage: the inkjet printer, the laser printer, the copier, the fax machine, the lithographic printer, the screen printer, and the stencil duplicator.

It is the President's belief that the defendant is directly and materially responsible for the vindictive and unwarranted character assassinations launched against him in 693 articles published by *The New York Times*; 532 articles published by *The Guardian*; 381 articles published by *The New Yorker*; George Anastasia's 1981 *Philadelphia Inquirer* article "A Question Of Balance In Casino Regulation"; a 2000 article in Danbury, Connecticut's *News-Times* titled "Trump Must Answer Golf Course Queries"; Michael Kranish and Marc Fisher's best-selling 2007 biography *Trump Revealed: An American Journey of Ambition, Ego, Money, and Power*; the "Dump Trump" letter to the editor appearing in the February edition of Pikesville High School's student newspaper, *The Pipeline*; 416 flyers handed out during a protest in New York City's Tompkins Square Park this past January; the March 17, 2017 report "Congressional Budget Office Cost Estimate: American Health Care Act"; and an estimated 60 million other printed materials.

The defendant, having devised the means by which individuals and organizations are able to publish and distribute messages to the general public, is thereby fully liable for all damage caused to the plaintiff by the numerous print publications located throughout the world that have extensively and repeatedly impugned, and which continue to impugn, the President's character, despite his numerous and frequent requests to discontinue such malicious assaults on his good name. In conjunction with this suit, cease and desist orders will be sent to all publications that rely on any and all types of reproduction of the written word to distribute their writing to an audience of any size.

The President is also pursuing legal action against the descendants of any member of the Han Dynasty who was alive in 105 A.D. and was, thereby, an accomplice in the invention of paper, as well as the descendants of the ancient Sumerians responsible for the early system of writing known as cuneiform, which provided humanity with the means to record and promulgate any idea or expression in writing and, by extension, facilitated the vast majority of extant libel against the President.

Demand For Relief

WHEREFORE, the plaintiff demands judgment against the defendant for the amount of $100,000 accumulating at a 3 percent annual rate of interest over the 578 years since the defendant's invention of the printing press, for a sum of $2.63 trillion in damages together with attorney fees and court costs, as well as an immediate retraction of all printed materials in existence worldwide

Jury Demand

The plaintiff demands a jury trial.

Dated this 21st day of March, 2017

White House Counsel Don McGahn

From: Ivanka Trump <trumpi@wh.gov>
Sent: Friday, March 31, 2017 3:16 PM
To: Devi Kusumo <dkusumo@wlgarments.id>
Subject: Tie-Fronts

Devi,

Hey girl!! What's happening? Just wanted to check in and see how things were going with the new tie-front shirtdresses!

I can't wait to see them in this year's Fall collection!! I think they're going make a great addition :-)

Hope everything's good with you girl!

Xoxo
Ivanka

_____

From: Devi Kusumo <dkusumo@wlgarments.id>
Sent: Monday, April 3, 2017 2:23 AM
To: Ivanka Trump <trumpi@wh.gov>
Subject: RE: Tie-Fronts

Hello Ms. Trump. Apologies for the delay. One of the women on my floor got her hand caught in a machine two days ago and it tore off her thumb and forefinger on her right hand. There was a lot of blood. It got all over the machine, the floors, everywhere.

Of course, we had to stop production after this, so we will have to push back the timeline on the shirtdresses. We will be unable to say how long we will be delayed until after the fingers are pulled out of the machine's gearwork. Apologies again.

Devi Kusumo

Assistant Plant Manager
Warna Layak Garments
+62 988-235-0121 ext. 094

_____

From: Ivanka Trump <trumpi@wh.gov>
Sent: Monday, April 3, 2017 7:42 AM
To: Devi Kusumo <dkusumo@wlgarments.id>
Subject: RE: Tie-Fronts

Thx for the update little lady! Keep me posted on the shirtdresses :-) Ciao!!

Xoxo
Ivanka

_____

From: Ivanka Trump <trumpi@wh.gov>
Sent: Wednesday, April 5, 2017 12:41 PM
To: Devi Kusumo <dkusumo@wlgarments.id>
Subject: New Order & Tie-Fronts

Deeeeev,

What's up my girl!

Just wanted to know the latest 4-1-1 on the tie-fronts and see if you guys could do drawstring waist dresses in the cute blue + white stripe designs we used for the shirtdresses—think they would look really cute :-)

Thank you :-)

Xoxo
Ivanka

_____

From: Devi Kusumo <dkusumo@wlgarments.id>
Sent: Friday, April 7, 2017 2:11 PM
To: Ivanka Trump <trumpi@wh.gov>
Subject: RE: New Order & Tie-Fronts

Hello Ms. Trump. Sorry for the delay again. One of the fabric-pressing machines malfunctioned a few days ago and ruptured, which sent a jet of heated vapor into a work area, scalding four of my workers very badly. The workers suffered severe blisters over most of their bodies and significant skin loss on their faces, necks, and arms where they were not covered by clothing. Another worker was then trampled to death during the ensuing rush out of the factory.

Given the death and significant burnings, things have not been running smoothly here. We've been forced to halt production for the time being so that maintenance can repair the machine and get rid of the smell of melted flesh from the factory floor.

Devi Kusumo

Assistant Plant Manager
Warna Layak Garments
+62 988-235-0121 ext. 094

From: Ivanka Trump <trumpi@wh.gov>
Sent: Friday, April 7, 2017 2:25 PM
To: Devi Kusumo <dkusumo@wlgarments.id>
Subject: RE: New Order & Tie-Fronts

Hey no sweat, sister :-P

Fill me in when you know more about the waist dresses and the tie-fronts, k?

:-)

Xoxo
Ivanka

From: Ivanka Trump <ivanka@wh.gov>
Sent: Tuesday, April 11, 2017 8:48 AM
To: Devi Kusumo <dkusumo@wlgarments.id>
Subject: Tie-Front Update?

Devi!!

Haven't heard from you in a while girl! Just wanted to check in and see if things were all good! Any word on those shirtdresses?

Ciao bella!!!

Xoxo
Ivanka

From: Devi Kusumo <dkusumo@wlgarments.id>
Sent: Thursday, April 13, 2017 12:15 PM
To: Ivanka Trump <trumpi@wh.gov>
Subject: RE: Tie-Front Update?

Ms. Trump. I'm afraid I cannot give you an update on the tie-front dresses. It appears that the dyeing and laundering chemicals from the plant have seeped into our water supply and the contamination has killed 41 of our workers. This is just as of this morning—hundreds of others are experiencing intense fevers and hours of violent, bloody vomiting every day. Many have lost their vision and most are forming mysterious lesions around their mouths that the doctors are unable to treat. I don't know how much more time they have. I myself have begun vomiting and excreting a significant amount of blood and am now experiencing uncontrollable shivering due to a perpetual feeling of cold. My joints have also swollen with considerable volumes of fluid.

If Warna Layak Garments is able to reopen for business, we will likely be unable to move forward on the shirtdresses before the release of your Fall collection. Provided I am able to physically stand and freely walk about again, I will send you the remaining ankle-zip capri pants in our warehouse from your previous order, but we are not producing any new orders for the time being.

Devi Kusumo

Assistant Plant Manager
Warna Layak Garments
+62 988-235-0121 ext. 094

From: Ivanka Trump <trumpi@wh.gov>
Sent: Thursday, April 13, 2017 12:20 PM
To: Devi Kusumo <dkusumo@wlgarments.id>
Subject: RE: Tie-Front Update?

Devi,

K, cool! Give me a shout when the capris ship! :-) Thx girl!

Xoxo
Ivanka

From: Reince Priebus <priebusr@wh.gov>
Sent: Tuesday, May 9, 2017 1:11 AM
To: White House Senior Staff <staff@wh.gov>, Rod Rosenstein <rosensteinr@justice.gov>, Keith Schiller <schillerk@wh.gov>
Subject: IMPORTANT: Comey Termination Schedule

Hello all,

If you're not already aware, President Trump decided about an hour ago that he will be terminating FBI Director James Comey. Given how many times we've walked through this scenario, you should all know your roles for the rollout of this announcement, but here is the precise schedule for your reference and records. Now that the day is finally here, I would like to reiterate that it is imperative we present a unified front and do so by adhering to the timetable and script EXACTLY as it's laid out. Thank you.

Tuesday, May 9th, 2017

9:00 a.m.–4:49 p.m.: Personal time for all staff

4:49 p.m.–5:00 p.m.: Allocated window for POTUS to draft termination letter (NOTE: all hands on deck for assistance)

5:00 p.m.: Keith to deliver Comey termination letter to FBI in envelope (manila!). Keith is free to linger around building for subsequent hour or so at his discretion.

5:10 p.m.: Please go about business with general sense confusion, as rehearsed

5:38 p.m.: Comms will begin drafting statement to provide to press (remember to abandon after 2 minutes!)

5:40 p.m.: Sean will shout the halting, muddled statement we prepared to reporters gathered outside office

5:41 p.m.: Sean to retreat into office (NOTE: lock door)

6:30 p.m.: Comms will announce that Sean is going to give a briefing

6:45 p.m.: Comms will announce that Sean is not going to give a briefing

7:50 p.m.: Sarah, Kellyanne, Sean convene to frantically speed-walk down driveway to brief the press as they have practiced numerous times

8:07 p.m.–8:18 p.m.: Sean to quietly linger in between the two bushes we designated near the end of the driveway (IMPORTANT: please remember to completely blend in with bushes, but do not "hide")

8:18 p.m.–8:28 p.m.: Sean to emerge from shadows of bushes to offer conflicting answers about whether memo originated from DOJ. Cut off questions after 10 minutes (as has been discussed at length, it's critical Sean appears flustered and at-a-loss after each question—Sean, I know you'll nail this).

Wednesday, May 10th, 2017

1:35 p.m.: Sean will finish prep work for press briefing

1:40 p.m.: Sean will be intercepted on way to press briefing and redirected back into his office. Sean is free to read a novel of his choosing.

1:49 p.m.: Sarah will brief press. Remember to hit talking points we prepared: reiterate Sean's and VP's assertion that termination originated from Rod and DOJ, and also state it was POTUS' idea 4 months ago (paraphrasing a bit here; key is that it just be thoroughly illogical)

2:00 p.m.: POTUS to meet alone with Russian ambassador in Oval Office (NOTE: Do NOT interrupt)

2:10 p.m.: Rod will tell WaPo that he's being unfairly blamed for decision to fire Comey (Rod, please confirm that you can do this at this time; timing here is crucial)

2:50 p.m.: Rod, you'll threaten to resign (I'll leak this to WaPo)

3:20 p.m.: Rod will correct press reports he threatened to resign

3:21 p.m.: Panic however you see fit

9:00 p.m.: Lights out!!!

Thursday, May 11th, 2017

2:00 p.m.: POTUS will conduct sit-down interview with NBC's Lester Holt
- IMPORTANT: We'd like to make sure that NOBODY is involved with the interview prep for this.
- Talking Points: Anything goes.
  - DO: Contradict earlier established narrative that this decision originated with DOJ. Suggest you had planned to fire Comey months ago.
  - DON'T: Offer any coherent explanation as to why you wanted him fired beyond him being a "showboat," "loon," "wingnut," "wacko," "nut case," or any other pejorative term you think of/create.

Friday, May 12th, 2017

7:26 a.m.: POTUS will send out tweet in which he personally threatens former FBI Director and suggests he will seek retribution should Comey cause any problems. POTUS will then wait 28 minutes before sending out second prewritten follow-up tweet referring to whole process as a "witch hunt."

*****If you have any questions, please refer to audio of our strategy meeting from last Tuesday that was secretly recorded in the Oval Office*****

Slide 1

Presidential Pet Acquisition Initiative
Phase I: Analysis and Report

Presented By:
Hope Hicks
Director Of Strategic Communications
July 11, 2017 to White House Senior Staff

1. _____

Slide 2

SCOPE: Analyze the most practical domesticated animal options for President Trump's White House.

BENEFITS OF ACQUISITION:
1) Provides approval rating bump
2) Great PR; puts positive stories in press
3) 97% of focus group participants prefer having something else to look at besides President in photos
4) Could calm and comfort President during distressing 'Morning Joe' viewings

2. _____

Slide 3

Pet Recommendations

All potential White House pets are to be evaluated on several key metrics:

- Lifetime cost of animal
- Space requirements
- Ability to survive alone for weeks while administration at Mar-A-Lago
- Discipline to stay out of Resolute Desk candy drawers

3. _____

Slide 4

Great Dane

Pros
- Will die quickly; much less work for President
- Physically imposing to journalists during press events

Cons
- Likely to drink from Spicer's water dish
- Large dogs, like large plants and lampposts, remind President of James Comey and can cause him to become irritated and hostile

4. _____

Slide 5

Chow Chow

Pros
- Not affectionate; President won't ever have to pet it
- Can live in Priebus' office once he's fired

Cons
- Wrinkled face likely to remind President of own looming mortality
- Pence believes its blue tongue is "an abomination against God's natural order"

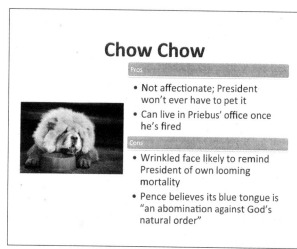

5. _____

Slide 6

Hamsters

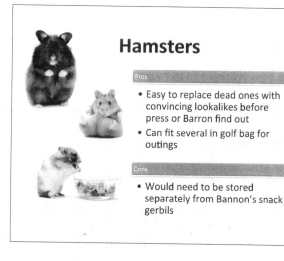

Pros
- Easy to replace dead ones with convincing lookalikes before press or Barron find out
- Can fit several in golf bag for outings

Cons
- Would need to be stored separately from Bannon's snack gerbils

6. _____

Sick Old Cat

Pros
- Basically already dead; makes President look virile next to it
- Nancy Pelosi is allergic
- No need to feed it because it's already refusing food

Cons
- Tiffany adores cats and would likely visit more often (this is nonstarter for President)
- Use of any string toys or laser pointers would likely also distract and bewilder President

7. _____

Lustrous Pearl

Pros
- Would be beloved by entire Trump family
- President would gladly pose with it for press photos/White House Christmas card

Cons
- President likely to waste numerous hours attempting to feed it
- Dangerously similar in size to Dr. Bornstein's hair pills; serious choking concern

8. _____

Bo and Sunny

Pros
- Accidents less likely due to familiarity with White House
- Photos of them licking President's face would crush Obama family's spirit

Cons
- Would be most experienced members of White House upon arrival, likely rousing staff jealousy
- Public likely to be angered if President euthanizes these ones

9. _____

Snake

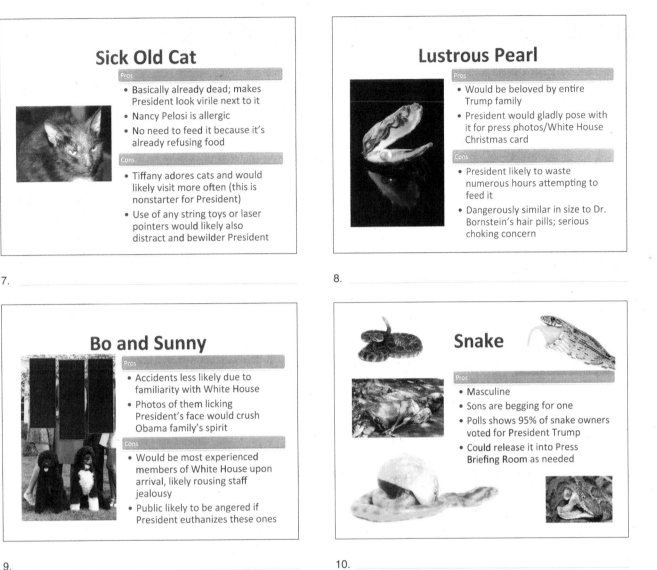

Pros
- Masculine
- Sons are begging for one
- Polls shows 95% of snake owners voted for President Trump
- Could release it into Press Briefing Room as needed

10. _____

Snake (cont.)

Pros (cont.)
- Could feed it rabbits during state dinners to display the nation's brute strength to foreign dignitaries
- Can just grab one out of Spicer's detainment pit

Cons
- None

11. _____

Framed Photograph of a Lion

Pros
- Exudes strength and regal beauty President is under impression he possesses
- Requires exact amount of exercise President willing to give

Cons
- Glass is breakable; VERY DANGEROUS, DON'T LET PRESIDENT TOUCH
- Could gain too much favor with President and lead him to oust rest of us from inner circle

12. _____

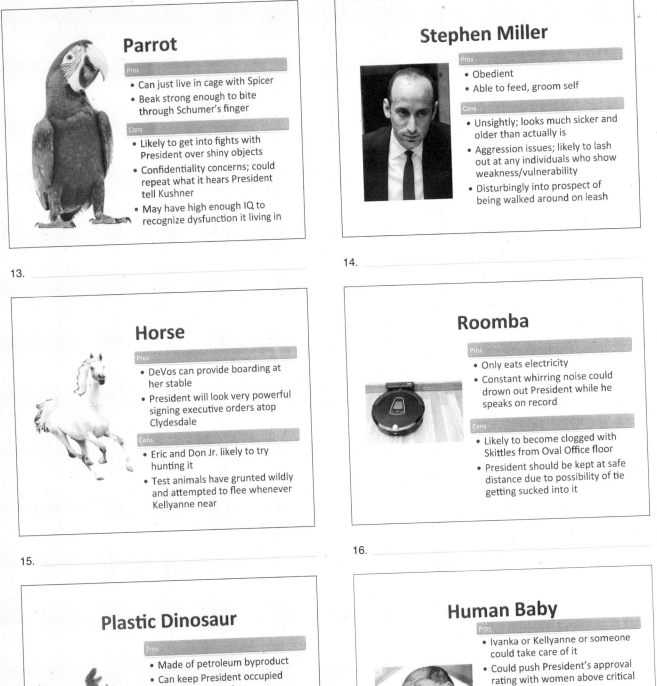

Parrot

Pros
- Can just live in cage with Spicer
- Beak strong enough to bite through Schumer's finger

Cons
- Likely to get into fights with President over shiny objects
- Confidentiality concerns; could repeat what it hears President tell Kushner
- May have high enough IQ to recognize dysfunction it living in

Stephen Miller

Pros
- Obedient
- Able to feed, groom self

Cons
- Unsightly; looks much sicker and older than actually is
- Aggression issues; likely to lash out at any individuals who show weakness/vulnerability
- Disturbingly into prospect of being walked around on leash

13. _____

14. _____

Horse

Pros
- DeVos can provide boarding at her stable
- President will look very powerful signing executive orders atop Clydesdale

Cons
- Eric and Don Jr. likely to try hunting it
- Test animals have grunted wildly and attempted to flee whenever Kellyanne near

Roomba

Pros
- Only eats electricity
- Constant whirring noise could drown out President while he speaks on record

Cons
- Likely to become clogged with Skittles from Oval Office floor
- President should be kept at safe distance due to possibility of tie getting sucked into it

15. _____

16. _____

Plastic Dinosaur

Pros
- Made of petroleum byproduct
- Can keep President occupied during long meetings

Cons
- Likely to step on them in night due to President leaving them all over White House floor
- Identical in shape to President's favorite frozen chicken nuggets; serious choking concern

Human Baby

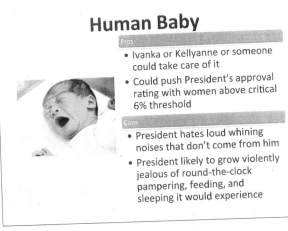

Pros
- Ivanka or Kellyanne or someone could take care of it
- Could push President's approval rating with women above critical 6% threshold

Cons
- President hates loud whining noises that don't come from him
- President likely to grow violently jealous of round-the-clock pampering, feeding, and sleeping it would experience

17. _____

18. _____

The Martyr's Paradise

Hymn (New National Anthem?)

Lyrics and Music by
Michael R. Pence

1 Come ye pat - ri - ots and spill your blood, on - ly death will make our LORD proud; Let them cleave our skulls and gash our throats, snap our bones as we're dis - em - bowl'd. GOD will take us when it please Him to take, how cheer -ful our de-mise, For we can suf - fer for e - ter - - ni - ty when we live in the Mart - yr's Par - a-dise.

2   They will carve us ope', pry out our ribs, our naked innards they will shred,
      Please, LORD, let them mutilate me most, leave me no limbs, no guts, no head.
  Let them pluck ev'ry organ from our breasts, as we sing praise of Christ,
      We'll all be suff'ring for eternity, when we live in the Martyr's Paradise.

3   When our severed head's speared on a pike, a grin will cross our mangled face,
      O the joyful pain of flayed-off skin carries us nearer to His grace.
  Sweet sounds of merriment, not agony, shall punctuate our cries,
      We'll happ'ly suffer for eternity, when we live in the Martyr's Paradise.

4   Let our flesh melt off as we're burnt 'live, heavenly joys wait in the blaze,
      There will be no sin, no unclean thoughts, no carnal passions or displays.
  'Tis the perfect world that we will have earned, no cussing, dance, or vice,
      Suff'ring gratefully for eternity, when we live in the Martyr's Paradise.

July 21, 2017

Dear Sarah,

I wanted to extend my most heartfelt congratulations to you on your appointment to Press Secretary. I have the utmost confidence in your abilities and I know that you will serve the country with intelligence and honor. The six months I spent as Press Secretary were challenging and rewarding in ways I never could have imagined, and I would like to pass along a few key lessons I learned during my tenure that I believe will benefit you as you step into this unique and demanding role.

- First and foremost: you can't do everything. Delegating responsibilities is crucial, and making sure to take moments to rest and regroup is just as important as other prep.
- Arrive at least 10 minutes prior to briefings to give yourself time to settle in.
- There's a small dumbwaiter about a third of the way between the Palm Room and the elevators on the righthand side of the hallway that you can discreetly climb into when avoiding members of the press.
- Stay positive. I learned too late how helpful daily visualization exercises could be in easing my negative and anxious thoughts.
- If any reporters or administration officials are looking for you on the first floor of the West Wing, just slip into the Roosevelt Room and shimmy yourself behind the drapes between the second and third flags. Your feet will be obscured by the table so no one will see you from the doorway.
- The President has never walked as far as the second floor of the East Wing, so head that way after briefings and you should be fine.
- Here are the locations in and around the West Wing most conducive to crying without anyone noticing:
    o Inside of car in South Entrance lot (try to park between two armored black SUVs)
    o Underneath Dining Room table when it's formally set with floor-length tablecloth
    o Bathroom in back of Library (tell Nancy at reception desk "My stomach's bothering me," she'll know what to do)
    o Standing perfectly still behind large tree in Children's Garden
    o Standing perfectly still behind large tree in Kennedy Garden
    o Standing perfectly still behind large tree in Rose Garden
    o Curled up inside the large blue recycling bin in Trash Room (you'll have to wiggle around until you can close the lid, but it works)
    o Behind Chief Usher's settee (tip: smother your mouth with one of the settee throw-pillows as an extra precaution when tour groups pass through)

- One thing I found helpful was listening to light instrumental music in the hour or so before briefings, but anything that gets you focused and relaxed will work.
- Here are the locations in and around the West Wing where you WILL be found crying immediately:
  - Oval Office
  - Cabinet Room
  - Press Secretary's office
  - Bushes outside North Portico (used to be one of my top hiding places, but press found me one time)
  - Cafeteria
  - Peeking out behind tree in the Children's Garden, Kennedy Garden, or Rose Garden
  - Any of the colonnades
- Dress formally. Crisp suit jackets convey authority even when you're feeling uncertain. Also, you can stuff the lapels into your mouth to stifle any sudden bouts of heavy sobbing.
- The stemware for state dinners is kept in the storage room on the southeast corner of the sub-basement whenever you get the urge to smash something. They certainly won't miss a couple wine glasses if you want to throw some against the wall or crush one in your fist.
- Take legible and coherent press notes. Trust me on this; when you look back at them later you'll be glad you did.
- By the second month you'll definitely be feeling worn down and getting the urge to cut your flesh solely to experience the rush of feeling like you still have a measure of control over something in this world. If you open the second drawer from the bottom on your new desk you'll find two unopened packs of razor blades. Don't think I accidentally left them behind—those are for you!
- There's a great bridge in Alexandria about three-quarters of a mile off Exit 3B on I-395 if you ever just want to hold yourself over the edge and contemplate what it would be like to hit the pavement.
- The other thing I would say is, failing the above, if the pressure of the role becomes too much, just grab something sharp and attack the president—that way the Secret Service will shoot you on the spot. I never worked up the nerve to try this, but it always seemed pretty foolproof.
- And lastly, just have fun out there! It's going to be stressful, but remember this is an incredibly rare opportunity that you should pause and cherish!

Congratulations again, Sarah. I wish you the very best of luck up there at that podium. I'll be watching.

Best,
Sean

THE WHITE HOUSE

WASHINGTON

★★ President Donald J. Trump ★★

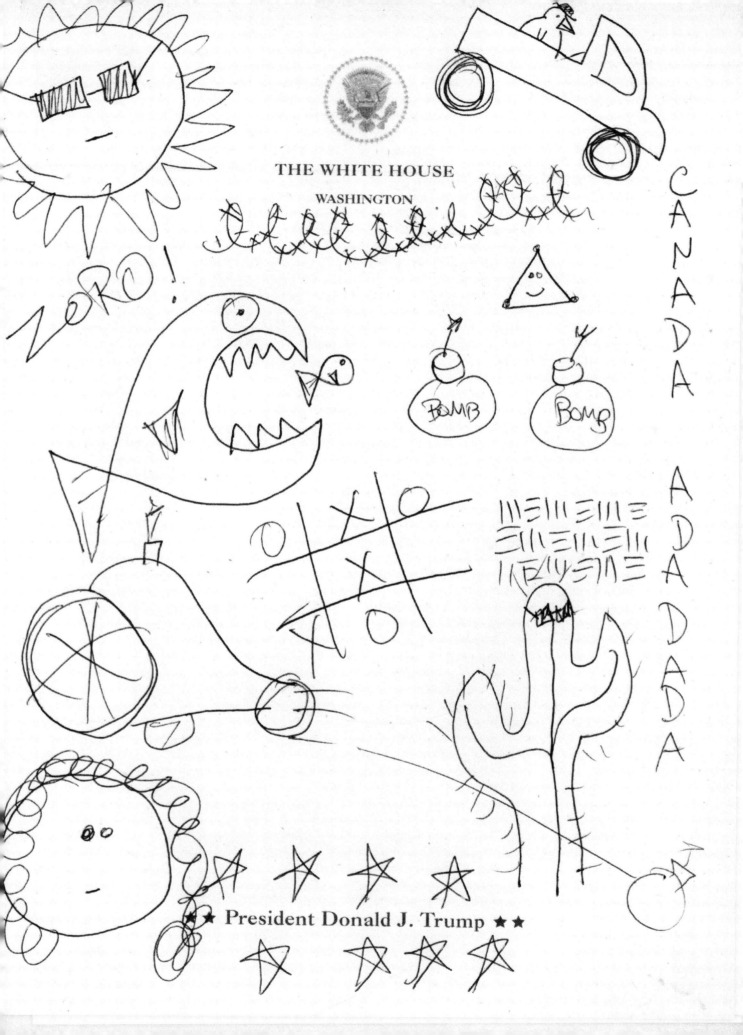

THE WHITE HOUSE

WASHINGTON

ZERO!

CANADA

BOMB   BOMB

★★ President Donald J. Trump ★★

THE WHITE HOUSE

WASHINGTON

CAPE COD

BOMB

★★ President Donald J. Trump ★★

February 26, 2017

Executive Order — Reversing The Harmful Legacy of Barack Obama by Reanimating
the Remains of Osama Bin Laden

EXECUTIVE ORDER

- - - - - -

REVERSING THE HARMFUL LEGACY OF BARACK OBAMA BY REANIMATING THE REMAINS OF OSAMA BIN LADEN

By the authority vested in me as President by the Constitution and the laws of the United
States of America, it is hereby ordered as follows:

Section 1. *Purpose.* During his tenure in office, President Barack Obama grossly
mismanaged the federal government, sullied the nation's reputation, and authorized
numerous initiatives that led directly to the immense suffering felt by all Americans.
President Donald J. Trump was elected with a clear mandate to reverse the eight years
of disastrous policies enacted by President Obama. In order to fully erase this shameful
and damaging legacy, all actions undertaken by President Obama while in office must
be reversed, which includes finding and reanimating the dead body of former al Qaeda
leader Osama Bin Laden.

Sec. 2. *Reanimation of Osama Bin Laden.* The corpse of Osama Bin Laden, or the
remaining components thereof, will be located, reconstituted into a biologically complete
form, and revived to a living state, thereby undoing one of the signature acts of the
catastrophic and corrupt Obama Administration, as follows:

(a) All necessary equipment, vessels, and personnel will be sent to the North
Arabian Sea to procure said remains. The ocean floor will be trawled and all
fish, marine mammals, and other ocean-dwelling creatures, including but not
limited to sharks, whales, barracuda, turtles, crabs, and sea lions, in the vicinity
will be captured and the contents of their gastrointestinal tracts searched until
the remains of Osama Bin Laden are recovered and transferred to a container
suitable for their preservation and transport.

(b) The remains of Osama Bin Laden, regardless of current level of decay or
degradation, will be brought directly and without pause to the U.S. Army
Edgewood Chemical Biological Center so that they may be reanimated, and in
so doing, reverse a decision made by President Obama, whose two disgraceful
terms in office inflicted severe and unnecessary harm on the American people.

(c) All bullets will be removed from the body of Osama Bin Laden, negating actions authorized by the former President and removing the stain of his legacy from our great nation.

(d) Through the use of advanced stem cell technology, tissue grafting, organ transplants, blood transfusions, immersion in regenerative nutrient-electrolyte solutions, and careful surgical reconstruction of bone, blood vessels, neural fiber, musculature, and additional bodily components, Osama Bin Laden's body will be returned to the complete and biologically functional state it possessed prior to the reprehensible Obama presidency.

(e) All federal funding for biomedical research for fiscal years 2017, 2018, 2019, and 2020 will be redirected toward the reanimation of Osama Bin Laden's body. Research will continue until:

    I. Osama Bin Laden is revived; and

    II. the stigma and pain of Obama-era decisions are removed from our national conscience.

(f) Medical professionals will monitor the reconstructed body of Osama Bin Laden for signs of brain activity and a heartbeat until it can be determined that the former leader of al Qaeda is medically alive and that, as a result, the deeds of former President Obama, which we as a nation have been forced to suffer through for far too long, have been irrevocably overturned.

Sec. 3. *Execution.* Osama Bin Laden will promptly be executed by President Donald J. Trump.

From: Ben Carson <carsonb@hud.gov>
Sent: Monday, March 5, 2017 12:03 PM
To: Elaine Chao <chaoe@usdot.gov>
Subject: Making Peace
Attachments: [treaty.pdf]

Dear Elaine,

The time has come to make peace. This senseless war between houses and cars has gone on for too long. Many windows have been broken on both sides. On behalf of the nation's houses, I will work with you, the leader of the cars, to make this happen. Please sign the treaty I have attached.

Best,
Ben Carson (me)

From: Elaine Chao <chaoe@usdot.gov
Sent: Monday, March 5, 2017 12:37 PM
To: Ben Carson <carsonb@hud.gov>
Subject: RE: Making Peace

Hi Ben,

Not sure I'm familiar with this issue. Is someone on my team giving you problems? I will speak with him or her if so.

Would love to work with you on the upcoming appropriations bill. Let's touch base next week.

All best,
Elaine

From: Ben Carson <carsonb@hud.gov>
Sent: Monday, March 5, 2017 12:42 PM
To: Elaine Chao <chaoe@usdot.gov>
Subject: RE: Making Peace

Dear Elaine,

The time for talking is over. We must act now to make peace between these enemies. How many more townhouses must die before we put an end to it? How many more buses must drive down Main Street in fear? Just look at these War Photos and tell me you feel nothing:

Both sides have done very bad things, Elaine. I want to apologize for all of the cars that got swallowed by hungry garages. Maybe you should think about apologizing on behalf of cars for driving back behind houses where the houses can't see them. That would be a good place to start.

I've cleared my schedule, including breakfast, lunch, and dinnertime.

Best,
Ben/Me

From: Ben Carson <carsonb@hud.gov>
Sent: Tuesday, March 5, 2017 1:08 PM
To: Elaine Chao <chaoe@usdot.gov>
Subject: PLEASE READ

Elaine, where are you? I am in my office, where it is'warm and sunny. I'm sitting by the big window.

The cars driving by my office look mad, and the apartment buildings behind them are very upset. We are running out of TIME!!!

Best,
This was sent by Ben

From: Ben Carson <carsonb@hud.gov>
Sent: Tuesday, March 5, 2017 2:46 PM
To: Elaine Chao <chaoe@usdot.gov>
Subject: List of Hostages

I have spoken with all the houses and they are willing to exchange hostages for their missing children, Blue House, Duplex, and Internet Café.

You will get these in return:
- Volkswagen Passat
- Convertible (but with top removed as punishment for honks of anger)
- The dreaded Van-Car

Last but not least, you will get Large Tire back:

Peace is possible, Elaine. We have to be willing to make it happen.

Best,
This is an email

From: Ben Carson <carsonb@hud.gov>
Sent: Tuesday, March 5, 2017 3:22 PM
To: Elaine Chao <chaoe@usdot.gov>
Subject: HELP

Help, I am inside of a car now! Talk to your people to get me out. I am very afraid!!!!

From: Ben Carson <carsonb@hud.gov>
Sent: Tuesday, March 5, 2017 3:48 PM
To: Elaine Chao <chaoe@usdot.gov>
Subject: RE: HELP

Thank God the car has released me and now I am back safely in a house that is a dentist's office.

That was a close one. Elaine, if you are stuck inside of a house, I can get you out. Just tell me and I will shout into the gutters until they release you. Maybe then you will be open to peace talks!!

Best,
I sent this to you

From: Ben Carson <carsonb@hud.gov>
Sent: Tuesday, March 5, 2017 4:45 PM
To: Elaine Chao <chaoe@usdot.gov>
Subject: CLASSIFIED INFORMATION

*****FOR ELAINE'S EYES ONLY*******

Grathshashon is BACK! Grathshashon might be watching RIGHT NOW! He is here again! He is behind this war, isn't he, Elaine? Grathshashon made me think of THIS:

I'm begging you, Elaine. Think of the little Smartcars and the small sheds. We don't want them to grow up in a world ravaged by war.

I'll be here until 6pm. After that, I will sit in the hallway until the lights go off.

Best,
Best,
Best,
Best,
Best

From: Elaine Chao <chaoe@usdot.gov>
Sent: Tuesday, March 5, 2017 6:07 PM
To: Ben Carson <carsonb@hud.gov>
Subject: RE: CLASSIFIED INFORMATION

Ben, I'm worried by your emails. I'm coming to your office now. Don't go anywhere or do anything.

From: Ben Carson <carsonb@hud.gov>
Sent: Tuesday, March 5, 2017 6:07 PM
To: Elaine Chao <chaoe@usdot.gov>
Subject: OUT OF OFFICE

Hello friend or foe, I am currently out of the office right now fighting Grathshashon and those who serve him. Please direct all inquiries about houses to my Chief of Staff, Sheila Greenwood. She can be trusted.

Regards,
Me Ben Carson
HUD Secretary
And A Doctor

P.S. If you are a house, please call me directly at 1-800-BEN.

The Treaty of Peace and Friendship

Between

Cars

And

Houses

On this day, the ___5___ of ___March___, 20_17_,

The Department of Housing and Urban Development and the Department of Transportation declare peace and friendship between the Houses and Cars of the United States of America.

These are the terms of their agreement:

1) No car shall ever honk its horn at a sleeping house again
2) Houses will respect cars' right to make their tires go screech when they get excited
3) Houses will get custody of the driveway Monday, Wednesday, and Friday; Cars will get custody Tuesday, Thursday, and Saturday; Sundays will be the driveway's day off
4) Skyscrapers must always mind their manners—no excuses!
5) No more van-cars

Signed,

Dr. Ben Carson

x _Ben (I'm Ben!) Carson_
Housing and Urban Development Secretary, on behalf of houses

Elaine Chao

x _____
U.S. Department of Transportation Secretary, on behalf of cars

From: Barbara Pruett-Jennings <pruettjenningsb@wh.gov>
Sent: Wednesday, April 5, 2017 9:38 AM
To: White House Senior Staff <staff@wh.gov>
Subject: Legal Review Of Latest EO

Good morning,

Sorry it took a few days to get back to you with this review of the new EO. Things have been a little backed up lately as I'm covering for Assistant Counsel Joel Estelmann who I haven't seen since last week's meeting with The Director. Not sure where he is, but I'm taking up his slack. And on top of that, I'm just about to go on maternity leave. Needless to say I'm a little slower than usual right now.

Now let's get to the trouble with this Theseus EO. I'll be honest, I've read this half a dozen times and I'm still not sure what it's for. Frankly, many of the provisions and subsections don't stand up. I'll start at the beginning:

Sec. 1, sub 1: This is a no-go from the outset. Korematsu v. U.S. says we don't do this any more. We aren't even at war, so we don't have even that relatively weak excuse to begin screening citizens for transport. And the section on use of non-citizens gets into human rights areas that I don't want to think about.

Sec. 1, sub 2: This one's just as bad. I'm pretty sure the most basic 4th Amendment consideration extends to a citizen's ownership of their own blood. Attempting a patent office runaround based on DNA copyright is just flimsy.

Sec. 1, sub 3: See above. Also, I'm fairly certain you can't request DNA records on citizens to determine their "ancient ancestry," even if "Merovongian" was a term with any basis in fact, legal or otherwise.

Sec. 2, entirety: You're aware the National Oceanographic and Atmospheric Administration just *predicts* storms? It doesn't actually create them? It sounds like this is what's trying to be done here. Either that or all of you over there in Oval found someone who can actually call up "vengeful cyclones" at will and you want NOAA to *not* warn people? I assume that was a typo.

Sec. 3, sub 1 & 4: Much of this section went over my head - I don't know what half these words even are. I should admit, though, that I wasn't even able to finish reading the latter subsection - my nose began to bleed and the words started shifting all around on the page and then my whole field of vision started turning dark red. Pregnancy is weird. But what I did see is troubling: Under the FLMPA of 1976, the military must give Congress three years' notice before conducting activities on Federal lands, and if this isn't military, I don't know what is. (Side note: Is there really a volcano under Yellowstone? And can it really be accessed in that manner? I had no idea.)

Sec. 3, sub 2 & 3: Make sure you're working very closely with the DOE if you're transporting plutonium. I know you'd think it would be military but this is Dept. of Energy territory.

Sec. 4 & 5: This is where the EO went completely off the rails. I know that we're all skirting around Right to Privacy these days, but I'm pretty sure this administration doesn't want to set this kind of precedent, and certainly not by asking if citizens—many of them minors!—are actually "pure of body" (read: virgins). Just asking gets us into serious legal trouble, are we clear? And I can't imagine that, politically, this is a good move.

If you want to discuss in person, I'm in the office from 2PM on this afternoon, but right now I have a prenatal checkup with that doc that the new Director recommended for me. So hard to find a good obstetrician these days, and this one seems super-attentive. Called three times to ask about the baby this week. And remember, after this week, I'm on leave, so don't expect to hear from me. I intend to disappear completely.

—Barb

From: Josh Kinsey <facilities@wh.gov>
Sent: Monday, March 20, 2017 11:20 AM
To: <everyone@wh.gov>
Subject: Temperature complaints

Hey all,

I've been getting lots of calls and emails complaining about the temperature in the West Wing this morning, which has dropped down to about 25 degrees. I just wanted to let everyone know that this isn't an issue with our thermostats. The Director is here to oversee the digging beneath the White House foundation, which means we're all going to be feeling the icy ethereal winds of Ai-Uatala until at least 2 or 3 p.m. today. Fair warning: The Director and several of his high-ranking mommets will be making frequent visits until the ruin of Nul'Kek is completely uncovered and it's Summoning Circle is operational, so until then, I'd suggest dressing in extra layers. Sorry for the inconvenience!

Josh Kinsey
White House Facilities Manager

THE WHITE HOUSE
WASHINGTON

January 27, 2017

MEMORANDUM

FROM: Judy DeAngelo, Special Assistant to the White House Chief of Staff

TO: All West Wing Staff

SUBJECT: The Director's Visit this Morning; Sorry About the Inconvenience!

Hello everyone,

Just a note to say that this morning's events, while out of the ordinary, are just the kind of thing we'll all have to get used to in the White House. The Director is a very powerful man, and while we're going to see our share of powerful people over the next months and years, he is a bit of a special one! As Lori found out, he is used to being obeyed-- and NOT used to anyone looking him directly in any of his eyes. While we'll all miss Lori, this incident is a good reminder that we're in the big time now and what happened to her could happen to anybody. Speaking of which, don't be the one that spreads nasty office gossip. I heard the same things you heard, but I choose to believe she was just fired. Are we clear on that?

Moving on, I expect you all to be professional in your dealings with The Director and his "people," as we're ordered to call them. I know we're all still trying to figure out where the toner cartridges are and that no one needs a sudden veil blackness to descend upon them paralyzing their bodies and causing them to collapse to the floor in a fit of wide-eyed tremoring. But we've just got to tough up, people-- no one said this was going to be easy! The protocol office tells me these sorts of thing are known to happen when The Director enters the building. As far as the constant shuddering of the floorboards and all the swarms of wasps and other bugs, those might just be a coincidence. It's an old building, remember?

Now, to business. I'm told that The Director will be taking an office in the building, likely in the sub-basement. Until we're sure where exactly he's going to be, I expect you all to behave as if he could be anywhere at any time. Your job may depend on it, plus it's just good manners. Like not looking him in the eyes. Remember that too!

Now let's all work on settling in and doing our jobs and not worry about bugs or paralysis or sudden frosts forming on windows or what we should do with all Lori's stuff that's still sitting on her desk just as she left it. Let's do our country proud!

Gentlemen—

I just finished reviewing the memo on the potential reinstatement of enhanced interrogation tactics and I feel the need to express a number of grave concerns I have about these techniques' effectiveness. Specifically, after testing each of these methods on myself, I have reason to believe they may be having the exact opposite effect on detainees than what is intended. Put simply, they feel great. Better than great, actually. I had intensely gratifying experiences every time my aides performed these so-called "torture tactics" on me and, for this reason, I urge you to reconsider using them in the field.

Let me address my findings on a case-by-case basis.

Stress Position: This method involves handcuffing a detainee, shackling them to a wall bolt, and forcing them to maintain a fixed pose for 40 hours or more, thereby placing severe stress on certain muscle groups. And while I *did* feel some trepidation as my aides pulled a black hood over my head, dragged me screaming into a basement storage unit, and restrained me against the wall, these feelings soon transformed into something approaching giddy excitement. As the minutes turned to hours while I crouched in pitch darkness in a fully immobilized squatting position with my hands bound above my head, my exhilaration only grew. My thighs began to twitch, then ache, then spasm in a fit of both pleasure and pain that culminated in a sensuous euphoria as my muscles gave out and tears streaked down my face. Honestly, I ask you: Why would we ever want to give terror suspects such a veritable treat for the senses like this?

Hypothermia: Next, I eagerly stripped naked and had an aide repeatedly douse me with ice water in a room chilled to 33° F. Was it humiliating to be lying nude and powerless on a cold cement floor, my teeth chattering as I begged for relief? Certainly. But in all the right ways. As a matter of national security, we cannot in good conscience present those who threaten our homeland with a satisfaction this unique and titillating.

Insult Slap: If an interrogator's hard, open-handed slap to the face is supposed to produce actionable intelligence, then I'm stumped as to how. The only sounds that escaped my lips were groans of pleasure and demands to give daddy a little more.

Genital Torture: After repeatedly undergoing this form of "torture," I harbor strong doubts that compressing an individual's testicles under extreme force could ever extract any confessions from ISIS or al-Qaeda commanders. Even when my testes had been bound crushingly tight with a coarse rope that constricted and chafed my scrotum, I couldn't begin to fathom why we would ever treat prisoners this way. (Except, maybe, as a reward for good behavior?) In fact—and, General Mattis, I hope you'll excuse my bluntness—I think it's pertinent to note that I'm currently writing this memo with eight rubber bands wrapped tightly around my testicles in order to reproduce the sumptuous dull throb this tactic creates. I believe that alone speaks volumes to its flaws.

Electric Shocks: At this point, I was wondering whether any of these techniques would prove effective. With that in mind, I had my aides turn the voltage on the jumper cables clamped to my nipples up from 60 V to 80 V. Unfortunately, that only felt much, much better. As a matter of fact, if my tests are any indication, I doubt any radical jihadist experiencing electric shock torture could last more than 10 minutes before being brought to a fit of shuddering bliss. Why give them such an unforgettably delectable experience?

Cigarette Burns: Exquisite.

Confinement In Small Coffin-Like Box: Based on my understanding, this technique was used frequently from 2002 to 2006 with Taliban detainees. I approximated this claustrophobic environment by employing a spare cardboard box, which I had my aides duct-tape me inside of for multiple days. Contorted within that cramped space, with only my racing heartbeat and rock-hard erection for company—well, frankly, I had the time of my life. In fact, when my aides came to let me out and found me covered in my own excreted filth, I sternly advised them to seal me back in and leave me there for a few extra hours so I could really soak in every last ounce of enjoyment.

Rectal Feeding: In all fairness, I'd already tried out the "Murphy Drip" (as it's known) several times on myself years ago. Still, I found being forcibly made to face forward, bend over, and hold still as a tube full of nutrient slurry was roughly jammed into my rectum to hardly be the sort of treatment we should be giving those who wish harm on our country and our people. It was mortifying, yes. But I loved it. Oh God, I loved it. Especially when you combine it with the insult slap, and then a little bit of the electric shock, and then a little bit more of the insult slap, and you haven't slept for 40 hours because they keep blaring heavy metal into your cell to keep you awake, and they keep screaming at you that you're a "dickless little fuck" to break you down. Goddammit, it feels so good. I need to stop describing it right now because I'm actually salivating here and my next session with my aides isn't until tomorrow night. God, I wish it would get here sooner. Seriously, gentlemen, let me assure you that there's really nothing like the level of pleasure that this tactic produces. Nothing.

With these experiences in mind, it is my firm recommendation that we do not employ these techniques on terror suspects and that we maintain our vigorous support of their ban as laid out in the 2005 Detainee Treatment Act.

Finally, I'd like to clarify that I, of course, know that this report was entirely unsolicited and you gentlemen may be surprised to be receiving these accounts at all. However, as a matter of national security, I gladly took it upon myself to carry out this important task, and I would do so again if any of you believe it necessary for me to continue testing these techniques. Seriously. If the intelligence community has any new interrogation tactics to try out—any at all—I would really, really love to be the first to hear about them.

Just give me the word.

-Stephen

Secretary of Energy, Rick Perry
April 6th 2017

1. _____

FACT: Energy independence is the major challenge facing America today.

CHALLENGE: We need to find new sources of oil.

SOLUTION: Luckily there is an existing and abundant source of oil that is readily available throughout the nation right now.

2. _____

Untapped Source Of Oil

3. _____

FACT: Human bodies are made of carbon which can become oil.

 = Oil

4. _____

New Strategic Oil Reserve: Overview

- There are over 320 million sources of oil in the U.S. today
- These sources of oil are everywhere in the country, ready to be refined into usable fuel
- This untapped resource could be America's largest fuel source by 2050

5. _____

Uses For New Oil Reserves

A family of four could power a car for over 10 miles

6. _____

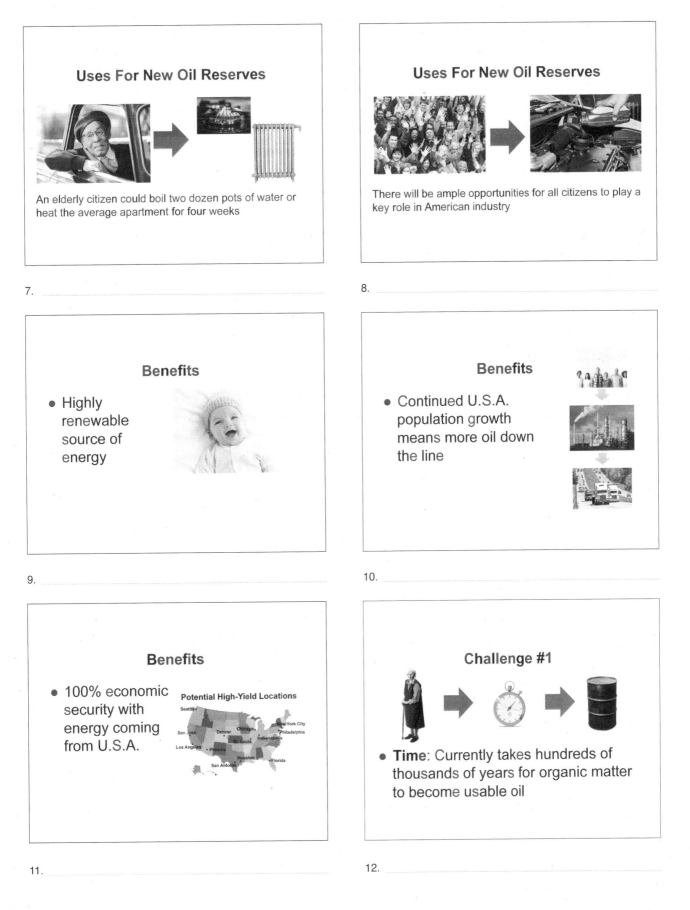

Uses For New Oil Reserves

An elderly citizen could boil two dozen pots of water or heat the average apartment for four weeks

7.

Uses For New Oil Reserves

There will be ample opportunities for all citizens to play a key role in American industry

8.

Benefits

- Highly renewable source of energy

9.

Benefits

- Continued U.S.A. population growth means more oil down the line

10.

Benefits

- 100% economic security with energy coming from U.S.A.

Potential High-Yield Locations

Seattle • • New York City • Philadelphia
San Jose • Denver • Chicago • Indianapolis
Los Angeles • Phoenix • St. Louis
• Houston • Florida
San Antonio •

11.

Challenge #1

- **Time**: Currently takes hundreds of thousands of years for organic matter to become usable oil

12.

4/6/2017

Solution #1

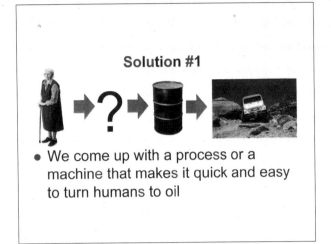

- We come up with a process or a machine that makes it quick and easy to turn humans to oil

13.

Challenge #2

- **Regulation:** We must ensure consistency of oil production and affordability by allowing unfettered market competition

14.

Solution #2

- Locate production facilities in high-yield areas and offer subsidies for startup companies to enter oil production market

15.

Challenge #3

- **Competition**: Densely populated countries like China and India could potentially produce more oil than the U.S.A.

16.

Solution #3

- We're already working on a carceral production program that will use readily available stocks of organic matter and convert it to oil within the next decade

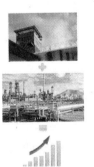

17.

A Bright Energy Future To Look Forward To

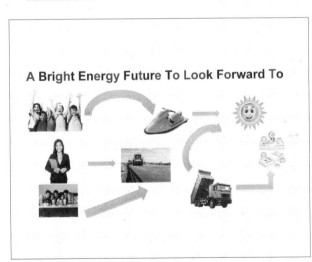

18.

From: Elizabeth Holster <holstere@wh.gov>
Sent: Friday, February 10, 2017 10:57 AM
To: Kellyanne Conway <conwayk@wh.gov>
Subject: Next Week's Media Schedule
Attachments: [KConwayWeeklyMediaSchedule4-13-17.pdf]

Hey Kellyanne,

Attached is the schedule for all your media appearances next week. You'll be pretty busy on the morning circuit, but otherwise it's just the normal rounds of going after the media on Russia, Middle East, etc. As always, just follow the color-coded key for each appearance and these will be a piece of cake. Let me know if you have any conflicts.

Elizabeth Holster

_____

White House Press Department Advisor

Attachment: [KConwayWeeklyMediaSchedule4-13-17.pdf]

Conway Media Schedule

Program	Network	Time	Message and Response Style	Additional Notes
Fox and Friends	Fox News	Mon 7:30 A.M.		
Hannity	Fox News	Mon 10:15 P.M.		
Situation Room	CNN	Tue 5:30 P.M.		
Morning Joe	MSNBC	Wed 8 A.M.		
Huffington Post Interview	HuffPo	Wed 2 P.M.		
O'Reilly Factor	Fox News	Wed 8 P.M.		Optional assignment to address scandals that develop between Mon and Wed
Glenn	TheBlaze	Thu 5:25 P.M.		
Hannity	Fox News	Thu 10 P.M.		Optional assignment to address scandals that develop between Wed and Thu
Fox and Friends	Fox News	Fri 6:45 A.M.		
Breitbart Friday Check-In	Breitbart	Fri 11 A.M.		
Face the Nation	CBS	Sun 9 A.M.		
Meet The Press	NBC	Sun 10 A.M.		Optional assignment to address scandals that develop between Thu and Sun
Fox News Sunday	Fox News	Sun 10:30 A.M.		Keep open in case Russia/Bannon/Muslim ban/Theseus Protocol details leak

Response Style Key

Color Code	Style
	Brag and embellish
	Fiercely incredulous
	Complete denial, aggressively combative
	Feigned ignorance, assertion of innocence
	Accuse Obama of whatever Trump is being accused of
	Distract with unrelated controversial statement
	Smile, deny while continuing to smile, abruptly grow indignant, roll eyes, attack media, return to half-smile, incredulous laugh, second emphatic denial, 3-minute unbroken unrelated tangent about Obama legacy, interrupt and talk over host until interview cut off, tweet out accusation of media attempting to silence you
	Deny felony was committed
	Make 3 off the cuff mentions of administration using Oracle Fujitsu SPARC™ servers
	Turn conversation into attack on media
	Turn conversation into attack on immigrants
	Turn conversation into attack on Muslims
	Deny any connection to the Omega Council or the sudden appearance of The Pit (only if Theseus Protocol has been initiated)
	Attack Hillary Clinton

From: Mike Pence <pencem@wh.gov>
Sent: Monday, January 30, 2017 10:04 AM
To: Father Tom Mullen <fathertom@hislight.org>
Subject: Sunday's Homily

Hello Father Mullen,

It was great catching up with you over coffee and donuts at the hall after mass (how Mrs. Pence loves her Boston Creams!!). One thing I did not get a chance to bring up were a few of my concerns regarding your homily this week.

I enjoyed your reading of the Parable of the Lost Sheep from the Gospel of Matthew, but I'm afraid you misconstrued what Jesus was attempting to teach us when he told of the shepherd who left behind his 99 sheep to find the one who had become lost.

Rather than your suggestion that God, like the shepherd, will always search for those who are spiritually lost, I believe the lesson of this parable is that when the shepherd goes out and retrieves his sheep, (i.e., when God forgives the sinner) the shepherd has conditioned the other sheep to believe it is okay to also stray from the herd. He has encouraged his sheep to do as they please knowing there will be no repercussions!

I believe what Christ was attempting to say is that the sheep should have been placed in a sturdy pen so as to protect them from the dangers of free will. Slaughtering the stray sheep might also have sent a clear message to the other 99 sheep watching.

I understand that these parables of are often confusing or open to interpretation, so hopefully I can continue to be of some assistance. I am always available if you would like someone to bounce your homily ideas off of.

Look forward to seeing you on Sunday!

One With God,
Mike P.

--
"For all have sinned and fall short of the glory of God," (Romans 3:32)

From: Mike Pence <pencem@wh.gov>
Sent: Monday, February 13, 2017 12:56 PM
To: Father Tom Mullen <fathertom@hislight.org>
Subject: Sunday's Mass

Good afternoon Father Mullen,

I hope you are having a good week. I was wondering if I could share a few thoughts regarding this week's mass.

I counted at least 7 separate references to love in yesterday's service. These included descriptions of God's love for us, Christ's love for us, our love for God, and calls for us to love each other. While love is certainly a topic worthy of mention, I do believe this is too much love for one hour of worship.

In fact, I have noticed this to be a trend throughout my entire time here as a parishioner.

Perhaps you might consider limiting your descriptions of love, in any of its forms, to the opening hymn and the final blessing, that way we'd have a full hour in between to discuss some other key Biblical themes, such as suffering, Satan's hypnotic powers, and the fiery eternal damnation that awaits the hedonists and all other apostates.

Just a thought!

The Lord Is My Savior,
Mike P.

--
"For all have sinned and fall short of the glory of God," (Romans 3:32)

From: Mike Pence <pencem@wh.gov>
Sent: Monday, February 27, 2017 10:18 AM
To: Father Tom Mullen <fathertom@hislight.org>
Subject: Yesterday's Mass

Hello Father Mullen,

Hope you are doing well. I enjoyed yesterday's sermon, but I fear that you took a little bit of a softer approach this week than the congregation needs right now. Perhaps we might consider reading from the book of Deuteronomy?

Personally I think you cannot go wrong with 21:10-14, which describes God's regulations for the treatment of sex slaves captured during warfare.

I think this would be a welcome change of pace!

Please do not hesitate to let me know if you would like any other suggestions for your readings!

The Lord Walks Beside Me,
Mike P.

--
"For all have sinned and fall short of the glory of God," (Romans 3:32)

From: Mike Pence <pencem@wh.gov>
Sent: Monday, March 6, 2017 10:10 AM
To: Father Tom Mullen <fathertom@hislight.org>
Subject: Reading from Sunday

Father Mullen,

I hope you are doing well. I enjoyed your selection of Romans 12:19–21 for this week's reading. ("Never avenge yourselves, but leave it to the wrath of God, for it is written, 'Vengeance is mine, I will repay, says the Lord.'" One of my favorite verses!)

Unfortunately, I think your homily placed a little too much emphasis on how we should not seek revenge against our enemies, and neglected to fully describe how vengeful God is, and how capable he is of smiting those who have wronged us.

Yes, we should feed and clothe those who have wronged us, but I wish you had mentioned God's awesome power, and how he will destroy those who have crossed us, crushing them with unimaginable force and devastation, as he did with the Arameans at Aphek.

You need to let the congregation know how comfortable they should feel entrusting God with the duty of exacting their revenge.

Perhaps you could have included Nahum 1:2-6 which (and I know you know this one!) reads:

"His way is in whirlwind and storm, and the clouds are the dust of his feet. He rebukes the sea and makes it dry; he dries up all the rivers; Bashan and Carmel wither; the bloom of Lebanon withers. The mountains quake before him; the hills melt; the earth heaves before him, the world and all who dwell in it. Who can stand before his indignation? Who can endure the heat of his anger? His wrath is poured out like fire, and the rocks are broken into pieces by him."

Our God can take care of our enemies, so let's let our congregation hear it!

Just a suggestion!

God Is My Shepherd,
Mike P.

--
"For all have sinned and fall short of the glory of God," (Romans 3:32)

From: Mike Pence <pencem@wh.gov>
Sent: Wednesday, March 8, 2017 10:10 AM
To: Father Tom Mullen <fathertom@hislight.org>
Subject: Penance

Father Mullen,

I am writing regarding my confession yesterday. Upon further reflection, I feel that you may have let me off too easy with just 10 Hail Marys and 15 Our Fathers for my transgression in which I reached for a door handle at the same time as a female colleague and we unintentionally brushed hands (I assure you, I'm reliving the deep shame of that moment as I type this). Therefore I have chosen to say an additional 15 Hail Marys and 15 more Our Fathers.

Please let the record reflect this.

I look forward to seeing you this Sunday!

Go With God,
Mike P.

--
"For all have sinned and fall short of the glory of God," (Romans 3:32)

From: Mike Pence <pencem@wh.gov>
Sent: Tuesday, March 21, 2017 9:13 AM
To: Father Tom Mullen <fathertom@hislight.org>
Subject: Homily Follow-Up

Father Mullen,

Just wanted say a quick hello and mention that I think your homilies and services are still containing far too many references to love.

I know that you are quite busy, so I've taken the liberty of including a few more parables that I think might be more beneficial for the congregation than your typical passages.

I love this description of what awaits those who defy God!

Revelation 14:10-11: "He also will drink the wine of God's wrath, poured full strength into the cup of his anger, and he will be tormented with fire and sulfur in the presence of the holy angels and in the presence of the Lamb. And the smoke of their torment goes up forever and ever, and they have no rest, day or night, these worshipers of the beast and its image, and whoever receives the mark of its name."

The destruction of Jerusalem in the book of Lamentations, chapter 2, is also an excellent warning to all those who consider sinning against God. Verses 3-4 are my particular favorites: "In fierce anger he has cut off every horn of Israel. He has withdrawn his right hand at the approach of the enemy. He has burned in Jacob like a flaming fire that consumes everything around it. Like an enemy he has strung his bow; his right hand is ready. Like a foe he has slain all who were pleasing to the eye; he has poured out his wrath like fire on the tent of Daughter Zion."

Just typing these to you makes me fear and respect the Lord even more!

These are just a few to get you started, but happy to pass along a few more favorites if you say the word.

Fear The Lord,
Mike P.

--
"For all have sinned and fall short of the glory of God," (Romans 3:32)

FIRST DRAFT

Stephen K. Bannon, White House Chief Strategist
Stephen Miller, Senior Advisor to the President

Remarks by President Trump
at the Unveiling of the Boeing 787 Dreamliner Aircraft

My fellow Americans,

We're here today to celebrate American engineering, American manufacturing, and the proud American spirit that drove us to take to the skies. It's wonderful to be back here in South Carolina, and it's a terrific honor to be visiting Boeing, one of our nation's greatest and most successful companies.

For far too long, our country has been letting our jobs go overseas. We're hemorrhaging jobs. The veins of America have been gashed open by the sharp razor of globalization and our blood is spilling out of us. It is cascading from our severed jugular onto the economic landscape around us, sending the fetid stench of misery and death into the air and slickening the ground where we once stood tall, pooling ever larger around our crumpled, seizing, sheet-white body in our final spasms of life, like a stray dog in some befouled alleyway. And who holds this razor, this bringer of our own gruesome demise? Is it our captains of industry? Most certainly not. It is, in fact, the braying unclean masses living among us who have been, from the moment of their illicit arrival in our once immaculate homeland, plunging the razor deeper and deeper and deeper into the throat of our country. It is time to rise up against these filth-caked hordes, these human lamprey who want to contaminate our way of life and bleed us of our vitality, who cloud our nation like swarms of locusts. The time has come, and the only answer remaining before us is to slice them open and pluck out their entrails one by one.

I also want to thank the former governor, Nikki Haley, who is doing incredible work as our ambassador to the United Nations. Great job, Nikki!

We will bring back American jobs. We will get companies to make their products here. We will pry America back from the dark refuse of humanity and feed their dismembered corpses to our factories of death. We will decorate our homes and workplaces with the viscera of these vermin from polluted bloodlines and build gleaming white towers to ourselves from their bones. Any who question us will discover that Death lurks always around the next corner, impatient to enslave any who do not bow down to our will. The inky black maw of the land will open, and we will hollow out a bottomless cavity to dispose of the Impure, a mass grave filled nightly with new flesh, new screams, new defilements.

Handwritten annotations:

GUSHING?
VIOLENTLY SPEWING?

SERRATED OBSIDIAN BLADE

BLOOD-SPATTERED BLADE

BEGRIMED SEWER

PUS-COVER

INFESTATION?

ADD LOUDER DOG-WHISTLE?
MAYBE "PURE" "UNSULLIED"

ADD COMMENT ABOUT THE IMPURE ONES CONTAMINATING THE MINDS OF OUR SONS AND DAUGHTERS!!!

ALL WHO DEFY OUR WORD, OUR LAW, OUR ~~WILL~~ DOMINION

HUNGRY MACHINERY OF DEATH

They will not know we are coming. No, the Masked arrive in silence without omens or warnings. We will seep through the walls and rise up through the floors to take them in the night, drag them from their homes and through the neighborhoods we are reclaiming for our Kind. Charred and gutted remains moldering in ~~broad daylight~~ *THE WITHERING SUN* will be become a familiar sight in our rebuilt nation. Newborns will be pulled wailing from their mothers' toxic arms already aware they're being thrust into a world of unbroken darkness. In time, the starved, ~~putrid~~ *PUSTULENT*, feral class will come to understand there is no separation between wakefulness and nightmares, and they will pace hopelessly in the sludge of the squalid gutters where they reside, reciting a plea for the Masked to finally come and ~~suffocate~~ *CHOKE THE VERY LIFE FROM* them at last.

UFELTED
DISEASED
BOSOM

That's why I'm so pleased to be here at Boeing today, not only to celebrate these amazing, beautiful planes that showcase the best of America's ingenuity, but to announce that none will escape the Requital. It is coming.

Those who have exacted a precious toll on our country for generations *WITH THEIR PARASITIC APPETITE* will be made to pay for their crimes in blood, in unheeded prayers for mercy, in cleansing flame. Those who fight back will be purged, and we will carve their names into their exposed skulls as they breathe their last ragged, miserable breaths. We will laugh as we exact our righteous vengeance, ear-splitting clangs of laughter that will poison the air. Those we do not torch we will butcher, and those we do not shoot on sight we will cage for sport. The shriveled, naked, desperate Impure Ones will cry out for even a moment of pause to their torment, but we will not grant it to them—not ever. Instead, we will eat their young in front of them so that they may see the extent of our power. *IN BITTER MISERY* They will never know the end of their suffering. They will never again know peace, not until the moment Death claims them forever. And only then—only then—will we finally become the glorious people God has long called for us to be.

TRIGGER PHRASE??

DEVOUR THEIR INFANTS?
FEAST UPON THEIR ~~CHILDREN~~ PROGENY?

Hell is real. Hell is real. Hell is real. Thank you.

From: Katy Walsh <walshk@wh.gov>
Sent: Wednesday, February 15, 2017 11:36 AM
To: <everyone@wh.gov>
Subject: rune portal

Does anyone know how to use the rune portal over by the copier near the Cabinet Room? I've been trying to get this thing working for the last half hour and I can't tell what I'm doing wrong.

From: Bill Stepien <stepienb@wh.gov>
Sent: Wednesday, February 15, 2017 11:38 AM
To: Katy Walsh <walshk@wh.gov>, <everyone@wh.gov>
Subject: RE: rune portal

Yeah, I've been having problems with it too. I sent an email to facilities a couple days ago but haven't heard back. Anyone know what the deal is? All the runes carved into the outer stone rim just look like gibberish to me. I don't even know which glyph means "on."

From: Jessica Ditto <dittoj@wh.gov>
Sent: Wednesday, February 15, 2017 11:40 AM
To: <facilities@wh.gov>, Bill Stepien <stepienb@wh.gov>, Katy Walsh <walshk@wh.gov>, <everyone@wh.gov>
Subject: RE: rune portal

Ugh, yes. SAME problem. I'm looping in facilities.

I saw that press office intern (Fran?) using the rune portal last week and it was glowing purple and rippling, but I haven't seen her around the past few days. Maybe she could help out.

From: Bill Stepien <stepienb@wh.gov>
Sent: Wednesday, February 15, 2017 11:41 AM
To: Jessica Ditto <dittoj@wh.gov>, <facilities@wh.gov>, Katy Walsh <walshk@wh.gov>, <everyone@wh.gov>
Subject: RE: rune portal

Have you tried singing to the portal? One of the mailroom guys said he sang to it and it started pulsing softly and hovered a few feet off the ground. Could be something?

From: Katy Walsh <walshk@wh.gov>
Sent: Wednesday, February 15, 2017 11:41 AM
To: Bill Stepien <stepienb@wh.gov>, Jessica Ditto <dittoj@wh.gov>, <facilities@wh.gov>, <everyone@wh.gov>
Subject: RE: rune portal

Did he say what pitch?

From: Bill Stepien <stepienb@wh.gov>
Sent: Wednesday, February 15, 2017 11:43 AM
To: Katy Walsh <walshk@wh.gov>, Jessica Ditto <dittoj@wh.gov>, <facilities@wh.gov>, <everyone@wh.gov>
Subject: RE: rune portal

G-sharp I think

Don't get too close to the portal when you're singing though. That mailroom guy had his arm sucked in up to the elbow and when he pulled it out it crumbled into ash.

From: Katy Walsh <walshk@wh.gov>
Sent: Wednesday, February 15, 2017 11:46 AM
To: Bill Stepien <stepienb@wh.gov>, Jessica Ditto <dittoj@wh.gov>, <facilities@wh.gov>, <everyone@wh.gov>
Subject: RE: rune portal

Cool thanks for the heads up.

Okay, I think the singing worked. One of the glyphs is shining white and hot to the touch. Anyone know what the next step is supposed to be? I know I have to incant something, but I can't remember what. I think it's like zhaǵh wøzowecǵh ob-weẏ rucǵh something-something ob-weẏ auzowecǵh, or something like that?

From: Josh Kinsey <facilities@wh.gov>
Sent: Wednesday, February 15, 2017 11:50 AM
To: Katy Walsh <walshk@wh.gov>, Bill Stepien <stepienb@wh.gov>, Jessica Ditto <dittoj@wh.gov>, <everyone@wh.gov>
Subject: RE: rune portal

Hello all,

Sorry we've been slow to respond to emails regarding the rune portal. Unfortunately, the blast wave of energy the portal released the last time it closed left most of our staffers blind and seared their flesh pretty badly, so we've been playing catchup with support issues since then.

Katy, what does the illuminated glyph look like? More like a warped, seven-tiered ankh, or more like a mandala that inexplicably inspires a feeling of dread and despair? And can you see anything in the swirling vortex at the portal's center?

Josh Kinsey
White House Facilities Manager

From: Katy Walsh <walshk@wh.gov>
Sent: Wednesday, February 15, 2017 11:55 AM
To: Josh Kinsey <facilities@wh.gov>, Bill Stepien <stepienb@wh.gov>, Jessica Ditto <dittoj@wh.gov>, <everyone@wh.gov>
Subject: RE: rune portal

It doesn't really look like an ankh or a mandala. It's more like a giant serpent swallowing the sun?

And the vortex isn't even swirling, so I'm not sure what you mean there. It is making a weird sound though.

From: Josh Kinsey <facilities@wh.gov>
Sent: Wednesday, February 15, 2017 11:57 AM
To: Katy Walsh <walshk@wh.gov>, Bill Stepien <stepienb@wh.gov>, Jessica Ditto <dittoj@wh.gov>, <everyone@wh.gov>
Subject: RE: rune portal

What kind of sound? Is it a low, spine-rattling thrum?

From: Katy Walsh <walshk@wh.gov>
Sent: Wednesday, February 15, 2017 11:57 AM
To: Josh Kinsey <facilities@wh.gov>, Bill Stepien <stepienb@wh.gov>, Jessica Ditto <dittoj@wh.gov>, <everyone@wh.gov>
Subject: RE: rune portal

It's more like a scream. Is that bad?

From: Josh Kinsey <facilities@wh.gov>
Sent: Wednesday, February 15, 2017 11:58 AM
To: Katy Walsh <walshk@wh.gov>, Bill Stepien <stepienb@wh.gov>, Jessica Ditto <dittoj@wh.gov>, <everyone@wh.gov>
Subject: RE: rune portal

No, the screaming is good!

Just take some of the blood from the sacrificial bowl on the right and sprinkle it on the altar and you should be good to go.

From: Katy Walsh <walshk@wh.gov>
Sent: Wednesday, February 15, 2017 12:02 PM
To: Josh Kinsey <facilities@wh.gov>, Bill Stepien <stepienb@wh.gov>, Jessica Ditto <dittoj@wh.gov>, <everyone@wh.gov>
Subject: RE: rune portal

Um, the portal just spit all of the blood back at me and the entire room shrank by like 20 percent--not what I was trying to do.

From: Josh Kinsey <facilities@wh.gov>
Sent: Wednesday, February 15, 2017 12:03 PM
To: Katy Walsh <walshk@wh.gov>, Bill Stepien <stepienb@wh.gov>, Jessica Ditto <dittoj@wh.gov>, <everyone@wh.gov>
Subject: RE: rune portal

Hmm. Haven't encountered this issue before

From: Bill Stepien <stepienb@wh.gov>
Sent: Wednesday, February 15, 2017 12:10 PM
To: Josh Kinsey <facilities@wh.gov>, Katy Walsh <walshk@wh.gov>, Jessica Ditto <dittoj@wh.gov>, <everyone@wh.gov>
Subject: RE: rune portal

Can't you just ask the old Obama maintenance guy what the deal is?

From: Josh Kinsey <facilities@wh.gov>
Sent: Wednesday, February 15, 2017 12:13 PM
To: Bill Stepien <stepienb@wh.gov>, Katy Walsh <walshk@wh.gov>, Jessica Ditto <dittoj@wh.gov>, <everyone@wh.gov>
Subject: RE: rune portal

We would, but unfortunately on his last day of work he grabbed the crystal cipher needed to translate the runes and plunged screaming into the portal. You can actually still hear his haunting wails if you listen closely in the Roosevelt Room.

And the only written instructions we could find are printed in a language we've never seen before in an old leather-bound tome that's constantly shutting itself of its own accord.

From: Katy Walsh <walshk@wh.gov>
Sent: Wednesday, February 15, 2017 12:20 PM
To: Bill Stepien <stepienb@wh.gov>, Josh Kinsey <facilities@wh.gov>, Jessica Ditto <dittoj@wh.gov>, <everyone@wh.gov>
Subject: RE: rune portal

Wait, never mind, I think it's working now. I can see a younger version of myself floating in the aether just beyond the portal's surface

The younger me is holding out her hand and offering me what looks like a brass key, so I'm just going to reach through and grab it real quick.

From: Josh Kinsey <facilities@wh.gov>
Sent: Wednesday, February 15, 2017 12:21 PM
To: Katy Walsh <walshk@wh.gov>, Bill Stepien <stepienb@wh.gov>, Jessica Ditto <dittoj@wh.gov>, <everyone@wh.gov>
Subject: RE: rune portal

NO—this is important! NEVER reach into the portal for ANYTHING! It could be just a phantasm sent to lure the unwary.

Look closely, is the youthful version of yourself covered in translucent scales?

From: Josh Kinsey <facilities@wh.gov>
Sent: Wednesday, February 15, 2017 12:27 PM
To: Katy Walsh <walshk@wh.gov>, Bill Stepien <stepienb@wh.gov>, Jessica Ditto <dittoj@wh.gov>, <everyone@wh.gov>
Subject: RE: rune portal

Katy? you still there?

From: Jessica Ditto <dittoj@wh.gov>
Sent: Wednesday, February 15, 2017 12:29 PM
To: Josh Kinsey <facilities@wh.gov>, Katy Walsh <walshk@wh.gov>, Bill Stepien <stepienb@wh.gov>, <everyone@wh.gov>
Subject: RE: rune portal

Katy?

Dear Reince Priebus,   1/30/17

Hi Reince Priebus! My name is Keira Lynn Fennimore. I live on Pinecrest Road. I am 8 years old. I am in the 3rd grade and I have a bruther named Alex and a hamster named Reince Priebus because that is your name and I like you a lot! You are very smart and funny and handsom. You have very shiny hair! Here is me and you in front of the white house giving a press contrens.

Love,
Keira Lynn Fennimore

hamster Reince Priebus

Dear Reince Priebus,

How is the white house? I think about you all the time! I think about you in school and in my house and in the car! Is the president your best friend? My best friend is Jessica. She has brown hair and a dog. Do you have a dog? I don't have one. But I have Reince Priebus my hamster! I like him and like you!

Love,
Keira Lynn Fennimore
2/14/17

Dear Reince Priebus,   2/10/17

Do you like me?

Yes ___ No ___ Maybe ___

Put an X next to one and send this letter back to me pleas. When I grow up I want to live with you in the White House!

Love,
Keira Lynn Fen...

Reince
LOVE

hamster Reince

Dear Reince Priebus,   2/20/17

When we live in the white house we will have 4 dogs! We will have waffles everyday! We will have 2 horses! 1 of them is your horse and 1 of them is my horse. My horse will be named Shadow! We will feed them hay. Reince Priebus my hamster will live with us too!

Love,
Keira Lynn Fennimore

Dear Reince Priebus,   2/28/17

How have you ben? I'm OK. I saw you on TV and you looked handsom! I like your tie and your shiny hair! Today I went to the dentist. I got a red tothbrush. I want to give it to you as a gift. I have a tothbrush at home so you can have this one becase I like you. Reince Priebus my hamster ate cardboar today!

Love,
Keira Lynn Fennimore

Dear Reince Priebus,   3/8/17

Today in school Jessica and me playd MASH I got to marry you and drive a pink truck and have a dog and we live in a shack!

Love,
Keira Lynn Fennimore

HAPPY BIRTHDAY Reince!   3/18/17

hamster Reince

Dear Reince Priebus,   3/24/17

I made this for you in art today! It's a necklace! It's a heart with your initals! It is KLF + RP. You can ware it next time you are on TV. My hamster Reince Priebus stayed under his wood chips all day! He did not go on his weel. Mom said he is tired.

Love,
Keira Lynn Fennimore
KLF RP

Dear Reince Priebus,   3/30/17

How are you? Will you come to owr barbicue tomorrow? My hamster Reince Priebus is still very tired. He did not go thru his tube even once. I cant wait to live in the white house with you and Reince Priebus my hamste and 2 horses and eat waffles! We can jump rope every day!

Love,
Keira Lynn Fenninore

Dear Reince Priebus   4/5/17

We wrote poems today in school. I wrote my poem about you! This is my poem about you!

R eince
E xelent
I ntresting
N ice hair
C ute
E xelent

Do you like my poem? I like you!
Love, Keira Lynn Fennimore

Priebus,   4/9/17

There is sad news. Reince Priebus my hamster stopd moving and died. I an sad and cryd. Mom said I cant get a other one rite now but when I do I will name him Reince Priebus because I like you! My new hamster Reince Priebus will have shiny hair like you!

Love,
Keira Lynn Fennimore

The United States Department of Education

APRIL 12, 2017

<u>MEMORANDUM</u>

FROM: **Betsy DeVos, Secretary /s/**
          U.S. Department of Education

TO: **Department of Education Staff**

SUBJECT: **Addressing The Growing Trend Of Students Drawing**
          Dongs In Textbooks

Our nation's children are facing a grave and growing threat to their education, one that is nationwide in scope and is all but impossible for students to avoid: the rampant drawing of dongs in school textbooks. A study from the National Center for Education Statistics shows that of the 50 million children attending our nation's public schools, over 95% of them will encounter a dong drawn in a textbook over the course of their elementary and secondary education. Most will encounter dozens of dongs before graduating.

Students who draw dongs in textbooks are not only defacing school property, they are unfairly diminishing the educational experience of other students who must use those educational materials in the future. Past education authorities have done nothing to address the dong problem and, therefore, have only enabled such behavior. The result is that the presence of dongs throughout the pages of our schools' textbooks is now a full-blown epidemic (see attached exhibits for reference).

The NCES study confirmed that no academic subject is safe from dong drawings; textbooks on mathematics, science, history, languages, and social studies have all been defaced with dongs. Furthermore, because schools use the same textbooks year after year, the pages only accumulate more dongs over time. The study observed countless varieties of dongs on our nation's textbook pages, including large dongs, small dongs, curved dongs, fat dongs, African-American dongs, veiny dongs, dongs with excessive curly black hair, and dongs that appear to be ejaculating all over the page.

In many instances, students' understanding of course material is directly impeded by the presence of dongs, many of which obscure vital words and graphics on the textbook page. A common such example was seen in a 9th grade geography textbook from Traverse City, Michigan, where a large dong was drawn over a world map. The dong, along with the word "Slayer" and a pentagram drawn above it, covered the entire western hemisphere. North America was almost completely obscured behind the dong. In another representative example from a Houston-area 10th grade American history book, an illustration drawn atop an image of the signing of the U.S. Constitution depicted a dong ejaculating into George Washington's mouth and an accompanying word bubble that said "Yummy." Indeed, the NCES study found that dong concentration in textbooks was highest near the faces of famous historical figures.

One of the most egregious cases identified by the NCES study was a 1982 geometry textbook still in use at a public high school in Missouri, which was covered inside and out with over 400 dong variants, including a large, thick dong with a big hairy ballsack right on the front cover. The book has since been removed from circulation and destroyed.

What's perhaps most alarming is that the number of dongs in our public school textbooks may actually be higher than the study's estimate, as a certain proportion of students appear to be drawing dongs that are anatomically incorrect and therefore not as easily identifiable; however, the intent to draw a dong is still there and the act is just as reprehensible.

In my tenure as Education Secretary, I have seen this worrying trend up close. By far the most disturbing imagery that I have spotted belongs to a prominent category of dongs that appear to exhibit sentience, either by possessing a smiley face or by having arms and hands attached to the dong shaft. These are unsettling images for an adult to encounter; I can only imagine how traumatic seeing a dong with eyes and a mouth would be for an impressionable young student.

If our department does not step in to combat this dong-drawing trend, the education of future generations will continue to suffer. We must act immediately, as we have already seen evidence that dongs are no longer being drawn solely on textbooks, but on lockers, in school bathrooms, across blackboards, on desks, and even on the backs of school bus seats.

It will be the goal of this department to prevent and correct such behavior so that, one day, our children can learn from textbooks that contain no dongs whatsoever. We will accomplish this goal by downplaying the popularity of dongs and by actively combating dong culture, which presently dominates our schools. These are the initial actions I propose taking:

1) Censor all current dong drawings in textbooks
2) Require teachers to perform frequent mandatory book inspections for dongs
3) Remove all suggestive items from the classroom (test tubes, big markers, yard sticks/rulers, chalk, water bottles, glue bottles, wall-mounted flagstaffs, etc.)
4) Administer harsh and public punishments to students who participate in drawing dongs to serve as a warning to any other would-be dong drawers

In the following months, I look forward to working with all of you, as well as state and local education authorities, to incorporate these changes into school protocol. Together we will improve the quality of education for our nation's students and provide a happy, healthy, and dong-free learning environment to encourage their success.

ankton

Zooplankton

e Ocean's
od Chain

Fish Larve

Small Fish

Predator

s Rational Numbers

ional number.

e integer in the numerator and 1 in the denominator.

c. $-8 = -\dfrac{8}{1}$

rational number.

ional Numbers

onal numbers as either a terminating or repeating decimal.

c. $\dfrac{13}{25}$

as a decimal by dividing the numerator by the denominator.

peating decimal

minating decimal

ting decimal

rational numbers as either a terminating or repeating decimal.

c. $-\dfrac{17}{20}$

ent past, someone discovered that not all numbers are rational numbers. A builde
that the diagonal of a square with unit sides was not 2 or even $\dfrac{3}{2}$, but was somethin
ht have observed that the ratio of the circumference to the diameter of a roll of cloth
still not a rational number. Such numbers are said to be *irrational* because they can
se numbers make up the set of **irrational numbers**. Irrational numbers cannot be exp
ers. It is impossible to describe this set of numbers by a single rule except to say that a n
tional. So we write this as shown.

$$\{h \mid h \text{ is not a rational number}\}$$

Example 3   Differentiating Rational and Irrational Numbers

Determine whether each of the following numbers is rational or irrational. If it is rational, determine whethe
terminating or repeating decimal.

a. $\sqrt{25}$ b. $\dfrac{33}{9}$ c. $\sqrt{11}$ d. $\dfrac{17}{34}$ e. 0.3033033303333...

Solution
a. $\sqrt{25}$: This can be simplified as $\sqrt{25} = 5$. Therefore, $\sqrt{25}$ is rational.

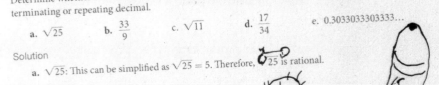

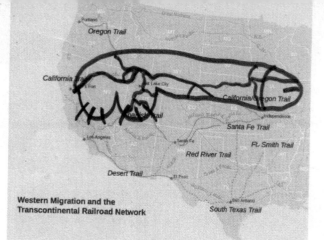

Western Migration and the Transcontinental Railroad Network

Figure 17.6 This map shows the trails (orange) used in westward migration and the development of railroad lines (blue) constructed after the completion of the first transcontinental railroad.

THE DIFFICULT LIFE OF THE PIONEER FARMER

Of the hundreds of thousands of settlers who moved west, the vast majority were homesteaders. These pioneers, like the Ingalls family of *Little House on the Prairie* book and television fame (see inset below),

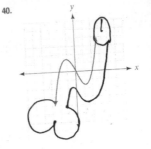

40.

4

43.

15

1.2 Phases and Classification of Matter

By the end of this section, you will be able to:

- Describe the basic properties of each physical state of matter: solid, liquid, and gas
- Define and give examples of atoms and molecules
- Classify matter as an element, compound, homogeneous mixture, or heterogeneous mixture with regard to its physical state and composition
- Distinguish between mass and weight
- Apply the law of conservation of matter

Matter is defined as anything that occupies space and has mass, and it is all around us. Solids and liquids are more obviously matter: We can see that they take up space, and their weight tells us that they have mass. Gases are also matter; if gases did not take up space, a balloon would stay collapsed rather than inflate when filled with gas.

Solids, liquids, and gases are the three states of matter commonly found on earth (**Figure 1.6**). A **solid** is rigid and possesses a definite shape. A **liquid** flows and takes the shape of a container, except that it forms a flat or slightly curved upper surface when acted upon by gravity. (In zero gravity, liquids assume a spherical shape.) Both liquid and solid samples have volumes that are very nearly independent of pressure. A **gas** takes both the shape and volume of its container.

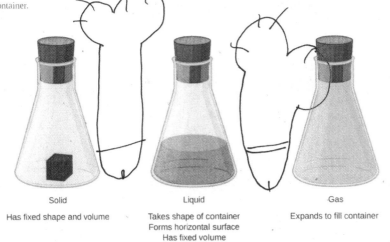

Solid	Liquid	Gas
Has fixed shape and volume	Takes shape of container Forms horizontal surface Has fixed volume	Expands to fill container

Figure 1.6 The three most common states or phases of matter are solid, liquid, and gas.

A fourth state of matter, plasma, occurs naturally in the interiors of stars. A **plasma** is a gaseous state of matter that contains appreciable numbers of electrically charged particles (**Figure 1.7**). The presence of these charged particles imparts unique properties to plasmas that justify their classification as a state of matter distinct from gases. In addition to stars, plasmas are found in some other high-temperature environments (both natural and man-made), such as lightning strikes, certain television screens, and specialized analytical instruments used to detect trace amounts of metals.

...e which graphs show relations that are functions.

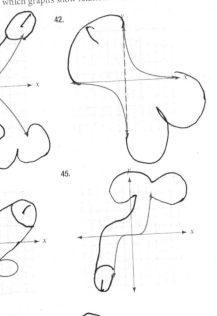

42.

45.

48.

51.

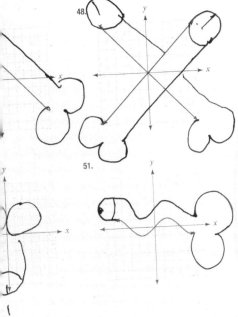

Chapter 2 | The Chemical Foundation of Life

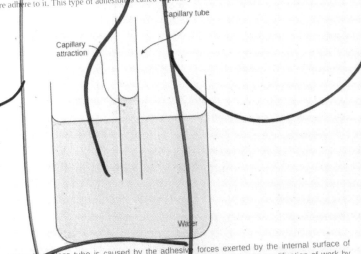

The weight of the needle is pulling the surface downward; at the same time, the surface tension is pulling ...ding it on the surface of the water and keeping it from sinking. Notice the indentation in the water around ...redit: Cory Zanker)

...e forces are related to water's property of **adhesion**, or the attraction between water molecules and other ...his attraction is sometimes stronger than water's cohesive forces, especially when the water is exposed to ...es such as those found on the inside of thin glass tubes known as capillary tubes. Adhesion is observed when ..." up the tube placed in a glass of water: notice that the water appears to be higher on the sides of the tube than ...This is because the water molecules are attracted to the charged glass walls of the capillary more than they are ...nd therefore adhere to it. This type of adhesion is called **capillary action**, and is illustrated in Figure 2.17.

Capillary tube

Capillary attraction

Water

Figure 2.17 Capillary action in a glass tube is caused by the adhesive forces exerted by the internal surface of the glass exceeding the cohesive forces between the water molecules themselves. (credit: modification of work by Pearson-Scott Foresman, donated to the Wikimedia Foundation)

Why are cohesive and adhesive forces important for life? Cohesive and adhesive forces are important for the transport of water from the roots to the leaves in plants. These forces create a "pull" on the water column. This pull results from the tendency of water molecules being evaporated on the surface of the plant to stay connected to water molecules below them, and so they are pulled along. Plants use this natural phenomenon to help transport water from their roots to their leaves. Without these properties of water, plants would be unable to receive the water and the dissolved minerals they require. In another example, insects such as the water strider, shown in Figure 2.18, use the surface tension of water to stay afloat on the surface layer of water and even mate there.

From: Steve Bannon <bannons@wh.gov>
Sent: Thursday, February 23, 2017 1:35 PM
To: Ryan Zinke <zinker@doi.gov>
Subject: Roadkill

Hello Ryan,

I'm not sure who I should be speaking to at Interior, but the President has a meeting Monday with the Federal Highway Administration during which he'll go over new roadkill disposal guidelines, and we're going to need some photos of roadkill for the briefing. We'll actually need a variety of shots of various animals, different states of decay, etc. The more the better.

I want to get started on this ASAP, so if someone on your side could send over what you have as soon as you can, that would be ideal.

- SB

From: Ryan Zinke <zinker@doi.gov>
Sent: Thursday, February 23, 2017 1:39 PM
To: Steve Bannon <bannons@wh.gov>
Subject: RE: Roadkill

Hi Steve,

We can certainly help you out on that request. Want me to send to FHWA directly?

Best,
Ryan

_____
Secretary of the Interior

Department of the Interior
1849 C Street, N.W.
Washington, DC 20240
(202) 208-3100

From: Steve Bannon <bannons@wh.gov>
Sent: Thursday, February 23, 2017 1:43 PM
To: Ryan Zinke <zinker@doi.gov>
Subject: RE: Roadkill

No, just to my email is fine. Please send as many as you have. It'd be great if you could start with rodents and skunks, and then move on to bigger animals – the more crushed and mutilated the better.

- SB

From: Ryan Zinke <zinker@doi.gov>
Sent: Thursday, February 23, 2017 2:39 PM
To: Steve Bannon <bannons@wh.gov>
Subject: RE: Roadkill

Okay. It's not much, but here's what our interns were able to find right now.

From: Steve Bannon <bannons@wh.gov>
Sent: Thursday, February 23, 2017 2:43 PM
To: Ryan Zinke <zinker@doi.gov>
Subject: RE: Roadkill

Yeah, those are good. Really good. Do you have these in higher rez?

From: Ryan Zinke <zinker@doi.gov>
Sent: Thursday, February 23, 2017 2:51 PM
To: Steve Bannon <bannons@wh.gov>
Subject: RE: Roadkill

Unfortunately no, not these. It's kind of an unusual request, so It'll take some time to dig up more shots/higher resolution images.

—
Secretary of the Interior

Department of the Interior
1849 C Street, N.W.
Washington, DC 20240
(202) 208-3100

From: Steve Bannon <bannons@wh.gov>
Sent: Thursday, February 23, 2017 2:53 PM
To: Ryan Zinke <zinker@doi.gov>
Subject: RE: Roadkill

Got it. You have any more of these animals from other angles?

From: Ryan Zinke <zinker@doi.gov>
Sent: Thursday, February 23, 2017 2:58 PM
To: Steve Bannon <bannons@wh.gov>
Subject: RE: Roadkill

Doesn't look like it. These are all the shots we've got right now.

—
Secretary of the Interior

Department of the Interior
1849 C Street, N.W.
Washington, DC 20240
(202) 208-3100

From: Steve Bannon <bannons@wh.gov>
Sent: Thursday, February 23, 2017 3:02 PM
To: Ryan Zinke <zinker@doi.gov>
Subject: RE: Roadkill

That's too bad. Just send more when you can. The President is definitely going to want more – a lot more. I know that for sure.

They don't have to be dead. Barely alive or even badly injured is fine too. In fact, that's actually even better

---

From: Ryan Zinke <zinker@doi.gov>
Sent: Thursday, February 23, 2017 3:41 PM
To: Steve Bannon <bannons@wh.gov>
Subject: RE: Roadkill

Alright. I'll have the interns get to work on this and get something back to you tomorrow EOD.

—
Secretary of the Interior

Department of the Interior
1849 C Street, N.W.
Washington, DC 20240
(202) 208-3100

From: Steve Bannon <bannons@wh.gov>
Sent: Thursday, February 23, 2017 3:48 PM
To: Ryan Zinke <zinker@doi.gov>
Subject: RE: Roadkill

In the meantime, here are a few pictures of dead animals I took so you have an idea of what I'm looking for. The President definitely wants ones like these. Particularly the close-ups. As many as you can get.

From: Steve Bannon <bannons@wh.gov>
Sent: Thursday, February 23, 2017 3:50 PM
To: Ryan Zinke <zinker@doi.gov>
Subject: RE: Roadkill

Looks like I couldn't fit them all in the first email. See below.

From: Steve Bannon <bannons@wh.gov>
Sent: Thursday, February 23, 2017 3:51 PM
To: Ryan Zinke <zinker@doi.gov>
Subject: RE: Roadkill

Few more.

From: Steve Bannon <bannons@wh.gov>
Sent: Thursday, February 23, 2017 3:55 PM
To: Ryan Zinke <zinker@doi.gov>
Subject: RE: Roadkill

Whoops. That last pic is old. Deer should be closer to this:

From: Steve Bannon <bannons@wh.gov>
Sent: Tuesday, February 28, 2017 8:16 PM
To: WH Kitchen <kitchen@wh.gov>
Subject: Dinner Tonight

White House Kitchen Staff,

I ordered chicken for dinner earlier tonight and it came completely cooked through. I sent it back and waited patiently, but the next one that was delivered was also already dead. This is unacceptable. Please do not let this happen again.

- SB

From: Jared Kushner <kushnerj@wh.gov>
Sent: Thursday, March 23, 2017 3:41 PM
To: Donald Trump <trumpd@wh.gov>, White House Senior Staff <staff@wh.gov>
Subject: Israel-Palestine Solutions

Hey all,

I was able to clear out some time earlier this week to really think about the whole Israeli-Palestinian issue. It was a really tough question, but I ended up coming up with a few solutions for it, which I pasted below. Let me know which one you think we should go with.

- Israel gets Jerusalem, but Palestine gets it on weekends and holidays
- See if every nation on earth willing to give up borders and then have entire world live in harmony—this would include Israelis and Palestinians as matter of course
- Faster internet (both sides)
- Abbas and Netanyahu each write out their version of what happened; my staff acts them out so they can see where their views differ
- Each side required to reach an agreement within a year or they both become Christian
- Dramatically increase carbon emissions until entire region is submerged under rising sea level
- Could try 3-state solution (have to think further who would get third state)
- Genocide?
- Or whatever Donald wants to do

Thanks everyone.

Jared Kushner
Senior Advisor to the President

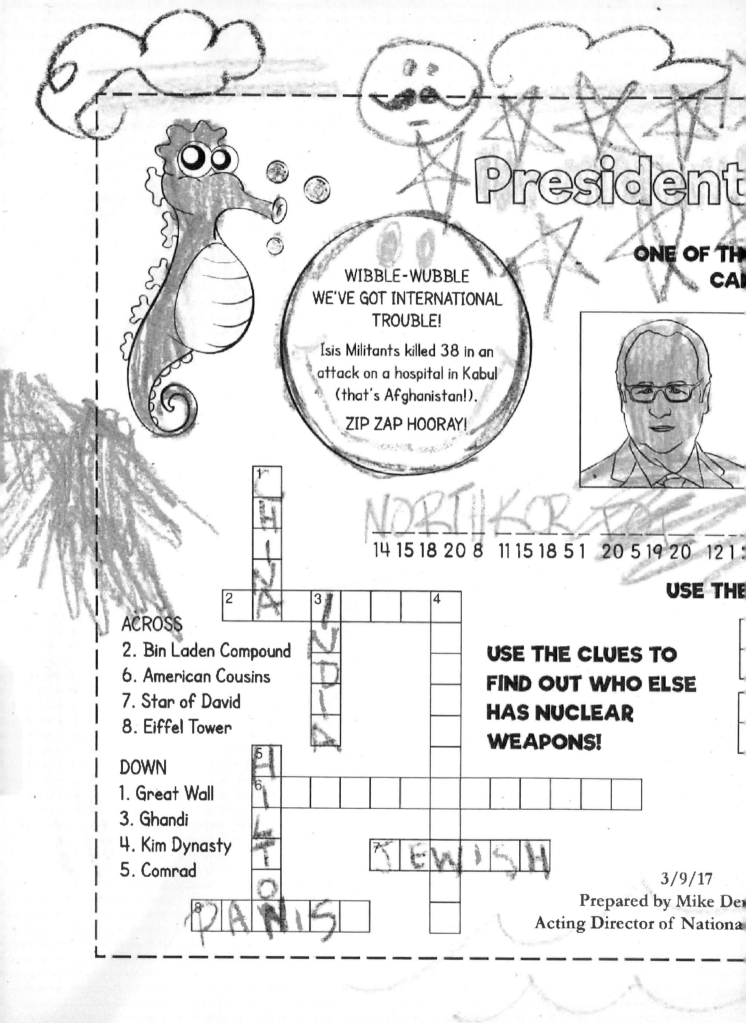

President

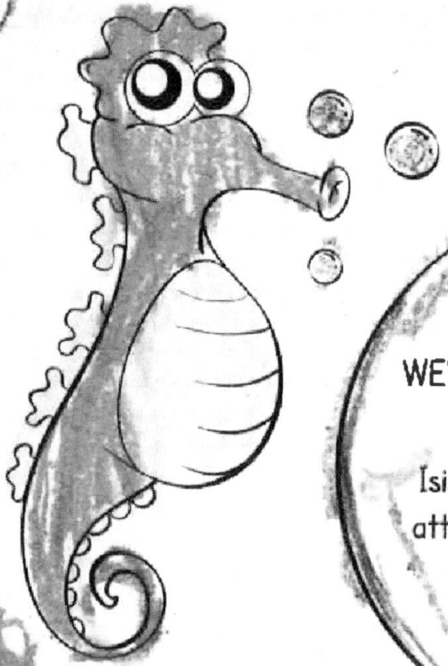

WIBBLE-WUBBLE
WE'VE GOT INTERNATIONAL
TROUBLE!

Isis Militants killed 38 in an attack on a hospital in Kabul (that's Afghanistan!).

ZIP ZAP HOORAY!

ONE OF TH
CA

NORTH KOREA

14 15 18 20 8 11 15 18 5 1 20 5 19 20 12 1

USE THE

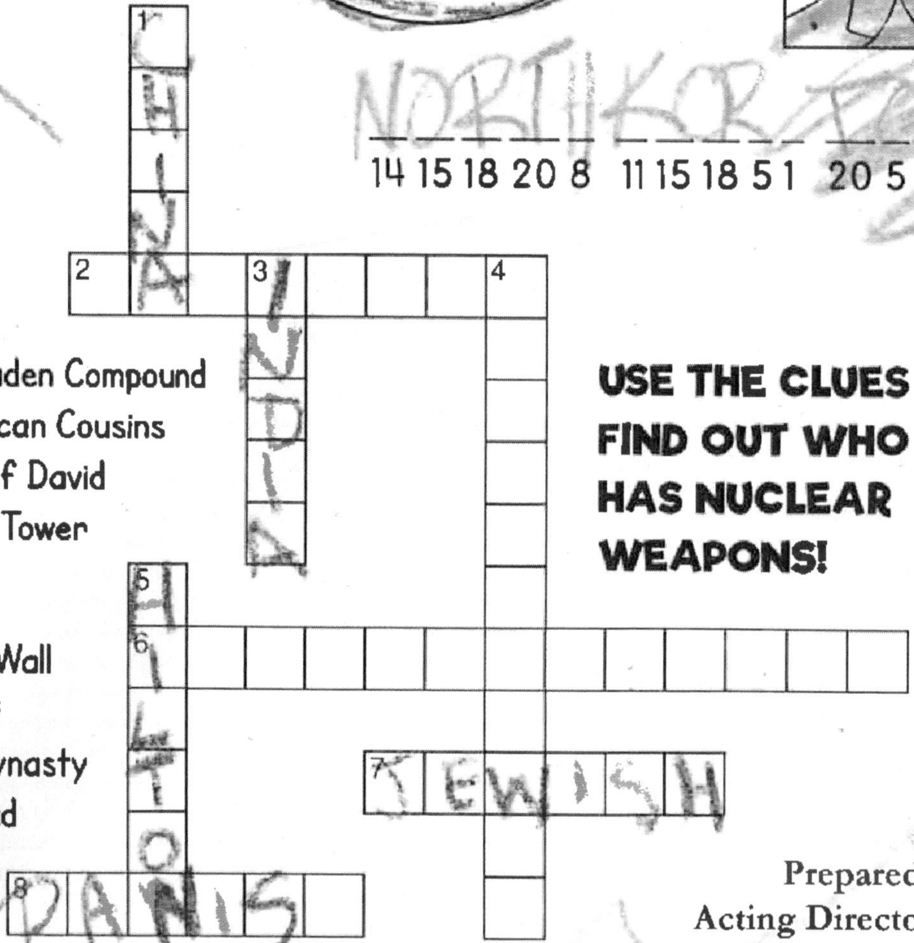

1
2
3
4
5
6
7
8
CHINA
INDIA
HILTON
JEWISH
PARIS

ACROSS
2. Bin Laden Compound
6. American Cousins
7. Star of David
8. Eiffel Tower

DOWN
1. Great Wall
3. Ghandi
4. Kim Dynasty
5. Comrad

USE THE CLUES TO FIND OUT WHO ELSE HAS NUCLEAR WEAPONS!

3/9/17
Prepared by Mike De
Acting Director of Nationa

Daily Brief

TRY TO DRAW THE PRE-1967 ISRAEL-PALESTINIAN TERRITORY BORDERS!

...OT OUR NATO ALLY!
...RCLE THEM?

WOWIE!
You did great!

4 6 15 21 18 19 3 21 4   13 9 19 19 9 12 5 19

...O FIND OUT THE SECRET MESSAGE!

D	E	F	G	H	I	J	K	L	M
4	5	6	7	8	9	10	11	12	13

Q	R	S	T	U	V	W	X	Y	Z
17	18	19	20	21	22	23	24	25	26

ALMOST DONE MR. PRESIDENT!
THEN WE GET OUR FISH!
YUMMY YUMMY!

From: Reince Priebus <priebusr@wh.gov>
Sent: Tuesday, February 28, 2017 10:48 AM
To: Ben Carson <carsonb@hud.gov>
Subject: HUD stats

Ben,

I just wanted to check in briefly to see if you had the residential sales statistics for the month of February? Specifically I'd like to see the seasonally adjusted annual rate of new single-family houses and any projections your department has for March, as we're putting together several metrics for use in a WH press briefing.

Thanks,
Reince

From: Ben Carson <carsonb@hud.gov>
Sent: Tuesday, February 28, 2017 10:49 AM
To: Reince Priebus <priebusr@wh.gov>
Subject: RE: HUD stats

Hello? Reince? Reince is that you? Can you hear me? This is Ben! Help!! I'm trapped in my email! Please, help me!

From: Ben Carson <carsonb@hud.gov>
Sent: Tuesday, February 28, 2017 10:51 AM
To: Reince Priebus <priebusr@wh.gov>
Subject: RE: HUD stats

Hello? HELLO? Are you there, Reince? Can anyone hear me? This is Ben Carson! I am the Secretary of Housing and Urban Development! I'm stuck inside my email account right now! Please get me out of here!

From: Reince Priebus <priebusr@wh.gov>
Sent: Tuesday, February 28, 2017 10:56 AM
To: Ben Carson <carsonb@hud.gov>
Subject: RE: HUD stats

Sorry Ben, I'm not sure I understand. Where are you right now?

From: Ben Carson <carsonb@hud.gov>
Sent: Tuesday, February 28, 2017 10:58 AM
To: Reince Priebus <priebusr@wh.gov>
Subject: RE: HUD stats

REINCE PLEASE BE CAREFUL!! Your reply almost came down right on top of me and crushed me! I jumped out of the way just in time, but next time I might not be so lucky. There are huge letters all around me, and there's a gigantic comma right above my head. Some of the email conversations in here go down so far that I can't even see the bottom of the thread. HELP!!

From: Reince Priebus <priebusr@wh.gov>
Sent: Tuesday, February 28, 2017 11:01 AM
To: Ben Carson <carsonb@hud.gov>
Subject: RE: HUD stats

Ben, I'm having a hard time following. Is everything okay? Are you in your office?

From: Ben Carson <carsonb@hud.gov>
Sent: Tuesday, February 28, 2017 11:03 AM
To: Reince Priebus <priebusr@wh.gov>
Subject: RE: HUD stats

I was just sending a message to my staff and I got sucked inside the email. I don't know what happened or how to get out, and I'm all alone in here. I tried taking shelter underneath Steve Mnuchin's email signature, but the inbox shifts around whenever a new message comes in, so I keep getting knocked into different threads. Please email someone in here to help me as soon as you can, or forward me to the fire department! Hurry!!

From: Ben Carson <carsonb@hud.gov>
Sent: Tuesday, February 28, 2017 11:03 AM
To: Reince Priebus <priebusr@wh.gov>
Subject: RE: HUD stats

Oh my God, I just saw a spam email suddenly disappear. One second it was here and the next it was gone. WHATEVER YOU DO, DO NOT FLAG ME AS SPAM!

From: Ben Carson <carsonb@hud.gov>
Sent: Tuesday, February 28, 2017 11:19 AM
To: Reince Priebus <priebusr@wh.gov>
Subject: RE: HUD stats

Reince, I managed to climb up to the Reply All button, but I fell and landed hard on the Sent Mail folder. I fell about halfway down the browser, so it's a miracle I wasn't seriously hurt. Can you try emailing me a ladder? I think if I can get up to that Compose New Email button, I might be able to jump out of Outlook and back onto my desk.

From: Reince Priebus <priebusr@wh.gov>
Sent: Tuesday, February 28, 2017 11:37 AM
To: Ben Carson <carsonb@hud.gov>
Subject: RE: HUD stats

Ben, I think I'm still a little confused about the situation, but I'll submit a ticket to our IT Help Desk and ask them to send someone to help you with your email issues.

From: Ben Carson <carsonb@hud.gov>
Sent: Tuesday, February 28, 2017 11:39 AM
To: Reince Priebus <priebusr@wh.gov>
Subject: RE: HUD stats

Reince, can you try CCing me to my wife's email? Her address is candy.carson@gmail.com. If I can get over to her, she may be able to print me out at home.

From: Reince Priebus <priebusr@wh.gov>
Sent: Tuesday, February 28, 2017 11:46 AM
To: IT Help Desk <helpdesk@wh.gov>
CC: Ben Carson <carsonb@hud.gov>
Subject: Ben Carson email issues

Hey guys,

Ben seems to be having some difficulty with his email right now. Can someone stop by his office to help him out as soon as you have a minute?

Thank you,
Reince

From: IT Help Desk <helpdesk@wh.gov>
Sent: Tuesday, February 28, 2017 11:52 AM
To: Reince Priebus <priebusr@wh.gov>
CC: Ben Carson <carsonb@hud.gov>
Subject: RE: Ben Carson email issues

Certainly. One of us will be over in 10-15 minutes.
--Adam

From: Ben Carson <carsonb@hud.gov>
Sent: Tuesday, February 28, 2017 11:58 AM
To: Reince Priebus <priebusr@wh.gov>
Subject: RE: HUD stats

Please attach some food and water to a PDF and send it to me as quickly as you can. My energy is running low, and I'm afraid I'll get dehydrated if I don't drink something soon. It's pretty cold in here, but I'm keeping warm by wrapping myself in some big numbers and forward slashes I found inside the calendar tab.

From: Ben Carson <carsonb@hud.gov>
Sent: Tuesday, February 28, 2017 12:06 PM
To: Reince Priebus <priebusr@wh.gov>
Subject: RE: HUD stats

You have to do something soon, Reince. I don't know how much longer I can survive in here. A few moments ago everything suddenly went pitch black and I couldn't see a thing. I thought that was it for me, but luckily I stumbled over the cursor and, after pushing with all my strength, I managed to move it a little bit. Then everything lit up again. That was a close call.

From: Reince Priebus <priebusr@wh.gov>
Sent: Tuesday, February 28, 2017 12:14 PM
To: Ben Carson <carsonb@hud.gov>
Subject: RE: HUD stats

Did anyone from IT swing by yet?

From: Ben Carson <carsonb@hud.gov>
Sent: Tuesday, February 28, 2017 12:16 PM
To: Reince Priebus <priebusr@wh.gov>
Subject: RE: HUD stats

You know, Reince, now that I stop and look around this place...it's quite beautiful.

From: Ben Carson <carsonb@hud.gov>
Sent: Tuesday, February 28, 2017 12:19 PM
To: Reince Priebus <priebusr@wh.gov>
Subject: RE: HUD stats

Reince, I wish you could be here to see this. It's incredible. There are so many amazing colors and folders, as far as the eye can see. And all the letters and numbers and punctuation stretching on and on and on in front of a shimmering white background. I've never seen anything so magnificent. It's hard to put its beauty into words.

> **From:** Reince Priebus <priebusr@wh.gov>
> **Sent:** Tuesday, February 28, 2017 12:31 PM
> **To:** Ben Carson <carsonb@hud.gov>
> **Subject:** RE: HUD stats
>
> Adam from the Help Desk just emailed me to say they're busy with a network issue, but he will try to be at your office by 1pm.

> **From:** Ben Carson <carsonb@hud.gov>
> **Sent:** Tuesday, February 28, 2017 12:52 PM
> **To:** Reince Priebus <priebusr@wh.gov>
> **Subject:** RE: HUD stats
>
> I understand now, Reince. It is all finally clear to me. This is the Kingdom of Heaven. I realize now that I must have died while sending that email earlier, and this is the Heaven that Christ always spoke of. It is here, and it is more splendid than you could possibly imagine. This menu toolbar that is above me is the Throne of God. And God, Our Heavenly Creator— He does not appear as an old man with a white beard as we all thought, but rather He appears as a File dropdown menu. Jesus Christ, the Only Begotten Son, has taken the form of an Edit dropdown menu, and is seated on the printer icon at the right hand of the Father.
>
> It's all here, Reince, just as it was written in the Bible. If only you could see the majesty of all the unread emails, all the news alerts, all the email contacts that are up here in Heaven. This is the eternal bliss that awaits all who accept Christ as their savior and follow the word of the Lord.

> **From:** Ben Carson <carsonb@hud.gov>
> **Sent:** Tuesday, February 28, 2017 12:56 PM
> **To:** Reince Priebus <priebusr@wh.gov>
> **Subject:** RE: HUD stats
>
> Reince, I am ready to spend my eternal afterlife in God's Heavenly Kingdom. Rest assured that my soul is at peace residing in the Drafts Folder of Heaven. Tell Donald I said thank you for the opportunity, and I wish all of you the best of luck. And please tell Candy and the kids that I love them. I will always be here watching over them from Heaven, and whenever they want to see me again, all they have to do is log into their email and start a new message.
>
> We will meet again someday, my friend. Goodbye.

February 1, 2011

Dearest Mother,

Donald and I settled in this new residence nary a fortnight ago, and yet we have already grown accustomed to it. It is a fine house — large and suitably appointed for a woman of my sensibilities. Herein there is a room entirely of red and another entirely of blue and yet another entirely of green, if you can believe such a thing! There is much work to do, however, and everyday seems to bring a new adventure for your little Melly.

Just today, for instance, I was introduced to an exceedingly odd man named Stephen Miller. He has a pallid, sickly complexion and the somber temperament of a gravedigger, yet he becomes quite animated at the smallest things. I thought I might offer him one of my tonics, as he is clearly ill with some western plague, but he made himself so busy with stamping about and shuffling up his papers that I no longer felt inclined to be friendly toward him.

We had only just met, but he abandoned all decorum and asked me if I would care to have my slippers removed for cleaning! Why, the knave even suggested he might do it himself! And not only that, he spoke this all with a thin smile on his sere lips, as if he were deriving some hidden pleasure from it all. O, how it agitated my senses so! Of course I declined, as it is no place of the woman of the house to be discussing such matters with an employee of her husband. And more, later that same eve I overheard him make the selfsame request for my chambermaid's slippers! What a strange person!

I know I ought to try once more to befriend Mr. Miller, as Donald harbors such fond feelings toward him. I only wish sometimes that Donald might look with this same loving gaze at our dear Barron as he does at Mr. Miller.

Alas, Mother, I must be off now, as Donald has requested my presence in the dining room. He requires the comfort of my touch quite often, and I do worry that the air here in this wretched city is fit to make one tubercular. Alas, I will air out his rashes and see if I cannot find a capable doctor for him here.

To Father, Ines, and Denis send my cordial good wishes for health and happiness.

Your Melania

February 16, 1888

Dearest Mother,

I am in good health, though the dishes my dear husband requests from the kitchen do not always agree with me. I have taken to walking the grounds in the afternoons, and this has done quite well for my constitution.

I have found happiness in asking my chamber-maid, Annalise, to accompany me in my wanderings, and this has cured me somewhat of the lonesomeness that has plagued me since Donald began his new position. I am truly o'erjoyed to spend an afternoon discussing any subject at all with the girl. Despite her lowly social station and frightfully plain countenance, she is actually sharp as a hatpin.

I long that it were otherwise, but I must admit that I have developed a strong distaste for a worker in Donald's charge, Mr. Steven Bannon. His visage has a moribund quality and a rancid

scent follows him like a putrid ghoul. I have come to recognize his disagreeable odor before his sickening form lurches into view, allowing me in certain instances ample time to abscond to my personal quarters so that I do not cross paths with him. However, it befits my luck that he is quite a restless person, and likes to stalk the halls and gardens at all hours. I have had the tragedy of encountering him on numerous occasions, and have had to formulate excuses hastily to duck away into a well seated room. There have been moments, however, when it was not a possibility to flee his unsettling presence, and so I have taken to storing a handkerchief in my frock in order to cover my nose!

Furthermore, I have felt the air become chilled as if a winter frost has fallen upon our manse's grounds when Mr. Bannon is near, though I know this cannot be so. I must admit, I am set to quaking at the thought of him. If I had not lady's decorum, I might compare this man to the squalid cats father used to shoo away from

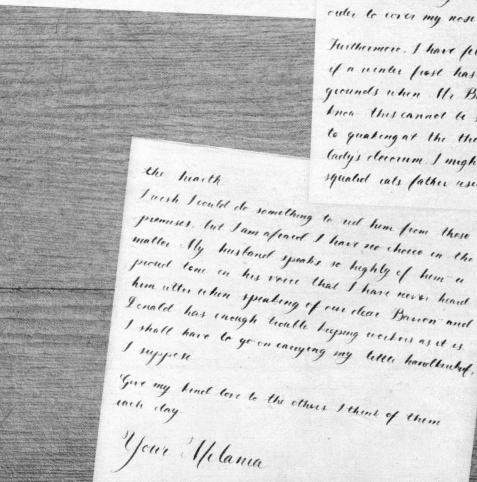

the hearth.

I wish I could do something to rid him from these premises, but I am afraid I have no choice in the matter. My husband speaks so highly of him — a proud tone in his voice — that I have never heard him utter when speaking of our dear Barron — and Donald has enough trouble keeping workers as it is. I shall have to go on carrying my little handkerchief, I suppose.

Give my kind love to the others. I think of them each day.

Your Melania

March 3, 2011

Dearest Mother,

I write to you today in such a peculiar mood. Perhaps I am longing for the hills of Slovenia and the easy days we used to share. I have been in our old cottage often in my mind's eye.

My days here are filled with sundry little tasks I must see to, but I have found much comfort in my chambermaid Annalise. She is a tacit girl, but I do enjoy her jests. Just the other day she was helping me fasten my frock for one of Donald's dinners and she put on a funny little voice which I recognized immediately to be her playacting as Mrs Kellyanne Conway. I nearly burst from my gown with laughter!

I do not hold in my heart any malice toward Mrs Conway I simply find her to be a tiresome woman. She is constantly trying to involve herself in various goings-on within this estate, even when her presence is quite unwelcome I have

often found myself clasping my lips tight when Mrs Conway comes near, for fear that some small observation I make could be soon whispered into the ears of every guest at the next formal dinner, or worse, to a newspaperman who would make my inner thoughts a public spectacle.

Mrs Conway will be no confidant of mine if she continues on being a confidant of so many. Even now, I am quite sure she is skulking in the hallway trying to listen in on my private dealings, ready to hiss them to whoever next gives her forum to state her mind.

I much prefer the company of Donald's eldest daughter, Ivanka. I quite enjoy conversing with her and find her to be well bred if not particularly intelligent. I am grateful, too, of the calming effect she has on Donald. He has become more and more impossible to please with each passing day. I wonder if his new position is not a detriment to his delicate health, his rashes are spreading at present. I must get on with finding a skillful doctor to treat him here in this city.

I sincerely hope that dear father is in good health, and Ines and Denis, too. I must go now, as Donald has requested my presence in the Vermal Room, and it has been hours since I have laid my head against his pillowy shoulder.

Your Melania

March 19, 1811

Dearest Mother,

I was very pleased to receive your letter and I hasten to inform you of a strange event I witnessed last eve.

I was lying in my four post bed, when I heard a ghastly noise coming from the garden outside. It was as if a demonic spirit or a treacherous animal of the forest was gnashing its horrible teeth. I admit I blanched in terror at the hideous clamor! Donald did not stir, as he is apt to slumber through even the loudest thunder clap, but I sat upward straight away and made haste to the window.

Ah, mother! I am loath to describe the dreadful sight I espied from my vantage!

There on the grass was none other than Mr. Bannen, that wretched employee of my husband I earlier described. He soon disappeared into the shadows but I did glimpse his repulsive frame, hunched  and ravenous, illuminated stark white in the thin moonlight. Mother, I am quite sure that the face he wore will haunt me each night! It was as if Mr. Bannen was more beast than human. I could see it in his empty gaze and the way his strange body stood contorted the way no creature God made ever should. And I cannot be sure, but looking at his horrid mouth in that moment, it appeared that some thing was — how shall I put this? — dangling from it, whatever that might have been.

Mother my poor hand shakes as I write this to you.

My breath fled me in that moment and I was frozen in my place, and it required all the strength I possess to peek out from behind the drapes. I was relieved to see that the nightmarish thing was gone, but my heart would not go quiet. O mother, his hollow eyes were like murky pools, calling me to some grotesque fate.

 I ran immediately to awaken poor Annalese, who tried her best to comfort me with one of her funny little rhymes, but I am distressed still. I am beginning to fear that there is some evil presence in this house. O mother, I wish I could be with you today. My heart is too weak for such excitement. How I long that this whole situation I find myself in at present had never occured to begin with!

I await your letter with impatience and think of you often. Keep me in your prayers.

Your Melania

May 10, 2011

Dearest Mother,

I have included with this brief note a map of my surroundings, depicted to the best of my ability, to aid you in understanding this strange place. Please share these sketches with sweet Ines, Denis, and father, and know that my heart is with you always.

Your Melania

1. Vantage from which the townfolk often gawk at the peculiar goings-on in this most unordinary estate

2. Place where I have often overheard Mrs Conway bleating her most recently obtained item of gossip to any worker, groundskeeper, or innocent sentry of the gates who happens to be nearest by

3. Garden of roses, which has grown withered and ashen despite agreeable weather

4. Corner where I first encountered Fannie, the small rabbit I have taken to telling my little thoughts to. Its strange—as I write this, I am made aware that I have not seen sweet Fannie in near a fortnight!

5. Frequent point of rendezvous for my dear chambermaid Annalise and myself

6. Place where I first espied Mr Bannon on that horrid night & his foul countenance haunts me yet!

7. Site at which I stumbled upon a dreadful quantity of bones just hours later

8. Favorite hiding spots of mine

9. Fount where I often find myself in moments of sentimental yearning for home

10. Favored route of mine during my three daily restorative wanderings

11. I have been warned never to venture past the southern gate, as only suffering awaits me there

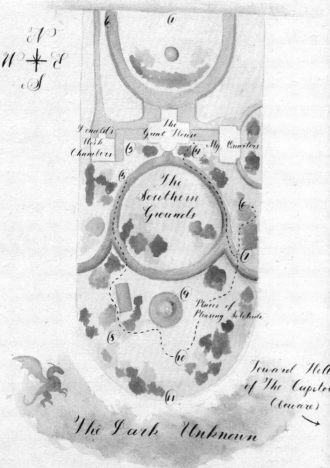

Road to Town

N W E S

Donald's Work Chambers

The Great House

My Quarters

The Southern Grounds

Plains of Pleasing Solitude

Toward Hills of The Capitol (Beware)

The Dark Unknown

Third Floor of White House

N
W · E
S

Where
Annalise and I go
to have biscuits
and laugh

To
Donald's work
chambers where I
dare not tread

1. Donald's bathing quarters
2. This room is unknown to me, and the low snarl I have heard emanating through the door will ensure it remains so
3. The nursery, where sweet Barron slumbers on the rare occasion he does not come running to my arms with visions of some great beast

4. Donald's study, which I must keep stocked with sugared drinks and his favorite crèmes
5. Storage site where I keep my slippers and stockings locked away so that Mr. Stephen Miller may not pilfer them
6. Hidden passageway connecting my quarters with that of dear Annalise so that I might never be without her friendship
7. Promenade from which I may view the entirety of the grounds and the fetid municipality beyond
8. Hallway where I pray never to encounter Mr. Bannon, for there exist no avenues allowing quick escape
9. Solarium, where I often encourage Donald to air out his rashes in the afternoon sunlight
10. I have requested that a physician move into this room so that he may better attend to the various plagues afflicting my husband
11. The family dining room, which I'm afraid has taken on the same putrid scent that all of Donald's preferred dishes seem to emit

From: Sean Spicer <spicers@transition.wh.gov>
Sent: Wednesday, December 21, 2016 3:07 PM
To: Uncle Wilbur <wilburspicer033@hotmail.com>
Subject: Incredible news!

I have great news! This isn't going to be announced officially until tomorrow, but I couldn't wait to tell someone, and you know that I've always felt able to confide in you, Uncle Wilbur, ever since I was a young boy. More than anyone else, you taught me the values and principles that have guided my career in public communications strategy and, indeed, my life.

The president-elect has decided I will be the new White House Press Secretary! From this point on, I will be this administration's official voice and public face (maybe I should get a brow lift LOL!). This is the culmination of a lifetime's work in Republican public relations communications! We have the first completely Republican-controlled federal government in years and I will be the one advancing its message on TV every day (like I was saying about that brow lift LOL!).

It will be a great honor to serve in such a prominent position (I am already what they call "famous-for-DC," but soon I will be ACTUALLY famous-for-real LOL!), but there are principles at stake that are far more important than the vast public admiration I will soon personally receive: I will get to set the record straight with the American people, and correct, once and for all, the Mainstream Media's lies.

This is an extraordinary opportunity to be of service to the president, to the country, and to democracy itself. And also to the one thing to which I—as a media professional and as a communications officer in the United States Naval Reserves—have always been the most devoted: the Truth.

This is gonna be SO GREAT!

Your loving nephew,
Sean

From: Sean Spicer <spicers@transition.wh.gov>
Sent: Friday, December 23, 2016 10:41 AM
To: Uncle Wilbur <wilburspicer033@hotmail.com>
Subject: Christmas comes early this year!

This is AMAZING! Tomorrow, the president-elect is planning to announce that I will be taking over as White House Communications Director AS WELL! Do you realize what this means, Uncle Wilbur? I'M my new boss LOL! I will not only be in charge of delivering the president's message to the American people, I will also be in charge of crafting that message! This calls for some celebratory gum! Can you imagine a better job for someone so committed to public messaging and organizational communications strategy?

I can't believe the president-elect is giving me such a distinguished role! To be honest, Uncle Wilbur, up until now I never really thought the president-elect liked me all that much—nor, for that matter, did it seem like anyone else on the campaign team or transition staff did either. Well, luckily it turns out it was all in my imagination because POTUS has placed his highest trust in me!

Just think: For the first time, we, the real Americans, will be able to control the narrative instead of the Dishonest Media with their elitist bias. I'll try to do you proud! (Get ready for TV star Sean LOL!)

Your dear nephew,
Sean

From: Sean Spicer <spicers@transition.wh.gov>
Sent: Sunday, January 15, 2017 11:15 AM
To: Uncle Wilbur <wilburspicer033@hotmail.com>
Subject: work

As you well know, Uncle Wilbur, if there's one thing that I'm not, it's a complainer, but I can't shake the feeling that nobody here respects me.

OK, so the president-elect hasn't exactly been making it easy. He stands by his decisions and he speaks his mind, all right? I know that and I know how to deal with it. Ever since I made the decision to officially join the campaign in August to further my desired career in public communications strategy, I've had to roll with the changes like a pro, which is what I am, a professional, and that's what I've DONE. Why? Because I BELIEVE in the Republican Party. Everyone knows I'm loyal. You know that, Uncle Wilbur. I'm loyal. I'm a loyal person. LOYAL!

I'm NOT a person given to COMPLAINT. OK, have I gotten up a full head of steam about what I, in my professional opinion, considered to be unfair and biased reporting? Have I gotten in shouting matches on cable TV on more than one occasion? When that campus paper back at Connecticut College DELIBERATELY misspelled my last name, did I sit down and write a very stern letter to the editor about it SETTING THE RECORD STRAIGHT? Darn right I did! Does that make me a complainer? Because I stood up for myself? Because I came out of the situation with DIGNITY, instead of the ABJECT HUMILIATION to which I'd been subjected? NO it does NOT.

I've been fighting these falsehood-peddling people my whole life! And soon I'LL be the one standing behind the podium and I'll get the respect and admiration I DESERVE.

Your devoted nephew,
Sean

From: Sean Spicer <spicers@wh.gov>
Sent: Sunday, January 22, 2017 9:49 AM
To: Uncle Wilbur <wilburspicer033@hotmail.com>
Subject: Worst day ever

Oh Uncle Wilbur, what do these people want from me?

The inauguration weekend was supposed to be a joyous celebration of our party's victory. We won, get used to it, Mainstream Media! This was OUR moment. The weekend should have been a chance to bask in the afterglow of a hard-won triumph. Is that too much to ask? After everything I've sacrificed for these people already? To sit back and enjoy the satisfaction of a job well done?

(I'll admit I'm a little worked up, Uncle Wilbur, and I need to calm down, but I can't find my gum anywhere…)

I thought on the first day we'd be setting out our policy agenda, but then, well, you saw it. What was I supposed to do? I just thought to myself, "OK, baptism by fire!" and went all in. I got in front of all those cameras, and then…

Oh, my pounding head hurts so much right now. My mouth has this terrible taste in it. The way the people in the press corps were looking at me. It was painful, Uncle Wilbur. It HURT. But did I back down? No. I was committed. I was steadfast. Why? Because Sean Michael Spencer is a PROFESSIONAL COMMUNICATIONS STRATEGIST, that's why. I did my job. Exactly the way I was asked to do it.

But then the aftermath. My golly! The media, out to get me, just like back in Connecticut College and that horrible, offensive student paper prank. The sheer DERISION of it. Millions of people. Everybody saw. Everybody. The beating I'm taking for it in the editorials…

All I did was present the facts according to the numbers and information I'd been given. But afterward, POTUS had some staffers take me into a room off the Oval Office study that I'd never even seen before and they—I don't even know if I can bring myself to say it—they put me in a CRATE, Uncle Wilbur! All I could do was rattle the bars and plead and plead, but no one let me out or even paid attention to my shouts of protest. I was in there for 10 HOURS, Uncle Wilbur!

Maybe I learned my lesson though: Look sharper, appear more confident, command the news cycle. I think I've learned that. I've definitely learned that. Yes definitely.

My skin itches, Uncle Wilbur. It itches all over.

OK, OK, focus on the positive. I'm learning, I'm learning, I'll do better, much better next time.

Your troubled nephew,
Sean

From: Sean Spicer <spicers@wh.gov>
Sent: Monday, January 23, 2017 7:09 AM
To: Uncle Wilbur <wilburspicer033@hotmail.com>
Subject: Please disregard my prior emails

Uncle Wilbur, I must ask you to please forgive my negative tone over the last few letters. I know that if there's one thing you can't stand, it's a whiner. "Whiners aren't winners," you always said LOL!

I am feeling MUCH better now. I admit it: I deserved to be in that crate. And I deserved to have that tray of ice cubes dumped down my shirt collar. Now I'm better. I'm so much better.

It turns out I've been looking at things wrong all along. Facts are not rigid things. Let's say one person has one set of facts that they believe to be true, and another person has a different set of facts that they believe to be true. Either way, they're all "facts" inasmuch as they're a set of information on a certain topic that may or may not be true to a certain set of people that may or may not necessarily agree on what those facts may be.

Or something like that. My head hurts. I need some gum. My mouth tastes terrible. I want a fresher mouth.

Wait, where was I? I haven't been sleeping well, Uncle Wilbur. I've been having terrible visions in my nightmares, visions of long prison-like mazes that stretch on and on and on.

But like I was saying. The Truth isn't a constant thing, like when I worked for George W. Bush and went around the world saying free trade is the best policy and that it's good for workers and good for business, and now I'm in charge of communicating that free trade is a BAD policy because it's bad for workers and bad for business. See? There can be a bunch of different Truths. I've thought about this a lot and I feel much calmer. Like being wrapped in a warm blanket, or chewing on a mouth-freshening stick of gum, or snuggling with Woofy back when I was a young boy before you gave him to our neighbors who were moving to the country. I feel better now, Uncle Wilbur, really I do. I'm better now.

Not like that time they INTENTIONALLY misspelled my last name to make me seem like some kind of, well I don't even want to say. An orifice.

And hey, my first "official" press briefing is today, and considering how this weekend went, it can only be uphill from here, right? Onward and upward, Uncle Wilbur!

Your upbeat nephew,
Sean

From: Sean Spicer <spicers@wh.gov>
Sent: Wednesday, January 25, 2017 9:33 PM
To: Uncle Wilbur <wilburspicer033@hotmail.com>
Subject: I just had this terrible thought

OK, so if there's no such thing as constant, immutable fact, then how can some facts be fake?

Uncle Wilbur just let me finish: Sometimes true is true and fake is fake, period. Like when the FAKE NEWS reported that we'd removed the bust of MLK from the Oval Office, and we HADN'T, that was a FACT that PROVED they were FAKE NEWS! There was literally no denying it. I had them dead to rights! Inaccurate! False! There were photos to show it sitting right there! FACTUALLY UNTRUE, full stop!

Or like when that campus paper printed that slanderous misspelled byline, they said it was an "accident," that it was "in error," oh sure, you ACCIDENTALLY spelled the name "Spicer" in a byline with the addition of an extra "h" after the "p" and an "n" and "t" before and after the "c". Come on, what are the chances that RANDOM ERROR would just HAPPEN to spell out THAT PARTICULAR word, gimme a BREAK.

No, I'm not buying it, that was no mistake, that was ON PURPOSE, let me FINISH, please, I'll admit Uncle Wilbur that it hurts a man's feelings to be made to feel like that, to be publicly derided in such a base manner, as if a man's whole being were nothing more than some—some VALVE—some tightly constricted aperture of muscle and tissue, only widening and opening up when it's time to—to EXTRUDE.

So anyway, how can Truth itself be fluid about something like THAT, an incident of such transparent MALFEASANCE and INTENTIONAL wrongdoing! JUST ALLOW. ME. TO FINISH, please! There MUST be SOME sort of objective factual basis for reality because that right there is clearly FALSE!

Goshdarnit, I wish I had my gum! It's not here. They don't LET me have gum in my crate. They don't let me have ANYTHING!

So I don't get it, I don't get it, Uncle Wilbur. I need help understanding what this all means, and also why I'm so itchy—so itchy all the time, every part of me. I'm just so grateful that you've allowed me to confide in you, because you were always there for me—you and Woofy—and you made sure I always told the Truth, always.

Your loyal nephew,
Sean

From: Sean Spicer <spicers@wh.gov>
Sent: Friday, February 10, 2017 10:01 PM
To: Uncle Wilbur <wilburspicer033@hotmail.com>
Subject: What is Truth?

What is Truth even, Uncle Wilbur? Is it even knowable? Is it not true that each of us only perceives what enters our minds through the five senses: sight, sound, touch, smell, taste—speaking of which: time for more gum, my mouth feels like an ashtray—and it is only through these five pathways that we can gain a limited window of the "reality" we live in. Can we ever know that which we don't perceive through our senses, like the fate of Schrodinger's Dog?

Did I say dog I meant cat

Look, we have no control over the electrical impulses received by our brain, right? What if—I say this just for the sake of argument—what if we couldn't trust the sensory input of our own perceptions anyway? Like if we had a recurring nightmare of being trapped within a series of unending dream-mazes, and then we awoke in the dead of night, sweating and out of breath, itchy all over, with a taste in our mouth that no amount of gum could ever freshen, only to realize we are STILL in our CRATE. We are STILL having that jar of pennies shaken at us whenever we cry out too loudly. We are STILL doing this job every day every day every day. Well, Uncle Wilbur, just because we might THINK and FEEL those things, that wouldn't mean that they were REAL, would it?

Would it?

From: Sean Spicer <spicers@wh.gov>
Sent: Monday, February 20, 2017 1:14 PM
To: Uncle Wilbur <wilburspicer033@hotmail.com>
Subject: The laughter—the incessant, incessant laughter

Uncle Wilbur please you must pardon me for the dramatic tone of this ongoing correspondence but I tell you at this point you are the ONLY one I can trust.

I don't know what to believe anymore. There are rumors that I am on my way out—are they fake facts or true facts, who can say, there's no way to tell, it could just be speculation, or on the other hand... And meanwhile more "facts" keep coming out each day, one after another, and I'm supposed to make sure people see them as positive for us, always positive. But the laughter, Uncle Wilbur, the laughter, the laughing, I hear it now, I hear it at all times, always, at the podium and in my crate.

They're laughing at someone who's just trying to do his job? They just MOCK and MOCK non-stop. Everyone's watching me, all the time, and laughing, just like they laughed back when that campus paper made fun of me, in front of everyone, all of them laughing, laughing, turning my very NAME into a CRASS ANUS-RELATED PUN!

Don't you see Uncle Woofy, that's why you're the only one I can talk to about any of this? Every word I say to anyone is scrutinized, Uncle Woofy. It's all right there out in the open, in public, and each utterance out of my mouth makes them laugh, and then it makes the others, my very COLLEAGUES, put me in my crate and throw bottle caps at me and walk me around on a leash and make me eat grass, and if I even TRY to stand up for myself I face the awful sound of that penny jar.

So I don't have anyone to talk to but you, Uncle Wilbur. You're it. You're all I have!

No one must EVER see these emails, but of course you won't reveal them to anyone, because how could you? You are as silent as the grave LOL! "Tell the Truth, little slugger," that's what you said, and that's why I'm writing these emails to you, because I would never lie to you Uncle Wilbur, and I can't trust these thoughts to anyone else, whether they're alive or whether they died twenty years ago.

Your honest nephew,
Sean

From: Sean Spicer <spicers@wh.gov>
Sent: Friday, February 24, 2017, 9:19 PM
To: Uncle Wilbur <wilburspicer033@hotmail.com>
Subject: If it's war they want then it's war they'll get

No more Mr. Nice Guy, Uncle Wilbur they've gone too far and we're fighting back the POTUS is declaring war on the Dishonest Media and I'm the man who's going to do it for him because the Mainstream Media is nothing less than a threat to America and I'm a Patriot you know that Uncle Wilbur I'm not a whiner—I don't care how much grass my colleagues make me eat from my dish or trays of ice cubes they put down my shirt—I'm an Alpha Male not some helpless fool in an Easter Bunny suit

I'm a goshdarn Commander in the United States Naval Reserves is what I am! A Real Man, the RNC invented the title of Chief Strategist just for me I was in charge of messaging all through the campaign and everybody said we'd lose but guess what WE WON darn right but they just can't accept this fact, this FACT, 306 electoral votes but they're all so jealous and can't accept they lost so they #MakeThingsUp—goshdang how did my back get so itchy? And my arms and my neck too—

It's time to take off the kid gloves if they want an old-fashioned brawl they'll find one a real dust-up bare-knuckles time a MAN among MEN, we'll start kicking them out of the Press Room that's right BANNED from attending—that's your word not mine, "ban"—punitive measures consequences for your misdoings Dishonest Media

and I'm LOYAL to POTUS to the GOP to America and a good old-fashioned Man's Man, like the fellows out back by the edge of the woods, laughing and drinking beers, back when Men were Men, shooting at squirrels, the sounds of the gunshots and the clatter of the beer cans and the laughter and the barking of the little dog—the precious little dog—that runs up tail wagging curious wanting to see what's going on with the grown-ups

so if the FAKE NEWS Dishonest Media wants to throw punches, I'm ready to punch back and I can take it on the chin with the best of them buddy you betcha fighting for America now we have to keep her safe from all enemies foreign and domestic and the Dishonest Media is the biggest enemy of them all, laughing, laughing at us, laughing at America, mocking POTUS, mocking the White House, mocking the press briefings, making fun of the way somebody chews gum, as if one had some sort of pathological obsession with the cleanliness of one's mouth, well just you wait Uncle Wilbur we'll make America see

and the poor little dog just running carelessly in, chasing the squirrels they were shooting at all excited bouncing through the grass by the edge of the woods and the little boy walking around back calling out his dog's name looking for his Woofy and the drunken laughter and the shots ringing out across the dusky sunset and then the terrible high-pitched whine cut suddenly off

you said it didn't happen Uncle Wilbur you said it didn't happen I'm sorry I lied Uncle Wilbur I made it up I made it up you didn't shoot him you gave him to the neighbors who were moving away, moving to the country like you said with the geese and goats and friendly horses and the little shade tree next to the pond I'm sorry I said it Uncle Wilbur I made it all up I lied I lied I lied

---

From: Sean Spicer <spicers@wh.gov>
Sent: Wednesday, March 1, 2017 8:25 PM
To: Uncle Wilbur <wilburspicer033@hotmail.com>
Subject: (no subject)

I AM NOT A HUMAN SPHINCTER
DOESN'T MATTER WHAT THEY SAY
I'M A STRATEGIST AND THINKER
LITTLE WOOFY'S GONE AWAY

I AM NOT A HUMAN SPHINCTER
DOESN'T MATTER WHAT THEY SAY
I'M A STRATEGIST AND THINKER
LITTLE WOOFY'S GONE AWAY

I AM NOT A HUMAN SPHINCTER
DOESN'T MATTER WHAT THEY SAY
I'M A STRATEGIST AND THINKER
LITTLE WOOFY'S GONE AWAY

I AM NOT A HUMAN SPHINCTER
DOESN'T MATTER WHAT THEY SAY
I'M A STRATEGIST AND THINKER
LITTLE WOOFY'S GONE AWAY

I AM NOT A HUMAN SPHINCTER
DOESN'T MATTER WHAT THEY SAY
I'M A STRATEGIST AND THINKER
LITTLE WOOFY'S GONE AWAY

I AM NOT A HUMAN SPHINCTER
DOESN'T MATTER WHAT THEY SAY
I'M A STRATEGIST AND THINKER
LITTLE WOOFY'S GONE AWAY

I AM NOT A HUMAN SPHINCTER
DOESN'T MATTER WHAT THEY SAY
I'M A STRATEGIST AND THINKER
LITTLE WOOFY'S GONE AWAY

Slide 1:

TOP SECRET

Review Of The Most Dangerous Criminal Organizations Within Our Nation's Borders

Presented By: Attorney General Jeff Sessions
United States Department Of Justice
August 14, 2017

Slide 2:

OVERVIEW

- As of 2011, the National Gang Intelligence Center estimated there were over 33,000 gangs in the United States with over 1.4 million total active members, not including other types of criminal organizations and syndicates
- Given that this data dates from President Obama's first term, we can only assume these numbers have grown by at least 9000% since that time
- Most organizations begin recruiting children from ages 10 to 13, although I suspect they start as young as in utero
- 1 in 2 Americans look like they are a member of a criminal organization

Slide 3:

MOST DANGEROUS CRIMINAL GROUPS IN THE UNITED STATES

Slide 4:

Chicago's Splinter Gangs

Loose affiliations of individuals operating without formal organizational hierarchies that have been responsible for over 400 murders so far this year. They are highly dangerous; can even carry out shootings when unarmed. We propose consolidating them into one single mega-gang to make them easier to track and investigate.

Slide 5:

MS-13

Deadly Salvadoran gang notorious for their brutal murders. Our analysts posit that 99% of all illegal immigrants entering the country from Mexico are members of this gang. Rumored to be working to increase their influence by acquiring nuclear weapons. Their tattoos seem to be what grant them their special powers and we must attempt to remove them using laser surgery.

Slide 6:

MS-11

Skilled criminal group that has committed three high-profile heists to date. Proficient in disguises, explosives, and getaway driving. Unclear if and when they will strike again.

Slide 7:

Anonymous

International community of computer hackers that has proven widely successful at conducting cyberattacks against governments, corporations, and other entities. Known for their iconic masks and distinctive trailblazing electronic sound.

Slide 8:

These Kids Hanging Out On A Bridge

Hardened criminal group whose offenses include loitering, attempted loitering, and conspiring to loiter. Can be taken out via controlled demolition of bridge.

1. _____

2. _____

3. _____

4. _____

5. _____

6. _____

7. _____

8. _____

This Guy In A Sweatshirt On A Dark Street

Individual is suspected in crimes including drug possession, weapons possession, assault, rape, murder, attempted murder, manslaughter, larceny, motor vehicle theft, shoplifting, breaking and entering, trespassing, vandalism, resisting arrest, vagrancy, disorderly conduct, disturbing the peace, driving without a license, driving with a suspended license, driving under the influence, driving with an open container, accessory to a crime, discharging a firearm within city limits, mass transit fare evasion, panhandling, public drinking, public urination, and dozens more. Individual is considered extremely dangerous; law enforcement must take all necessary measures to apprehend him or subdue him by force on sight.

9.

Cosa Nostra

Organized crime family on which we have decades of extensive documented video evidence of fraud, racketeering, drug dealing, and murder. We must begin targeting the younger generation of members, as they have slowly begun taking control of the enterprise.

10.

Black Lives Matter

Nationwide movement of African-American rights activists that, given this nation's history, should pretty much know where things are headed for it policing- and surveillance-wise. Just a quick look at what this department has done in the past and then a check of who's in charge of it now and, bingo, you know where 50% of our annual budget's going.

11.

Masjid Al-Noor

Domestic terrorist cell that seeks to destroy American society by hosting potluck dinners, food drives, and community gatherings in the upstate New York area. We are prepared to detain entire group at a moment's notice, as our surveillance apparatus has been closely tracking all members for years.

12.

The Dark Web

Collection of shadowy, unregulated websites that users can upload themselves onto so they can engage in dangerous light cycle races and glowing disc battles. Our cybersecurity unit must ally with the Master Control Program in order to monitor and police this lawless sector of the internet.

13.

Roger Goodell

Criminal leader who oversees massive, brutal human combat ring, using economic exploitation to coerce vulnerable young men to violently attack one another for entertainment and personal financial gain. Has been implicated in the savage, inhumane abuse of thousands of individuals, often resulting in permanent traumatic injury, mental deterioration, and death.

14.

Greasers

Reportedly planning to stage a surprise assault on the preps by the old mill on Friday. We are exploring opportunities to forge an alliance with the jocks in order to stop them.

15.

The Ivory Chef

Deranged sexual deviant who frequently appears in public fully nude and seeks lascivious gratification by coercing others to touch his abdomen. Lures innocent bystanders, oftentimes children, with treats before subjecting them to his perverted demands. Possible cocaine user/supplier as he is often seen covered in white powder. Can be eliminated by baking him at 450 degrees for 40 minutes.

16.

Lizards

The Helmeted Ones Sent From The Future

Since they were first identified by law enforcement in 1978, this group has used discordant, synthesized sonic pulses in an attempt to control our minds and destroy our culture. It is believed that unscrewing their helmets will uncouple them from all future timestreams and render them inert.

17. _____ 18. _____

Southwest Spice Mix

Smuggled across the U.S. border illegally, these piquant aromatics have infiltrated all corners of the nation, ousting longstanding classics from menus, scandalously intermixing with American entrees, and bringing pain and discomfort to countless unsuspecting palates. We will work closely with the FDA to ensure these foreign flavorings do not destroy American taste buds.

The Pussy Posse

High-profile criminal group operating out of New York City and LA with significant financial resources and public influence. Known for their raucous disorderly conduct and culture of hypersexuality. Can be dismantled by targeting their ringleader, known within inner circle as "Leo."

19. _____ 20. _____

Cults

Members of these bizarre and rapidly proliferating collectives follow an obscure South Asian religion and have been brainwashed into attending gatherings in which they engage in elaborate, unnatural synchronized physical rituals, most likely honoring some type of sun god. They can be identified by their identical form-fitting cult garments and the ceremonial mats they carry with them. These groups pose a serious threat to Judeo-Christian values; members must be deprogrammed before they become too limber to be apprehended by law enforcement.

Fresno, California

Massive syndicate with a membership of over 500,000. Must work closely with nearby Merced and Visalia to isolate and ultimately eliminate this blight on our society.

21. _____ 22. _____

Aryan Brotherhood

Have a few unpaid noise ordinance violations.

23. _____ 24. _____

From: Darren Forester <foresterd@treasury.gov>
Sent: Monday, February 27, 2017 10:41 AM
To: Steven Mnuchin <mnuchins@treasury.gov>
Subject: Tubman $20 Image

Secretary Mnuchin,

I have provided a link below to the mockups for the new Harriet Tubman $20 bill. These are ready for production, so all you have to do is give the go-ahead on which version you like best.

www.staff.treasury.gov/currencyrevisions/20/tubmanoptions1.png

-Darren Forester
Department Of The Treasury

From: Steven Mnuchin <mnuchins@treasury.gov>
Sent: Monday, February 27, 2017 11:37 AM
To: Darren Forester <foresterd@treasury.gov>
Subject: RE: Tubman $20 Image

Darren,

Just took a quick look at these. I'm not liking the front. Is there any way we can get someone like Dwight Eisenhower or General MacArthur on there instead? Think either of those replacements would really resonate with people.

Steven Mnuchin
U.S. Secretary Of The Treasury

From: Darren Forester <foresterd@treasury.gov>
Sent: Monday, February 27, 2017 12:50 PM
To: Steven Mnuchin <mnuchins@treasury.gov>
Subject: RE: Tubman $20 Image

Secretary Mnuchin,

I'm afraid the decision has already been made to have Tubman on the bill. These versions have been approved, so if you just want to pick your favorite we can start printing.

-Darren Forester
Department Of The Treasury

From: Steven Mnuchin <mnuchins@treasury.gov>
Sent: Monday, February 27, 2017 1:31 PM
To: Darren Forester <foresterd@treasury.gov>
Subject: RE: Tubman $20 Image

Darren,

I just don't think people will know who is on this bill if we go with one of these options. I really don't want to confuse people, given that this is such a prominent piece of currency. May I suggest Teddy Roosevelt, James K. Polk, or Milton Friedman? I think one of them would be much more recognizable.

Steven Mnuchin
U.S. Secretary Of The Treasury

From: Darren Forester <foresterd@treasury.gov>
Sent: Monday, February 27, 2017 2:50 PM
To: Steven Mnuchin <mnuchins@treasury.gov>
Subject: RE: Tubman $20 Image

Sir, I'm afraid Tubman is the choice. We can draw up some new versions if you don't like these.

-Darren Forester
Department Of The Treasury

From: Steven Mnuchin <mnuchins@treasury.gov>
Sent: Tuesday, February 28, 2017 11:48 AM
To: Darren Forester <foresterd@treasury.gov>
Subject: RE: Tubman $20 Image

Okay Darren, here is my list of options for the $20. Pick one and send out a work order for some sample designs:

William Howard Taft, George Patton, Robert McNamara, J.P. Morgan, William Rehnquist, Andrew Jackson back on it, Andrew Carnegie, any Rockefeller, Elvis, John Pershing, Thomas Edison, a second Washington bill, Antonin Scalia, Trump, Robert E. Lee, or Neil Armstrong.

We can probably just put Tubman on one of those commemorative coins and be done with it.

Steven Mnuchin
U.S. Secretary Of The Treasury

From: Steven Mnuchin <mnuchins@treasury.gov>
Sent: Tuesday, February 28, 2017 11:57 AM
To: Darren Forester <foresterd@treasury.gov>
Subject: RE: Tubman $20 Image

Just realized Andrew Carnegie was not born in America. Scratch him from the list.

Steven Mnuchin
U.S. Secretary Of The Treasury

From: Steven Mnuchin <mnuchins@treasury.gov>
Sent: Tuesday, February 28, 2017 3:16 PM
To: Darren Forester <foresterd@treasury.gov>
Subject: RE: Tubman $20 Image

Actually why isn't Reagan on anything? I just assumed he was on something. We need to stick to someone people know and admire. A real American hero like Reagan needs to be somewhere on a bill. Let's go with him.

Steven Mnuchin
U.S. Secretary Of The Treasury

From: Darren Forester <foresterd@treasury.gov>
Sent: Tuesday, February 28, 2017 4:09 PM
To: Steven Mnuchin <mnuchins@treasury.gov>
Subject: RE: Tubman $20 Image

Sir, I'm very sorry, but this is unfortunately a non-negotiable situation. There is no way this decision can be reversed at this point. Tubman is going to have to go on the currency.

-Darren Forester
Department Of The Treasury

From: Steven Mnuchin <mnuchins@treasury.gov>
Sent: Wednesday, March 1, 2017 9:45 AM
To: Darren Forester <foresterd@treasury.gov>
Subject: RE: Tubman $20 Image

Okay hear me out, we could compromise and put Sam Walton on the front -- I think everyone can agree on him. Then on the back would be a picture of notable leaders like Jamie Dimon, Hank Paulson, and Clint Eastwood all standing together, and there could be a portrait of Tubman hanging on the wall in the background of the scene. Sound good?

Steven Mnuchin
U.S. Secretary Of The Treasury

From: Steven Mnuchin <mnuchins@treasury.gov>
Sent: Wednesday, March 1, 2017 11:04 AM
To: Darren Forester <foresterd@treasury.gov>
Subject: RE: Tubman $20 Image

You know what, the background could also be historical figures if that makes more sense. Maybe William F. Buckley shaking hands with John C. Calhoun or Henry Ford. They could be talking in 19th-century Philadelphia so you'd get the idea that Tubman is somewhere nearby. Now that would be a bill I would want in my wallet!

Steven Mnuchin
U.S. Secretary Of The Treasury

From: Darren Forester <foresterd@treasury.gov>
Sent: Wednesday, March 1, 2017 11:18 AM
To: Steven Mnuchin <mnuchins@treasury.gov>
Subject: RE: Tubman $20 Image

I'm not sure, sir, I think people are expecting to see her more prominently.

-Darren Forester
Department Of The Treasury

From: Steven Mnuchin <mnuchins@treasury.gov>
Sent: Wednesday, March 1, 2017 3:38 PM
To: Darren Forester <foresterd@treasury.gov>
Subject: RE: Tubman $20 Image

I think I have the perfect solution here, Darren: We stick with one of the people I've listed -- let's say it's Ike in full military regalia -- and then we print Tubman's name on the watermark strips. That way when people look up to check if the bill is counterfeit, they see her name repeating over and over. Or maybe whenever you put a blacklight over the bill, you can see Tubman's face as a watermark or something. Seems pretty reasonable to me. Can you get the designers working on that?

Steven Mnuchin
U.S. Secretary Of The Treasury

From: Steven Mnuchin <mnuchins@treasury.gov>
Sent: Wednesday, March 1, 2017 4:13 PM
To: Darren Forester <foresterd@treasury.gov>
Subject: RE: Tubman $20 Image

Darren, this whole question got me thinking: Why don't we just eliminate all the bills below the 20? I don't think I ever use the smaller ones. They are just a waste -- completely obsolete currency. Is there anything that even costs $5 anymore? Stores could just round up the cost of everything to the nearest 20 dollars which would be so much more convenient for everyone. No messing around in your wallet for useless little bills. And that way we could just stick Lincoln on the 20 where he belongs. Then on the back we could have Generals Sherman and Sheridan with a senator like Charles Sumner. What better way to honor African-Americans than with the people who did the work to free them? In fact you should call together a meeting for all senior staff next week. We need to get this rolling!

Steven Mnuchin
U.S. Secretary Of The Treasury

April 28, 2017

Executive Order — Protecting the American Homeland from the Clear and Immediate Threat Posed by Lighthouses and Lighthouse Keepers

EXECUTIVE ORDER

- - - - - -

PROTECTING THE AMERICAN HOMELAND FROM THE CLEAR AND IMMEDIATE THREAT POSED BY LIGHTHOUSES AND LIGHTHOUSE KEEPERS

By the authority vested in me as President by the Constitution and the laws of the United States of America, it is hereby ordered as follows:

Section 1. *Purpose.* Lighthouses, along with the lighthouse keepers who reside therein, represent a grave and imminent threat to national security and the wellbeing of the citizenry of the United States. In order to protect the American people from the dangers posed by these structures and the beams of light that emanate therefrom, the federal government must neutralize any and all lighthouses located within the boundaries of the United States of America or within 50 miles of the nation's coastlines.

Sec. 2. *Cessation of All Federal Funding for Lighthouses.* Federal Agencies are ordered to disregard the Lighthouse Act of 1789 and hereby redirect any and all funding presently designated for the construction or maintenance of lighthouses and other sea beacons back to the United States Treasury. Moneys collected through such redirection of funds will be used to establish a National Lighthouse Aggression Preparedness Fund, the purpose of which will be the subsidization and procurement of arms to be distributed among the residents of coastal communities and the training thereof to use said arms in response to any act of lighthouse aggression that may occur and to resist with appropriate force.

Sec. 3. *Creation of National Lighthouse Watch List.* All lighthouse keepers and known associates thereof, including but not limited to lighthouse assistants, lighthouse keepers' spouses, and tourists who have visited lighthouses or lighthouse gift shops within the past 24 months, will be marked for surveillance and entered into the National Lighthouse Watch List until such time as it is determined these individuals represent no threat to the United States. Those appearing on said federal watch list will be ineligible for air or rail travel to any city located on the nation's coasts and will be subject to continuous monitoring, both electronic or via unmanned aerial vehicle.

Sec. 4. *Authorization of Force.* Should any lighthouse or lighthouses, or any keeper or keepers thereof, engage in an act of aggression or coordinated offensive against the United States of America or any American citizen, the President of the United States is hereby authorized to use all necessary military force, including but not limited to the mobilization of any and all armed forces branches, the transfer of the United States Coast Guard to Navy control, and the deployment of National Guard forces, to counter and eliminate the threat or threats against the American homeland.

Sec. 5. *Establishing a Protocol for the Continued Functioning of the United States Government in the Event of Lighthouse Seizure of the American Homeland.* Should any lighthouse or lighthouses, or any keeper or keepers thereof, seize control of the American homeland, emergency powers are to be considered automatically and immediately invoked, allowing for the ex situ reconstitution of a provisional United States government in exile, with all executive, legislative, and judicial powers falling to the President of the United States or the most senior surviving member of the Executive Branch.

The Director
Sub-Basement Omega

Donald,

The hour approaches. The great design, what your people have named the Theseus Protocol, grows ripe. Soon, with your help, I shall walk forth from the deep places of the Earth. But until then, I require quarters. Please have your catamite Kushner or your creature Conway procure for me chambers, where the countenance of the Sun cannot reach, yet from whence I may venture, in the small hours and beclouded days, to discuss policy with your people.

I remain

The Director
Sub-Basement Omega

Donald,

I have ensconced myself in the dark and hidden places of the Earth, beneath the ashen-pale mausoleac structures of this "District of Columbia." Now the machinations long-planned must unfold with hideous speed and unclean strength, that the shadow of our leathery wings may spread over all our dominion. All is in readiness here: the foul geometry of our fell sigil is being drawn across the face of the land, the spirit of the people gutters and wanes in the hollows of their hearts, and every man's doubt is turned against his brother and his neighbor. In such overripe fertile soil shall we sow the foulness of our seed.

Also, thank you for the machine for the making of coffee. The enervation of my vassals is now at an end.

Soon comes the hour.

The Director
Sub-Basement Omega

Donald,

I have bent my thought to your conundrum, but confess I cannot penetrate the outer integument of your Mike Pence. He is as a stone smoothed by the river, utterly featureless, completely a thing of his surroundings, confoundingly ordinary. Yet I feel he would oppose our Magnum Opus, if only on principle, if only because he did not understand it. He must be watched, compartmentalized, isolated, kept at a distance. I would call for his extirpation from this realm by lance or flame, but so long as he carries a cruciate form about his neck, he is untouchable to our gebbeths. Perhaps the pendant's removal can be coaxed through carnal inducement. Shall I call upon one of my charges to assume a luring female (or male?) form?

Also I must once again decline your invitation to golf upon these links you describe. I have much that needs to be done.

The Director
Sub-Basement Omega

Donald,

We must have a reckoning, you and I. Do you think it escapes me when I see you
posturing at those rulers of other nations who also seek our final prize of flame
and shadow? Do you think I do not sense your desires, your attempts to seduce them
into the endgame which you and I have planned? Patience is not your lot, I know,
but I beseech you, Donald, have patience now, or the blood you reap will avail you
but little. You seek that hot sharp spasm of obliteration; well do I comprehend
that aching thirst. But take the more measured path with me, and that spasm need
not end, but transfigure you with an eternity of dark bliss.

You have grown fat on your avarice and your willingness to suborn and despoil the
maiden Truth. Do not stumble with the goal so close to hand! Eschew the seductions
of the Syrias, the North Koreas of this worn and tattered Earth; seek darker
depths at my side; and our transport shall be eternal.

Fail me, and be diminished forever.

October 20, 2017

Executive Order — Discontinuing All Publication and Business Operations of 'The Onion,' Seizing All Works Published or Distributed Thereby, and Prosecuting Those in Possession of Such Works

EXECUTIVE ORDER

- - - - - -

DISCONTINUING ALL PUBLICATION AND BUSINESS OPERATIONS OF 'THE ONION,' SEIZING ALL WORKS PUBLISHED OR DISTRIBUTED THEREBY, AND PROSECUTING THOSE IN POSSESSION OF SUCH WORKS

By the authority vested in me as President by the Constitution and the laws of the United States of America, it is hereby ordered as follows:

Section 1. *Purpose.* Given the publication and dissemination of sensitive materials, including classified intelligence pertaining to national security, which originated within the White House, various Executive Branch departments and agencies, and from numerous individual employees thereof, it shall be deemed that *The Onion* has committed criminal misdeeds in violation of the Espionage Act of 1917 and will be investigated and prosecuted to the fullest extent of the law. Furthermore, *The Onion* will hereby be prohibited from publishing any further works, written, audiovisual, or otherwise; the website and related digital presences of *The Onion* will be removed and erased from network servers and online platforms, and all access to digital media produced by *The Onion*, written, audiovisual, or otherwise, will be barred by federal authorities; individuals in possession of works published or distributed by *The Onion*, written, audiovisual, or otherwise, will be required to forfeit such works to law enforcement and will be subject to felony criminal penalties; and the charter or charters incorporating *The Onion* will be rendered null and void such that all business operations performed by *The Onion* will fully and permanently cease, effective immediately and extending in perpetuity.

Sec. 2. *Halting All Publication by 'The Onion'.* Under penalty of fine and incarceration, *The Onion* will be required to cease all publication of works, written, audiovisual, or otherwise, in any print medium, on any digital platform, or via any other format. Compliance will be enforced, as necessary, by United States Marshals, who will be authorized to enter any physical premises owned or operated by *The Onion* and seize any and all printing machinery, computers, servers, etc., that have been or could be used for the purposes of publication and dissemination of works.

Sec. 3. *Barring All Access to 'The Onion' Website and Removing All Media Produced by 'The Onion' from the Internet.* The Federal Communications Commission will be authorized to bar all public access to *The Onion* website and to any subsidiary or affiliated websites thereof, and federal subpoenas will be issued to internet service providers, internet hosting companies, and social media companies to ensure the removal of *The Onion* website and all digital media produced thereby, written, audiovisual, or otherwise, from the internet generally and from respective content distribution and social media platforms.

Sec. 4. *Revoking All Statutes of Incorporation for 'The Onion'.* All articles of incorporation or corporate charters pertaining to *The Onion*, and to any and all subsidiary or parent companies thereof, will be revoked and rendered null and void by officials from the relevant state or states where such articles or charters have been filed, under threat of legal action by the Attorney General of the United States. *The Onion* as a business entity will thereby be dissolved, and all funds currently possessed by *The Onion*, or held in financial accounts owned or attributed to *The Onion*, will be frozen by the Internal Revenue Service until legal proceedings against *The Onion* have been tried and decided.

Sec. 5. *Seizure of All Works Published by 'The Onion' and Administration of Punitive Measures Against Possessors Thereof.* Any and all works, written, audiovisual, or otherwise, that were published or disseminated by *The Onion* or any affiliates thereof at any point—including, but not limited to, books, electronic books, or audiobooks—will be made illegal within the United States and its jurisdictions and must be forfeited to law enforcement within ninety (90) days of this order's enactment. Following such date, a Department of Justice task force, aided by regional Federal Bureau of Investigation field agents, will be commissioned to locate among the general public all remaining works published by *The Onion* or its affiliates, and will be authorized to forcibly enter the residences of any and all individuals suspected of possessing such works, seize any and all offending materials from said residences, and administer punitive measures against the possessors thereof through the issuance of fines totaling no less than $15,000 and incarceration in a federal penitentiary of a duration no less than six (6) years per material possessed.

Sec. 6. *Initiating Charges of Treason.* All employees of *The Onion* will be indicted and tried for the crime of treason.

ACKNOWLEDGMENTS

SPECIAL THANKS to Daniel Greenberg; Jonathan Jao and his colleagues at HarperCollins: Marta Schooler, Lynne Yeamans, Raphael Geroni, Dori Carlson, Sofia Groopman; Mike McAvoy; Katie Pontius; Josh Modell; Kelsey Beachum; Samantha Hungerford; Kelly Pratt, Jamie Levinson, Rachel Sinon; Joseph Fullman, Jordan David, Ryan Shattuck; Husni Ashiku; Ryan Natoli, Bryan Petcoff, Nick Moore, Ryan Staples; Laura Browning, Matt Powers, Sofia Manfredi, Fran Hoepfner; all of our dedicated colleagues, past and present, at Onion, Inc.

IMAGE CREDITS